Mary Horlock worked as a curator at the Tate Gallery Liverpool and Tate Britain, and has written widely on contemporary art and artists. Her first novel, *The Book of Lies*, was longlisted for the *Guardian* First Book Award. She lives in London.

JOSEPH GRAY'S CAMOUFLAGE

A Memoir of Art, Love and Deception

Mary Horlock

Unbound

This edition first published in 2018

Unbound
6th Floor Mutual House,
70 Conduit Street, London W1S 2GF
www.unbound.com
All rights reserved

Text design by Ellipsis, Glasgow

A CIP record for this book is available from the British Library

ISBN 978-1-78352-468-6 (trade hbk)
ISBN 978-1-78352-467-9 (ebook)
ISBN 978-1-78352-469-3 (limited edition)

Printed in Great Britain by Clays Ltd, St Ives Plc

1 3 5 7 9 8 6 4 2

MIX
Paper from
responsible sources
FSC
www.fsc.org   FSC® C018179

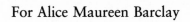

For Alice Maureen Barclay

Patron
Fiona Paice

With special thanks to
Darian Leader
Paddy Whitford

Dear Reader,

The book you are holding came about in a rather different way to most others. It was funded directly by readers through a new website: Unbound. Unbound is the creation of three writers. We started the company because we believed there had to be a better deal for both writers and readers. On the Unbound website, authors share the ideas for the books they want to write directly with readers. If enough of you support the book by pledging for it in advance, we produce a beautifully bound special subscribers' edition and distribute a regular edition and e-book wherever books are sold, in shops and online.

This new way of publishing is actually a very old idea (Samuel Johnson funded his dictionary this way). We're just using the internet to build each writer a network of patrons. At the back of this book, you'll find the names of all the people who made it happen.

Publishing in this way means readers are no longer just passive consumers of the books they buy, and authors are free to write the books they really want. They get a much fairer return too – half the profits their books generate, rather than a tiny percentage of the cover price.

If you're not yet a subscriber, we hope that you'll want to join our publishing revolution and have your name listed in one of our books in the future. To get you started, here is a £5 discount on your first pledge. Just visit unbound.com, make your pledge and type **gray5** in the promo code box when you check out.

Thank you for your support,

Dan, Justin and John
Founders, Unbound

Contents

Preface

This story starts with a picture: a vast turquoise sky, an endless yellow beach, a mother and her child playing in the sand.

My grandmother lifts a trembling hand and points towards the smallest figure.

'That is me.'

She now has a room measuring nine feet by five. There isn't much wall space, so the picture hangs in the corridor outside, beside the sign: 'No. 18: Maureen Barclay'.

Maureen Barclay is a widow and there are many here. Some don't know where they are, nor do they remember the lives they have lived. Maureen is different; she remembers plenty. But with this blessing comes a curse: the older she becomes, the more she worries what she might soon forget. She has moved into a nursing home quite by her own choice, but as she downsizes, reducing her life to the essentials, the more she is stripping back memories, the memories embedded in clothes, objects, papers and pictures.

There simply isn't room for them here.

The only solution is to pass them on to the people she trusts. She has given me many things over the years – her love and time above all else – and now she surrenders a most treasured possession. It is a pencil-drawn self-portrait of her father and my great-grandfather, Joseph Gray. This is the man who first painted that small child playing on the beach.

Joseph Gray is an artist most people have never heard of, but for much of my early life he was the only artist I'd ever heard of. His paintings filled all the rooms of my grandparents' flat and much of my own family home. Smoke-filled streets and blitzed churches lined our staircase, thickly painted still lifes crowded in corners, restless seas churned over each mantelpiece. While the houses of my friends contained candy-coloured Impressionist prints or tastefully anonymous landscapes, we had this curious mix of styles and subjects, all courtesy of an artist I'd never even met.

But at least I knew what he looked like. I would stare for hours at this pencil-drawn self-portrait: darkly piercing eyes under hooded lids, a wide curving nose, a proud, rounded jaw. With a crumpled hat pulled low on his head, Joseph Gray stood straight and returned my gaze. Now that's what an artist should look like, I thought.

The first time I met Joe was through this drawing, and the first time I saw London was through his paintings of the Thames. I was told he'd been a war artist and because of the prints on our staircase – images of St Paul's ablaze, a city in ruins – I assumed this meant the Second World War. I was wrong. Joe had fought in the trenches of the First World War and, once invalided out, had become an official war artist to *The Graphic* newspaper. He was later commissioned to paint battle scenes and portraits of fallen heroes, with his prints and drawings making their way into museums up and down the country.

Now, as Maureen's life shrinks – she has one cupboard to hang her clothes, one chest of drawers – so mine must expand. On each visit she surrenders new memories. First she hands me a file of old art reviews from the 1920s ('Mr. Gray has done wonders', 'Mr. Gray may be ranked with the great battle painters.'[1]); the next week there are photographs of actual paintings with titles like *A Ration Party* or *After Neuve Chapelle*. Then comes a huge cardboard roll jammed full of newspaper articles: sheet curled upon sheet ('June 1916 – A Day in the Life of a Trench, by our correspondent, Joseph Gray'[2]).

I think again of the pencil self-portrait, dark eyes haunted by what he's seen.

'It *is* a shame,' Maureen tells me. 'Nobody knows about him now, nobody remembers him. He lived such a life, he did such extraordinary work.'

I nod slowly, familiar with that lament, and reach over to give her hand a gentle squeeze. Despite the passing of the years there is something unresolved at her core, a sadness buried deep within. Maureen has lived a vivid life, created a large and loving family who adore her, but sometimes I catch a glimpse of the little girl on the beach, still looking for her father.

She refers to Joe often, as a war artist, a painter and etcher of note, and reminds us how successful he was once. That *once* was long ago, but it is what she clings to. She cannot really grasp the rest; why she never saw him after, where he went and what he did.

'There was, of course, another war.'

She uses her long ebony stick to prod at an ominous file abandoned at her feet.

'To serve in two world wars. It's hard to understand. Can you take this, please. I'm sure you'll find a use for it.'

I lean casually to pick up the file but am instantly defeated. It spews yellow papers and is as heavy as a brick. It bears the cryptic label: 'Steel Wool: Camouflage'.

'Camouflage,' I repeat, as if it is a question.

Joseph Gray was a good artist. My grandmother maintains that with a little more luck he might have been great. She is frustrated by the injustice of it all, by his failure to find a proper context. She has a point. After risking his life in one war Joe shouldn't have had to struggle through the next decade, fighting to get his paintings seen.

But just because something can't be seen doesn't mean it isn't there. For the uninitiated, the word 'camouflage' can be traced to seventeenth-century France: 'camouflet' was a slang word that meant a puff of smoke blown into someone's face to dupe them.[3] Another derivation is the French verb 'camoufler', which originally meant to make up for the stage.[4] The *Oxford English Dictionary*'s first example of published usage is when, on 25 May 1917, the *Daily Mail* reported, 'The act of hiding anything from your enemy is termed "camouflage".'[5] This makes it sound so simple, but camouflage is never just a matter of concealment; it is fundamentally about deception. You must fool someone with a surface resemblance, make them *think* they understand what they see, yet what they see is a lie.

All the facts sit in this heavy file, crammed full of reports and memorandums, photographs and drawings. I'm not sure how much of it Maureen has actually read, but I kiss her goodbye and take it away, struggling down the stairs that only the care-home staff ever use. I pass a few elderly residents slumbering in their comfy chairs. One pale, hairless gentleman repeatedly wipes at an invisible smudge on the table in front of him. I think of the stories lost, or so well hidden they will never be told.

Later, in my own home, I confront the file of scraps and secrets. There's a photograph of Joe in what I'd guess as middle age, standing on a grassy hillside. He is smiling coyly and if I look closely I can see why. It's not a grassy slope at all but a canopy of fake undergrowth hiding something. What? There are three more photographs showing a vast framework under construction, and hundreds of bombs stacked below. The view from underneath is astonishing: a man balancing on a wire like a trapeze artist at the circus. There's so much more. I find drawings for 'dummy trees', 'dummy farmhouses', 'movable hedges'; more photographs of landscape which isn't really landscape. It's magic. No, it is camouflage.

Art and camouflage are not obvious allies – the former makes something unreal recognisable, the latter makes something real unrecognisable – but for my great-grandfather one paved the way to the other. Joseph Gray spent one war representing reality, and the next *mis*representing it.

Here, in this file, I find pages of a tattered manuscript entitled *Camouflage and Air Defence*. There are memorandums and reports written on War Office letterhead, addressed to 'Major Joseph Gray R.E.', a camouflage officer and adviser on matters of civil defence, an 'expert in structural concealment'.

Maureen is proud of her father's work, but by the time Joe wrote this book so much was being hidden. He would meet and fall in love with another woman, a woman some fifteen years younger than him. 'Concealment is an art, and like every other art reaches perfection only through much practice.'[6] So declared the War Office in 1937, at the very time when Joe was leaving his wife and only daughter, making himself disappear from the family he'd once been part of.

I have grown up with Joe's presence – in his paintings, prints, fragments of stories – but this only ever seemed to reinforce his absence. I want to find Joe for Maureen, to find the man and make him whole. It's the very least I can do, but it won't be easy.

A complete draft of *Camouflage and Air Defence* is lying sealed in a box in the Imperial War Museum. Dated 1935 it is marked 'SECRET', 'CONFIDENTIAL' and 'Not to be published by order of the War Office'. It was intended as a guide to concealment and deception in a modern, mechanised war and proposes a range of strategies to protect from air attack. Joe was one of the first British artists to be recruited to the cause of camouflage in the 1930s, and it became an abiding obsession. He went on to invent a new kind of covering material – steel wool – that could be used to create artificial landscapes, covering vital sites and protecting them from the Luftwaffe. There is a sample of this material in his archive – bristling papery fragments painted in greyish green – and more photographs, 'notes on research', testimonials that bear witness to his knowledge and expertise. It was presented by the woman who was for a time his most precious secret. Her name was Mary Meade, or rather, as I discover much later, Kathleen Mary Meade.

I am Mary Kathleen, which seems a strange coincidence.

Maureen had four daughters. My mother, Patricia, is the eldest. She was the only grandchild to meet Joe.

'Was I named after Mary Meade?' I ask, when I realise the connection.

There's a long pause down the telephone.

'Well, not really,' replies my mother. 'But I liked the name and I liked *her*.'

It takes a moment for me to understand.

'You knew her?'

'Oh, y-es, and so did your aunt Victoria. They became close after Joe died. In fact, Victoria has some of the letters that Joe wrote to Mary during the war, when they first met and fell in love. You should ask to see them, they are really wonderful . . . just don't mention it to your grandmother.'

My aunt Victoria arrives at my door within days, looking furtive and flustered. She hands me a bundle.

'They are love letters,' she says quickly. 'Mary kept all of them, but I haven't mentioned them to your grandmother and I'm not going to. I know she'd find it painful. I mean, she wouldn't *want* to read them . . . but I don't see why you can't.'

How swiftly I have become the repository of family secrets. I'm not sure if it's right, but I read the letters anyway.

'Darling Mary . . . I love you devotedly and entirely and until I met you I did not know what love was. I will never leave you unless you want me to go.'

'My dearest Darling . . . I was sorry if I was difficult but I can't camouflage what I feel and I won't try to. I am at the moment in a very vulnerable position. ~~Do you really love me~~ (I dare you to try not loving me and see what happens!)'

It seems deception was quite Joe's speciality, but was it an art he learned or a talent he was born with? I read and reread his letters then return to the Imperial War Museum and scour the archives of other camouflage officers, trying to fix him in a wider context. There are lecture notes on blending in and how to spot bad cover, private papers and photographs. 'Having two lives makes it so difficult,' notes one officer in his diary.[7]

I also find a poem. It is called 'The ABC of Camouflage' and is a jaunty alphabetical guide intended as an instructional tool to make troops 'camouflage-minded'[8]. It stays in my head so it's obviously effective. How I wish Joe's life could be made simple, broken down to an ABC. Perhaps I could try, using this poem as a starting point, and so I plot two intertwining histories – one personal and particular, the other more objective and collective – Joseph Gray and camouflage.

But how can I get close to a man who was so good at hiding, a man who had made camouflage the fabric of his life?

I begin with the first story I ever heard about Joe, from 1959. My mother, Patricia Barclay, was nineteen years old, a coltish teenager with kohled eyes and a pixie cut. Having secured herself a place at Glasgow School of Art, she had big ideas and a huge portfolio, which made her own mother anxious. Maureen feared her eldest daughter was making the wrong choice, and perhaps that history might be repeating. She felt out of her depth but was too proud to admit it.

'If you want to be an artist then we should go and ask one for advice,' she said. 'We shall go and see your grandfather.'

Patricia didn't hide her shock. She had assumed her grandfather was long dead, since nobody had ever told her otherwise.

Without further explanation they took a train from Paddington down to Marlow, the small town where Joe and Mary had made their home, and he was standing on the station platform, stick in hand, waiting for them patiently as if he'd been waiting half his life. As Patricia stepped out of the carriage and met his gaze, she felt certain they had met before, and then she realised it was only the shock of resemblance. Maureen and Joe shared the same eyes, the same nose and cheekbones; it was like pieces of a puzzle falling into place. After the briefest of introductions Joe took his daughter and granddaughter to his house to meet Mary, and they sat on benches in the rambling garden, drinking tea from mismatched china.

'I want to be an artist,' Patricia announced with some finality.

She hoped he'd be pleased, but her grandfather appeared to be quite mortified. His gentle face set into a frown. He levelled his eyes on Patricia then turned to her mother.

'*Art?*' he queried after a long pause. 'Art? What has *art* ever done for *us* as a family?'

It was a question that hung in the air between them, a question for which there was no answer. Maureen stared at her father uncertainly. What *had* art done? She couldn't say. Joe shook his head again and left it there. Patricia gulped her tea and wondered. She couldn't possibly grasp the hurt in her mother's eyes, or the true weight of the silence. What *had* art done? But she made up her mind there and then to visit her grandfather as often as possible.

After that she invited herself to Marlow every other weekend. She'd sit with Joe in his studio, perusing the creaking bookshelves and watching him at work. There were many canvases, stacked eight to ten deep, and none were ever finished.

'Not yet,' Joe said. 'They're not quite ready, they're not right.'

He worked on different paintings at different times, moving between them according to his own logic, adding little details, blending light and shadow. He would paint and paint and paint. What should art do? It shouldn't end.

Patricia became particularly attached to a painting of an almond tree in blossom. She could stare for hours at the glistening surface: the dappled sunlight on scattering petals, the delicate brickwork on the wall behind, and the white cat sitting at the base of the trunk, a small and silent spectator. She watched the painting move through various stages, and then on one visit the cat had vanished. She told Joe that this was a mistake. She suggested he put it back.

After a short debate he did as his granddaughter asked, and in a matter of a few moments its pale, glistening form was reinstated.

'Better,' said Patricia. 'Much better.'

But the next time she visited the cat had gone again.

'Now why have you done that?' she asked. 'I think the cat should go back.'

Joe eventually relented, only to remove it on another day and wait to see what happened. A shadow grew where the cat had sat, as the paint was layered over it. The cat came and went, and this game of hide-and-seek continued over months. It might have gone on for ever.

'But then I met your father and moved to Australia. I never came back, and neither did the cat.' My mother sighs at the memory. 'I inherited the painting, long after Joe had died, and I was sad to see the cat had gone.'

I smile and shake my head.

No, I tell her.

The cat didn't disappear. It was just very well hidden.

Let me explain.

A stands for Aeroplane: *his is the eye*
That Camouflage tries to defeat; this is why

They no longer looked like soldiers, at least not the kind of soldiers he had ever seen before. Their faces were smeared with dirt, their tunics stiff with mud, their heads and legs swathed in rags. Joseph Gray scanned his own filthy uniform. Was it enough? He took the badge from his bonnet and tucked it in a pocket, just as an extra precaution.

'We had heard that the sun's rays striking a badge or button had often been the cause of attracting fire.'[1]

It was 10 March 1915 – not a day for taking any chances; even if there was no sun, even if it had been raining non-stop for days, even if the landscape ahead looked so destroyed nothing could survive there.

He crouched low beside a man of the Second Black Watch. With a shaky hand he was lighting cigarette after cigarette, taking a puff or two on each, then throwing them away. To his left, another was emptying his pack.

He thrust something out.

'What is it?'

'Shirts and socks.' The man was digging into his pack. 'I don't want them. Here's a loaf, too!'

Joe knew what he was really saying, what he was really thinking, but he tried to push him off.

'Away! You're havering! You'll be laughing at this tomorrow.'[2]

He didn't sound much like a Scot, and he didn't look like much of a soldier. He was neither. Joseph Gray was from South Shields, and a year after graduating from its art school, he had moved to Dundee to work as an illustrator for the *Courier*. The son of a sea captain, he had already travelled plenty – to France, Spain and even Germany – so when the war broke out he saw it as another great adventure. He'd enlisted with his workmates; they all had the same idea.

'There were about twelve of us who called ourselves, from some headline, "Writers and Fighters Too". We were all from the news-paper offices in Dundee, and meant to keep together.'[3]

Lord Kitchener, the war minister, wasn't allowing any journal-ists on the Front, and the Official War Artists Scheme was at least another year away, but that didn't stop men from the *Courier*, the *Dundee Advertiser*, the *People's Friend*. They'd eagerly joined the 4th Battalion of the Black Watch and had every intention of reporting their experiences from the trenches. As they'd set off from Caledonian Station, people had shouted 'Keep it short!', the subeditor's nightly cry to reporters.

Yes, that was the plan. Keep it short.

When I first told my mother that I was going to write Joe's story, she said: 'Don't make him out to be some kind of hero.' I thought that very strange. She knew nothing about Joe's time in France. She remembered him only as the old man who'd cut him-self off from his only daughter, the old man who would endlessly fuss over his paintings, never able to say: 'Yes, it is done.' But if each painting was a battle, then Joe's first was Neuve Chapelle.

The 4th landed in France on 26 February 1915; eight days later they were in the trenches. Neuve Chapelle was a small village about twenty miles north of Ypres. If British troops could break through German lines and capture it, then they could push on to the higher ground of Aubers Ridge.

Yes, that was the plan.

It started with the ominous drone of British planes. They flew back and forth over the German trenches like giants birds of prey, checking and re-checking the enemy's positions. Neuve Chapelle was the first large-scale offensive by the British and the first time aerial photography was used. This meant the trench lines were known in advance. This should have made it easier.

But then a single gun boomed and any sense of a plan disappeared. Joe held his breath as the first bombardment began. He pretended to himself that he knew what to expect, yet it was beyond anything he had imagined. From that first warning signal he felt an assault on all of his senses. Shells and bullets whistled past, whipping up the earth and filling his nostrils, his mouth, making him choke. Shots from eighteen pounders screamed, explosives came like express trains. For a second he dared to peer over the edge of the parapet; he saw clouds of dust and smoke, continuous flashes of fire like a furious burning sunset. It was beautiful in all the ways it shouldn't be.

'Fourth Black Watch, move to the left in single file!'

Every order had to be screamed. Joe was blinking grit, following the man in front, barely able to see beyond him, barely able to see anything until he was clambering over it: burst sandbags, earth, the already dead and wounded. Bullets thudded into the ground on both sides, throwing up mud and burning his eyes. Surely he would die now. Through the smoke, blinking, he saw a stretcher-bearer drop like a stone, taking the man he carried down with him. Men were falling all around and the communication trench was filling up with bodies. Blood and mud. It turned out blood was more slippery, but still he was alive and still he followed orders. Those who were able inched their way towards Port Arthur, a ruin of a trench only forty yards from the German line. It twisted and turned like a Chinese puzzle, at times so narrow they had to squeeze their way along. Joe was on his hands and knees, moving inch by painful inch. The confusion and chaos engulfed him. The air was thick with smoke and the explosions didn't stop.

The battle was going on around him but without him. He accepted he would die, pushed himself flat on his stomach, and waited. A group of Seaforths appeared. Was this a sign of success? They brought with them a straggling band of German prisoners, wild-eyed and terrified.

'The remarkable thing is not that some were insane – but that any had retained their reason.'[4]

A few years ago my aunt Victoria visited a number of First World War battlefields in France. As she was shown around a workshop where they were making headstones, she explained to the guide that her grandfather had been at Neuve Chapelle.

'Oh,' he said, lowering his eyes. There was silence. 'I am so sorry.'

'No,' she replied. 'You don't understand. He *survived*.'

The guide looked up, shocked. 'Well, he was one of the very, *very* few . . .'

My mother's words come back to me: 'Don't make him out to be some kind of hero.'

Joe never claimed to be. When he wrote about Neuve Chapelle later he was clear about the facts: he was little use to anyone. The 4th had been in France no time at all and he hadn't yet fired his gun. When evening finally came, he was put to work repairing a dugout, the very one he'd built two days before. He had to step over still-warm corpses to do so, passing back and forth to reach the only working pump. Staying alive was, so far, his great achievement.

How to make sense of it? He wasn't sure, but as long as he was breathing he could draw, and there was no denying that these strange, unatural sights demanded it.

That night he was on sentry duty. 'As I stood at my post and looked over towards the captured positions, the scene, after darkness fell, was most dramatic. Ahead two farmhouses were burning furiously. From the blazing buildings crimson and golden tongues of flame arose that illuminated the rising billows of smoke. Our artillery still fired incessantly, filling the air with an infernal din. The heavy shells hurtled wailing over our heads, their bursting flashes cleaving the darkness . . .'[5]

He began sketching. It made him feel more in control. He drew the men of different regiments, the destroyed earth they hid in, the shells exploding in the night sky. He recorded colours and shapes and shadows. And as he worked he tried to imagine himself back in Dundee, in a future he didn't dare believe that he had.

Art was his escape. It gave him a purpose and helped make meaning, and it also offered respite. With pencil in hand Joe could be in two places at once, sunken deep in this ruined earth whilst floating free of it. If he died – which he knew was likely – then his drawings might survive. That was as close as he got to hope.

But if drawing gave him comfort, it was soon to become his job. Captain Boase had been in charge of the battalion since their first weeks in the drill hall in Dundee and he was aware of Joe's skill as a draughtsman. Early on, Joe had come under suspicion for his thick Northumbrian accent and his interest in German newspapers

– some of the men even thought he was a spy. Joe had had to explain about his background and his travels, how he had drawn many different landscapes. It was enough for Boase to set him to work as his observer, his scout, his extra pair of eyes.

Joe wasn't the first artist to find himself so employed. Commanding officers discovered, much to their surprise, that artists could be quite useful in wartime: 'Every artist is a trained observer,' after all. 'His profession has taught him to use his eyes more keenly than the ordinary man, and consequently the artist–soldier is particularly valuable for all reconnaissance and observation work. His ability to draw rapidly and accurately is helpful for many military purposes.'[6]

It was no sinecure. The observer had to be good at map-reading and judging of distance, have a keen sense of light and shade. He had to draw quickly, and under intense pressure. He often worked alone, and not only did he need to be attuned to every detail of the landscape, he also had to blend with it. There was no point gathering crucial evidence if it died with him in No Man's Land. He had to see without being seen.

By the end of March, Joe was regularly being sent on reconaissance, by himself or shadowing Boase. He perfected the art of crawling on his belly like a lizard, always moving slowly, taking advantage of the debris of the battlefield to make a shield. His uniform was already the colour of the earth, and his hands and legs were now bandaged in rags to protect them from cold as much as anything else. He looked more like an animal than a man, and that was fine, because that was safer.

Dawn or dusk were the best times since he needed light to work, although that increased the risk, and not just to himself. On Palm Sunday he angered an entire trench occupied by Indian troops. They initially 'seemed to derive considerable amusement from my sketching'.[7] But it didn't last long. 'I worked unmolested for five minutes, the Indians gathering round with sundry amused expressions, until a bullet thudded into the parapet about a yard to my right. This was at once followed by another, so I hastily sat down while a Boche across the way emptied his magazine without doing any damage.' Joe waited and tried again, tentatively lifting his periscope. More fire broke out, much to the disgust of those around him. He soon knew many swear words in Hindustani – 'at least it sounded more like bad language than anything else' as he carried on with his task.[8]

It helped to see the humour in it – to write letters home boasting about a luxurious billet and delicious food – since only the next night he was lost in the darkness, stumbling from shell hole to shell hole, trying to find his way to a new location. 'The whole ground was terribly torn up, and many German dead lay around.' Joe hid under corpses as shells exploded over him, trying not to look too long into their empty staring eyes. They were men just like him, the only difference being the colour of their uniform. 'Some lay peacefully in composed attitudes; others were twisted into grotesque formless heaps.'[9]

He had to wait for a long time until it was safe. The landscape always looked desolate and empty, but even when it *looked* empty he knew it never was. It was bristling with men poised to kill him. Joe hated the German snipers but had to admire how well they hid: under nets, in hollow trees. They were clever with their trenches, too, alternating different-coloured sandbags that made it harder to see the loopholes. He reported it all back to Boase. The British didn't understand such tricks, opting for one colour, neatly patted down to form a perfect line.

Tidiness didn't help anyone. There are no straight lines in nature, as every artist knows. There should be curves and dips, nothing too jarring. But Joe wasn't now thinking of marketable pictures and an audience back home. He was part hunter, part prey, and he tried to convince himself it would make him a better artist. One day.

But it wasn't just about making sketches from life. He had to read and replicate air photographs to make drawings of the German positions; he had to duplicate maps and plans of attack. Sometimes he knew what would happen ahead of time. Would that make it easier?

Joe Lee, an artist and poet, one of his fighter–writer friends, sought him out one bright May afternoon.

'We've got an important job to do in a hurry. We must have a secluded place to discuss it.'[10]

They took themselves off to an empty office and there examined the contents of a large brown envelope. It was a map, or rather a plan that showed the distribution of troops for their next engagement. They were now tasked with making exact copies for all commanding officers.

So it was that Joe knew the exact distribution of troops before the Battle of Festubert. The 4th were to be used in the assault on the German trenches in front of Aubers Ridge. He had a strong, abiding sense that it would be bad.

The following night, the night of 8 May, it was unseasonally cold. He would remember it years later. A strange wind moaned through the trees as they began marching to Lansdowne Post through darkness, the few lanterns casting ghostly shadows. It felt as if nature was offering a warning. Joe stayed at the head, close to Captain Boase, and in the pale light of dawn they first glimpsed the smoking ruins of the battlefield. It looked like a storm at sea, with clouds of dust and smoke that stretched to infinity.

Their communication trenches snaked towards the road, but the Germans had located every furrow and a barrage of shell fire had already begun.[11] The bombardment had started at four o'clock in the morning and showed no signs of relenting. The battalion couldn't get any closer. Instead they held back in the reserve trenches, trapped under constant fire. Every inch was jammed with men of different units; Seaforths and Gurkhas, most of them wounded. The smell of burning flesh became overpowering. Stretcher-bearers moved back and forth. Keeping low, Joe waited until the order came to move, but then he wondered how they would move since so many men crowded him. Boase ordered them forward. They stopped and started.

'The enemy reopened a fearful fire upon us. The range was accurate, the shells bursting in hundreds one after another. The concussion was fearful, one seemed to be torn asunder . . . the bombardment reached an awful intensity – we realised now what the Germans experienced at Neuve Chapelle.' They tried to keep moving. Then Boase stopped abruptly.

'I'm hit, Gray.'

As he said it, he was hit again.

The world sped up and slowed down. Joe was pulling out his first-aid dressings, wanting to stem the blood pumping from Boase's arm.

But Boase pulled himself up, insisting they continue.

Joe knew there was a medical officer, Major Rogers, just ahead. The problem was everyone in-between was wounded worse than Boase.

'It was impossible to move forward. Dead and dying choked the passage, so full was the trench in parts that one man, dead, stood erect, sustained by the pressure of the living, who themselves could not move. I assisted Captain Boase along the trench but soon he had to stop, for progress in the trench, slippery with blood and crowded with the living and the dead, was impossible.' Joe didn't know what to do. 'To step outside was suicide.' But step outside he did, using all his strength to drag Boase with him.

'After a desperate rush across the open we reached the first aid post.'[12]

A desperate rush. Open ground. Was it luck that kept Joe alive or was it something else? There was a skill to keeping low and moving fast. He was deaf to the noise, blinded by the smoke, but he managed to survive. They both did.

After he watched Boase loaded onto a stretcher, someone tugged at his tunic.

'What about you? You are wounded.'

Joe didn't understand until, looking down, he saw that he was covered in blood. But it wasn't his, it was the blood of other men.

Many soldiers, once they'd been through this war, would find it impossible to talk about. How to describe the horror, the despair, and then how to acknowledge the guilt that came with survival. Joe would make it back to Dundee, marry a beautiful woman and have a child, but in the one surviving photograph he's still in his Black Watch uniform, his eyes tired and troubled. He would remain buried in the trenches for another five years, 'slithering in mud' and 'soaked to the skin';[13] he would wake in the middle of the night in a sweat of panic, then be gripped by a coldness in his bones he couldn't shake.

Men fresh out of the firing zone would come to his studio, dazed, blinking in the sunlight of civilian life. He'd relive 'hot moments' with them and then make them pose as models, and as they talked, he'd sketch. Day by day, Joe reimagined action scenes and battle charges, he drew medical officers and stretcher-bearers carrying out their duties, different moments from trench life. And as he collected stories, so he gathered objects, paying well for billy cans, bayonets and belt buckles as props to furnish every picture.

Because Joseph Gray was still observing, and he had to be authentic.

He would be made official war artist to *The Graphic*, a popular rival to the *Illustrated London News*. Everyone wanted realistic front-line images and Joe offered that. There, alongside the photographic spreads of the Home Front and endless maps of France, were drawings by Solomon J. Solomon, Francis Dadd and Joseph Gray. His sketches brought to life what was happening in the trenches, illustrating the drama of specific offensives or different artillery and equipment. They had an immediacy and naivety which spoke of direct experience and so had huge appeal. Around half the working domestic population were now reading newspapers. This was the first mass-circulation war and artists' impressions were seen by a far wider audience than anything in a gallery.[14]

But a gallery would soon be needed.

The newly founded Imperial War Museum would purchase seven of Joe's pen-and-ink sketches, all of them 'drawn in the firing zone'. They were less idealised treatments than his sketches for the newspaper, depicting different corners of the Western Front and the battlefield after Festubert. Sir Martin Conway, the director-general, travelled to Dundee to open the 'Victory' exhibition of war relics at Kinnaird Hall, where he singled out Joe's drawings as 'a record of priceless value' and 'the work of a man who had fought'.[15] The two men took the time to discuss a larger commission.

'It will be called *The Ration Party*.' Joe already had the composition in mind, pinned to an actual event.

On the night of 11th March the artist was one of a party that left the trenches to bring up rations for the company. The night was wet and stormy and the flat ground was flooded. The only light was provided by bursting star shells. The picture shows the return of the ration party to the front lines. A star shell has dropped near to the men – Their position, now exposed, is swept by machine gun fire and they make a wild dash forward towards cover.[16]

Joe would depict the men 'who were actually present when the incident took place'. He had to 'make the painting accurate in every detail' and for all the survivors to pose as models '(but photographs will have to be used in the case of men who were killed)'.[17] He also supplied an outline sketch identifying each man. The first, the central character, was already a hero. Charles McCririck had fought with Joe at Neuve Chapelle and Festubert, earning the nickname 'McGurkha' for his bravery.[18] After losing a leg at the Somme, McCririck had been awarded a Military Cross, and though he never once talked about the war to his son or grandson, they treasured Joe's sketches of him. Because Charles came time and again to Joe's studio, and he stands at the centre in *A Ration Party*, a ragged spectre, pushing his way through the debris of No Man's Land as if wading through a fast-flowing river.

A Ration Party is an eerie painting, its bedraggled soliders half sunk in mud, half lost in shadow. They are caught in a kind of limbo, between light and dark, between life and death, and Joe is right there with them. I know it's him because he identified himself on his own list, but he is the most obscure figure in the corner, a face hooded and hidden in the shadows, almost invisible. Almost a ghost.

By going back over each moment of each battle, Joe was making sense of it, to make his subjective war objective, but the line between the dead and the living was less and less distinct. By the time he came to write up a history of the 4th for the *Dundee Advertiser* every family in the city had lost someone they loved. Joe would try to give a focus to their grief, filling his columns with vivid descriptions of each battle, reminding everyone this was 'the greatest test of all'[19] and it wasn't all a waste, but breaking up each column were the grainy, head-and-shoulder photographs of soldiers mentioned in the narrative – all either dead, wounded or missing. Their faces accumulated steadily and silently, saying far more than words ever could.

'Nothing in our time will haunt us like the War. Our dead comrades live on in our thoughts, appealingly, as if afraid to be forgotten.'[20] But forgetting wasn't an option. Joe knew that he had survived for a reason: to keep his friends alive.

Years later he wrote: 'In the last war, all of my best friends died alongside of me. As they went, one by one, all in their early twenties – all men of subtlety and imagination – really the best in the country – I remember the conviction that I formed that it was ridiculous and absurd to assume that because their bodies were shattered and finished that they were finished too. Of course they went on.'[21]

They went on in his paintings. He wouldn't let them vanish. But the Battle of Loos on 25 September 1915 would be his last.

It was just before six o'clock in the morning. A mine exploded beneath the German trenches, and the ground shook over half a mile away, where the 4th were waiting. Two minutes later British guns opened fire, the gas was turned on, and candles were used to thicken the great clouds of smoke, which billowed ominously across No Man's Land. Soon the enemy lines were blotted out behind dense yellow and black fumes.

And there was Joe again, charging over the parapet. He ducked close to the ground and tried not to look at the men who fell down on either side not to get up again.[22] It was impossible to see further than a few yards but he was one of a very few who stumbled into the first enemy trenches. Any Germans left alive were huddled in corners, gibbering and terrified, ready to surrender.

'Carry on!' came the order.

They tried, they really did, but the artillery fire was suddenly more brutal. The Germans had recovered from the surprise of the first onslaught and now aimed all their artillery on the captured trenches, blasting them to bits. Men's bodies were mangled in the earth. High explosives dived into the midst of little groups crouching in shell holes. Everyone was killed.

'The battleground was a bloody inferno. The dense clouds of smoke from the enemy's bombs filled the air; it was almost impossible to distinguish friend from foe.'[23] Reinforcements, so badly needed, would never come. Communication lines had been cut, shrapnel had ripped out the cables. When Colonel Walker tried to get word back, he was picked out and killed instantly.

The remaining men dug themselves in, preparing for the worst. Joe closed his eyes, waited, prayed. He couldn't hear the screams any more; he couldn't hear anything. It would be hours before the fire decreased. Only then the straggling band of survivors began edging back to their old front line. Some were blown apart as they crawled, literally obliterated by gunfire or grenades. 'It had been a grand advance but at great cost,' was how it was phrased in the battalion diary. Nothing, though, could summarise the nature of that cost, as the roll was called next morning.

The air was thick with smoke and guns still thundered. Mechanically the old orders were called and survivors lined up slowly and quietly. Joe found his place in line, yet it was barely even that. On either side were the spaces where his friends were meant to be. It hadn't hit him, not yet. He waited. Where were they? Surely they had overslept. Yes, that was it.

'One looks around to the billets. One's special pal is late for parade again – just as he ever is. In a moment he will peep carefully from behind the billet door. The sergeant's head is turned away; out he will run and slip stealthily with dancing eyes, and an adroitness that shows much practice, into a place in the rear rank.

'But he does not come – nor will he ever.'[24]

The 4th had lost their colonel and twenty officers of the twenty-two who had gone into battle. On the night of the 24th, 423 non-commissioned officers and men had marched to the trenches. From these trenches 167 remained.

One of Joe's journalist colleagues later wrote that 'the heavy proportion of officers killed arose from their wearing, as the other ranks did not, a ready mark for snipers, the gleaming red hackle of the Black Watch in their bonnets'.[25] It's hard to know if that's true, but as Joe stood quietly, looking around, trying to take in what was left of his battalion, he saw only empty spaces where his friends were supposed to be.

He had to wonder – how could he not? – if it wasn't just that the dead men were more visible, but that they had died *because* they'd been more visible.

B *is for Bomber: he's coming so fast,*
If he can't see you quickly, why, dammit, he's past

'It's him, surely that's him. Isn't it?'

I lean in to examine the hunched, shabby figure of the soldier. Dark hair, a moustache, and yes, the profile is almost right. A sudden breeze makes my skin prickle.

'It's possible,' I sigh. 'Yes, I suppose it *could* be Joe.'

Maureen has her arm looped through mine and we stand together for a moment, staring long and hard at the canvas in front of us. She screws her eyes up tight whilst mine drift along its length. It's impossible not to be drawn to every small detail: the light glinting off freshly cleaned bayonets, the rough grain on a wooden crate. I know I should be looking at the men, but the surface of the painting is so bristling and agitated it shocks me. Every small stroke of the brush registers. I step back because I need to, but Maureen won't. She presses down on her walking stick, smiling and leaning forward. She knows this painting well, this battlefield.

Like it is her own.

She turns to me, her voice suddenly bright.

'Come now, my dear, he did put himself in his paintings, didn't he?'

I nod, scanning the surface quickly to be sure.

'Yes he did.'

After Neuve Chapelle (10 March, 1915) was presented to Dundee City Art Gallery in 1922 and has hung here ever since. It's not exactly a battle painting, since it depicts the aftermath of the Battle of Neuve Chapelle; the gathering together of exhausted survivors, waiting for new orders from their lieutenant colonel. Harry Walker is issuing his directives, with Boase just behind him, listening intently, and Rogers, the medical officer, standing to one side.

Joe made sure every man was known and named. Beneath the painting a small plaque lists the main characters: Colonel Walker, Major Tosh, Captain Boase, Lieutenant Weinberg, Major Muir, Captain Rogers, Lieutentant Tarleton, Lieutenant Weinberg, Lieutenant Stephen, Lieutenant Stevenson, and Sergeant Major Charles. These are the men mentioned in Joe's newspaper articles, their postage stamp-sized photographs scattered through his narratives. The glorious dead. He captured each likeness faithfully. He knew each man, he knew their families, he had seen some of them buried: Walker and Tosh at Pont du Hem, Weinberg at Vieille Chapelle. Of the ten named, seven had been killed in action, so it was always going to be more than a painting. It was to become a shrine.

We stand and stare, quite in awe. The eye-watering detail pulls the viewer in, demanding full attention, but now this painting is posing a new question.

'So. Is that him?' Maureen is pointing to a kneeling figure in the foreground to the right.

I can't be sure, but how can I tell her that? We've made this epic trip for her, because we all know it's the last time she will see it. Perhaps, *because* it is the last time, she is trying to see something new here.

'Joe did put himself in *A Ration Party*,' I say. 'But he was right at the back in that, in shadow, so you couldn't even know it was him.'

That was more his style. The man who was so good at hiding wouldn't make himself too obvious. This creates fresh debate amongst our small group. My mother, my aunts, an uncle, a cousin – we've all come along to share this enounter. But is that Joe? Nobody can say for certain. I close my eyes, open them again and take another look. For a minute it's like I have lost my balance, then I really focus. If I look hard enough, the connections are there to be made. I see him.

'There!' I point. 'There!'

Of course it's him, I am sure of it now, but he's not where everyone thinks. He is not the crouching figure. He is neither in the foreground nor in the background, but sits on his own, bowed and thoughtful and almost in the middle, and of course his face is blurred. This I know is deliberate – whilst every other detail is precise, right up to the guns propped just in front of him.

'He's that figure in the middle,' I say. 'No doubt about it.'

After a few more minutes we all agree.

'Oh! Oh yes! Of course!'

We cluster around, pointing and chatting.

It's a cold and clear Saturday morning in March and we've come a long way for this moment, this meeting within a meeting. The gallery guide is intrigued and then excited to meet the daughter of the artist Joseph Gray.

'I used to come here all the time with my schoofriends,' Maureen tells her. 'I would show them the painting and say, "Dad painted that!" and everyone knew about it. I felt almost famous.'

I hold on tight to my grandmother as tears well in her eyes. She sniffs them away quickly.

'You must've been proud,' I tell her.

'People come here and stare at it for hours,' says the guide. 'There's so much to look at. And then of course there's the key.' She points to the sign under the painting. 'It's nice to know the names, I mean the people who really fought. It's all so true to life.'

I stare once more at the painting. The background is alive whilst the men themselves are still and solemn, their drab and ragged uniforms blending with the landscape. There's a rippling tension between light and shade; apart from dashes of yellow and white, the palette is mostly greens and browns. The colours, I note, of camouflage.

Khaki is an Urdu word from the Persian word 'khak' meaning dust. In 1846, in the Punjab region of Northern India, a British officer by the name of Harry Lumsden raised a unit of troops – the Corps of Guides – from local tribesmen. Following orders to have his recruits comfortably and suitably clad, Lumsden kitted his men out in smocks and wide pyjama trousers made of coarse home-spun material, a cotton turban and jerkins of sheepskin. All the cotton was dyed locally with the product of a dwarf palm, mazari, which turned the white cloth a dullish grey. Leather was stained with mulberry juice, which produced a yellowy drab shade. This was the first unit in a European army to wear a khaki uniform.

A decade later, during the Indian Mutiny, British soldiers aban-doned their red tunics in favour of the light-weight white clothes they wore in camp. During the fighting these clothes became dirty and some soldiers dyed them with tea or curry powder, thus improvising their own khaki-coloured uniforms. Then, during the Second Boer War, the British forces became known as Khakis because of their uniforms, and many European armies adopted more subdued colours. While Britain went with khakis and browns, the Germans dropped Prussian blue in favour of field grey.

But it wasn't easy, the abandoning of military splendour. In 1911 a proposal to replace the French infantry's blue tunics and red pantaloons with something less striking was greeted with outrage.

'Abolish red trousers?' the French war minister magnificently scoffed. 'France *is* red trousers!'[1]

It was only once the First World War began that attitudes had to change. For the first wave of troops who faced the front-line trenches, the expectation of a brief battle fought like heroes was quickly dispelled. This was going to be a slow war of attrition, and the advent of the machine gun and the siege-style skirmishes of the trenches meant invisibility was everything.

It happened almost naturally. After a few weeks exposed to the rain and the cold, thigh-deep in mud, soldiers were merging with their backgrounds – balaclava-clad, a battered greatcoat padded with various quiltings, canvas hoods and earth-coloured oilskins wrapped tight around their heads, puttees protecting their legs. One of Joe's pen-and-ink drawings shows a private of the Black Watch swaddled from head to toe. His kilt is shredded, his legs are covered in stained rags. 'The "4th" looked like a regiment of tramps – weary, battered tramps at that.'[2]

Joe quickly learned to blend with his background. He picked up tips from other soldiers, blackening his face and hands with burnt cork, swathing rags around his legs and head. This was his highly personal version of camouflage, often hastily improvised and adapted to each terrain.

But camouflage would happen by design as much as by accident. Back in England fellow artist Solomon J. Solomon wrote to

The Times just two months before the Battle of Neuve Chapelle with concerns over the question of 'Uniforms and Colour'.

> The protection afforded animate creatures by Nature's gift of colour assimilation to their environment might provide a lesson to those who equip an army. To be invisible to the enemy is to be non-existent for him ... A knowledge of light and shade and its effect on the landscape is a necessary aid to the imagination of a designer of the uniform in particular.
>
> For instance, the khaki tunic is good in summer – in winter it is too yellow – but the same colour cloth clads the whole man. Here a knowledge of light and shade comes in. The planes parallel to the source of light are the lightest, and they darken as they recede from that light source ... To obviate these adverse changes of tone it becomes necessary to clothe the lower limbs in a much lighter stuff than the body, and the cap and shoulders – the shoulder straps would suffice – in a darker, taking the tunic to be the normal tone aimed at.[3]

In response 'an artist and big-game shot' wrote in, agreeing with Solomon's points but adding to this the importance of breaking up the outline. 'However well the tone of the clothing of a man is made to agree with its surroundings, the outline of the man is apt to show ... I have found that if the waistcoat is one colour, the coat another, the leg coverings another, &c., its outline is less easy to make out.'[4]

This echoes the advice of experienced hunters like Reginald Ryves, whose essay on 'Skulking and Scouting' had first appeared in the *Field* magazine back in 1905 and was reprinted to incorporate his war experiences. 'It is worthwhile dividing the man visually. A jester in motley clothes would be far better dressed for scouting than men in some "sober" uniforms.'[5] Ryves suggested using faded rags of different colours, as perfected by the 'Ghillie suit', a ragged cape first used by ghillies and gamekeepers on Scottish estates. This shrubby overcoat allowed the wearer to blend into the undergrowth and functioned like a portable hide. It was latterly adapted to warfare when these same men were recruited into the Lovat Scouts, a regiment revered for their skill at stalking, hiding, blending and watching.

'The step between war and hunting is but a very small one,'[6] wrote Major Hesketh Vernon Hesketh-Prichard, a crack shot on the Western Front who was appalled by the poor standards of the British military. Prichard established the First Army School of Sniping, Observing and Scouting in an attempt to remedy this, and his curriculum included everything from map-reading and compass work, to the importance of camouflage. For sniper and observer alike it was better 'to obtain safety *by concealment* rather than by cover from fire'.[7]

Joe was never given formal instruction, as Prichard's men would be, on the importance of 'protective colouring and the choice of backgrounds',[8] but the best snipers and scouts shared the steely focus of the artist. Prichard believed a sniper had to be like an artist in love with his work, and even used artist–instructors, commending the Slade-educated Ernest Blaikley, who proved adept at teaching map-reading and drawing techniques, as well as demonstrating how to read aerial photographs.

'Lectures on aeroplane photographs were another side of our work, and one which was undoubtedly very necessary,' noted Hesketh-Prichard.[9]

Yes, hiding from the sniper at ground level was crucial, but a

fresh threat came from above – from aerial reconaissance and the
bombing airman. There were three major innovations of this war:
the machine gun, the tank and the aeroplane. The latter meant
large-scale covers would be needed to hide not just concentrations
of men, but all their new machinery. Solomon J. Solomon understood this. Before he'd written to *The Times* on the subject of
uniforms, he'd read reports of 'German airmen dropping bombs
on our trenches'.[10] Taking the initiative, he set to work inventing
covers of his own.

> In August 1914, my family and I were spending the summer
> months with my mother-in-law, who had taken a house with
> large grounds on the outskirts of St Albans, and I was scouring
> the town for all the butter muslin, dyes and bamboo canes I
> could afford. Amid the laughter of the rest of the house party, I
> littered the lawns and hung on the tennis net to dry, the canvas
> that I had dyed.[11]

The popular image of the artist as a romantic visonary, a single-
minded idealist, sits well with Solomon. It is easy to picture this
portly figure with his sleeves rolled up, painting canvas rags in
earthy shades and knotting them to muslin, draping them over
improvised trench lines and examining the effect.

For Joe in the trenches, camouflage was an impromptu scramble
for personal survival. For Solomon back in St Albans, it was an
extension of art theory. He noted how objects became blurred
under different screens and in different light. As in an Impressionist painting, figure could merge with ground. Solomon excitedly wrote up his discoveries to submit to the War Office and after

time and persistence was able to demonstrate his ideas at Wool-
wich dockyards for assembled military personnel. Although his
proposals weren't immediately taken on, towards the end of 1915
he was invited by the War Office to go to France.

The French were already ahead in the camouflage game, and
again it was artists who were taking the lead. That February, they
had established their own 'service de camouflage', headed by
Lucien-Victor Guirand de Scévola, another well-respected realist
painter. The story goes that Guirand de Scévola had been working
as a telephone operator for an artillery unit near Metz when he
realised the Germans were picking off men and machines with
shocking accuracy. 'It was from this moment that, in a vague form
at first, then in a more and more precise one, was born in me the
idea of camouflage. There must be, I thought, a practical way to
conceal not only our artillery . . . but also the men who served
it. My first thought was to make the equipment manifestly less
visible, if not invisible, in its form and colour.'[12]

Guirand de Scévola began painting large canvases with earthy
colours, dressing artillery men in smocks streaked with paint, and
covering cannons similarly. Although early attempts yielded mixed
results, he knew all the right people to curry favour, and the
pressing need for effective camouflage meant he was soon able to
form his own unit. He began by recruiting painters who were
exempt from active service – André Dunoyer de Segonzac, Louis
Abel-Truchet and Jean-Louis Forain to name but a few – and this
soon expanded to include professional house-painters, decorators
and carpenters. Although camouflage remained top secret, the
Graphic saw fit to praise French initiatives early in 1915, with a
spread entitled 'Campaigning Under Cover' and showing a photograph of 'masking one of the Famous French 75s' and another of

men building huts made from a timber frame, draped in undergrowth: 'A home from home on the battlefield – some of the ingenious war villas erected by the French at Woevre.'[13]

From the outset the French saw camouflage as an art form, with handbooks and memos citing Corot and Delacroix. Artist-camoufleurs were respected and valued, and were soon extending their skills beyond the painting of artillery, uniforms and vehicles to the concealment of transport routes, the construction of false war materials and the all-important observation posts, so crucial to scout and sniper alike.

But this was all a long way from life in the trenches, where the cold and the rats were constant companions. This was the life that Joe knew, and by the spring of 1916 it had taken its toll. He was badly deaf from the constant shelling and he'd suffered repeated bouts of rheumatic fever. Worse still, he had finally been seen. A German sniper had caught Joe as he was setting out across No Man's Land. He had managed to fling himself forward and avoid serious injury, but had flashed enough of his pale backside to warrant a bullet there. A good lesson in camouflage, he would joke.

Just as Joe returned from France, Solomon was creating his own little 'royal academy of camouflage'[14], settling into an old factory at Wimereux. His unit was given the mysterious title 'Special Works, RE' and fell under the control of the Royal Engineers, because 'they have materials for making replicas and deception targets', and 'engineers look at landscapes with a more understanding eye than most other soldiers do'.[15] Inevitably Solomon disagreed: 'The camoufleur is, of course, an artist, preferably one who paints or sculpts imaginative subjects, with some deductive faculties.'[16]

Solomon felt his experience as a volumetric painter meant he understood exactly what was required of camouflage. It is by variations of light and shadow, often very delicate, that one recognises how an object is a solid and detached from its background. Solomon's mission was to eliminate telltale shadows and so create an ideal screen: essentially fishing nets threaded with canvas and hessian rags with bunches of dried raffia. 'It could be stretched over guns – dumps, trenches, and over quite large areas; it would make no appreciable shadow on the ground – it was in fact the scientific solution to most of our camouflage problems.'[17]

The balancing of light and shade was the essence of Joe's life now, too. Concentrating on large works, he planned for weeks, first covering the whole surface of the canvas, and then sketching in his figures and building up the foreground. He'd do close work for days and then refocus on the background, adding shadows to deepen the perspective. He knew when to take a step back to see how tones blended into one another, where shadows or highlights were needed, and then he'd blend some more. Back and forth he went, pulling in close, then stepping back. It was a delicate dance, playing light against shade, foreground against background. Joe was determined to create something seamless, harmonious and entirely 'realistic'.

'Who says the painter can't organise?' asked Solomon. 'This seemed to be a military prejudice. When an artist is composing an imaginative picture his organising faculties are at full stretch.'[18] Soon his nets and screens were in widespread production, becoming a 'universal camouflage' material for the French and British, of which some 7 million square yards were used by the end of the war. But despite Solomon's considerable contribution, he couldn't adapt to the Army's way of doing things. 'Solomon was obstinately and sincerely convinced that the Army had everything to learn from him, and that he and his colleagues had nothing to learn from the Army; he was out to teach a new language in warfare without knowing a thing about the common language of his potential pupils.'[19] He was thus soon replaced as head of the camouflage section by the 'cheerfully derisive'[20] Colonel Francis Wyatt, a trained engineer and committed pragmatist.

Bruised but not beaten, Solomon returned to England and created a camouflage school in Kensington Gardens. He also went to Scotland to advise on camouflage in the Firths of Forth and Tay, and to Hull after it had been bombed by Zeppelins. These experiences confirmed for him the growing threat of aerial warfare and the need for large-scale camouflage.

'Great armies and all their movements are now overlooked as are ants crawling about on the ground, the mass of them attacked far behind the fighting line by bombing airmen, or by shells fired from distances varying from one to twenty miles or more. Those who consider defensive concealment unchivalrous can never have visualised the conditions of modern war.'[21]

Solomon had long worried what the Germans were up to, and after poring over air reconnaissance photographs taken by his nephew, Gilbert, he thought he had found the answer. His artist's eyes detected inconsistencies in the landscapes – how the shadows seemed to be wrong in relation to the sun, how certain fields looked odd for the time of year. This seemed to him to reveal the clues of German schemes: that the enemy had shrouded vast areas with camouflage covers that imitated both fields and farms in an attempt to hide the build-up of machinery and men.

Paranoia or prophecy? It was fiendishly hard to prove – after all, the most effective camouflage by its very nature evaded detection – and Solomon didn't help himself by persistently badgering all in the military about his great 'discoveries'. The war was finally drawing to an end, as perhaps was his field of influence. That he pushed ahead and published his findings is testament to his grandiose ideas, and he was widely ridiculed in the press. ('Camouflage Gone Mad'[22] ran a critique in the *Morning Post*, while the *Times Literary Supplement* concluded that 'His illustrations . . . will provoke the mirth of expert air photograph readers.'[23])

But laying aside its more extreme claims, Solomon's *Strategic Camouflage* made the point that the science of the interpretation of aerial photography was going to be the eye of the command for all future wars, and in this he was quite right. This war had ushered in a time of huge change, and the use of the camera was a central innovation. The camera essentially meant everything and everyone could now be represented, and in a world where everything could be represented, the struggle for control would be crucial.

C is for Camera. try to confuse
The enemy's reading of aerial views

They stood or sat in two simple rows. Most were in uniform, polished medals pinned onto their tunics, clattering against each other as they straightened their shoulders, striking a pose. The survivors of Neuve Chapelle. Joe sat front and centre, but he wasn't in khaki. Instead, he wore a new dark suit and silk cravat, resting his felt fedora casually on his knee. His handsome face seemed fuller, and his thick hair sprang up rebelliously. He stared straight ahead, keeping his dark eyes fixed on the camera. The artist was composing himself.

Then came a blinding flash and it was over. The photograph would appear in the paper that evening, with the headline '"DUNDEE'S OWN" – Famous Battle Picture Presented to City' and an accommpanying article had the same flourish:

Men like those, we can say of them: 'To live in hearts we leave behind is not to die'. Ages and ages ago – or so it now seems to those who were 'there' – on a dull desolate morning in March, the Battle of Neuve Chapelle was fought; and though kindly time has enveloped naked memories in as soft a mist as screened the dreariness of the landscape that fateful evening, Mr. Joseph Gray's picture of the 4th Black Watch bivouac on the night of the battle recalls the stark brutality of half-forgotten scenes and incidents with a vivid truthfulness which makes the picture a masterpiece of reality.[1]

'It shall take its place among the great battle pictures in the country.'

Sir Alexander Spence was peering at the painting through his round, thin-rimmed spectacles. Joe, in turn, was admiring the polish of his provost's necklace. He turned to survey the crowd in the gallery. It was full to bursting with every type of person: men in their battledress, war widows, young men and women, children. The atmosphere was heavy with emotion as everyone swarmed towards the painting, craning necks to catch a glimpse of it. Would they marvel at the detail? Would they recognise the men they knew?

'Ladies and gentlemen. May I have your attention?'

Spence cleared his throat and a gentle hush fell across the room.

'I am aware this ceremony may open wounds only partially healed,' Spence began. 'No picture is needed to remind people of the huge loss, the scale of human sacrifice.'[2]

Joe was no longer listening. He turned and studied the men of his old battalion – not the men who'd just sat for the photographer, but the soldiers he'd spent so many hours painting – Walker, Tosh, Boase, Weinberg – all of them dead. Seven years had passed, yet it felt like yesterday. And it looked like yesterday.

There were more speeches. Much was made of Mr Gray's remarkable ability to combine so many likenesses within a single picture, of his meticulous attention to detail. The architect Charles Soutar hailed him a genius, praising the painting's truth to reality. The fact that it represented a moment after battle caught something of the 'everyday dreariness'³ and exhaustion of the battle-field, which was often more testing than an actual attack. Such uncanny realism, he declared, could only have been achieved by an artist who had been there. Yes, Joseph Gray had been there, and now all he did was go back there, returning men to the midst of the action, making sure they were seen.

He would say it time and again: that he would only depict the war as it was. It wasn't glittering and glamorous – it was ruinous and wearisome, and the waste was appalling – but he wouldn't make it pointless. There was heroism in the perseverance. He wouldn't forget that, any more than he'd forget the friends he had lost, and really he was lucky: while some veterans struggled with their memories of the war, Joe was turning his into something as coherent as a picture within a frame.

The public unveiling of *After Neuve Chapelle (10 March 1915)* was, he felt, a huge success. People pressed forward and reached out to shake his hand, congratulating him on his achievement. So many years had passed, but the war was still on everyone's minds. Joe had sketched and etched it, written and painted it. He weaved his way through the crowds, smiling and nodding. He couldn't hear half of the compliments but he knew every face and name. This was Joe at his best; charismatic, vivacious, a real life force.

And his wife was the same: fluttering around him, luminous in his reflected glory. Within five months of returning from France they had married – perhaps that was a little hasty, but they loved each other deeply. Agnes was the third daughter of John Dye, a bank clerk and church elder, a respected pillar of the community. Having such a strait-laced father gave her plenty to rebel against, and she liked to do so in style.

Although working as a stenographer, Agnes spent all her evenings on stage, indulging a passion for amateur dramatics. The minute Joe had seen her under the floodlights he was caught. Agnes had more energy than anybody he'd ever met. She was dazzling, feisty (in fact, rather fierce). She could dance and sing and ski and ride (but never side-saddle, as a lady should), and she saw things in simple, direct terms. Having never really liked the name Agnes, it seemed right that Joe christen her Nancy. Nancy Gray, the artist's wife, was a thrilling new role to play.

They'd settled in a home close to her parents in Broughty Ferry, 'a very modern and cultivated circle',[4] and Joe had converted one room of their house into a studio. There was still space for a live-in maid, who became devoted to Nancy, who gave up work and soon produced a daughter. They named her Alice Maureen, though people only ever called her Maureen.

Born the same month as the Treaty of Versailles, Maureen represented a bright new beginning and was cherished all the more for it. There is a wonderfully informal photograph of Joe and a very young Maureen with her grandfather, John Dye. Dye is smiling indulgently as he holds up the little girl, and she affectionately wraps one arm over his shoulder, using her other arm to point at the camera. She is ecstatic, her little face screwed up in excitement, and Joe shares her joy, grinning broadly, dark eyes sparkling.

Joe still believed in love and romance, and this was going to be part of his problem. The signs were already there if he looked for them: ex-soldiers begging on street corners, shops and factories failing. It was soon going to be hard to make a living at all, let alone make a living as an artist.

A few months after the unveiling of his Neuve Chapelle picture, Joe travelled down to London. He'd been offered the chance to show some of his war works at a Bond Street gallery, a prospect that created much excitement. He felt he needed to spread his wings and reach a wider audience. Perhaps *this* would be his moment. And London seemed to offer all that he hoped and the fast pace of life appealed. He wrote to Nancy telling her that he'd had many visitors to the gallery and that his dealer was confident of sales and success. On paper everything looked good. the *Scotsman* reported that Queen Mary visited and had showed 'much interest' in his work'.[5] Joe wrote excitedly to his friend, the photographer Andrew Paterson, offering edited highlights from choice reviews: 'vigorous and clever – enveloped in atmosphere', 'Mr. Gray has done wonders.'[6]

But Mr Gray could never shake off that feeling that he didn't quite fit in. By London standards he was rough around the edges, quite without advantages. He had trained at South Shields School of Art, not the Slade. He was nuts and bolts, without wealthy patrons or private income. He'd even had to pay for his own advertisements, hiding the cost from his wife.

'I wonder what will be the result of the exhibition,' Joe told Paterson. 'I am full of beans and have every hope, as I shall be in a serious position if nothing comes of it . . . All the <u>right</u> folk come in and after all we only need <u>one</u> or <u>two</u> people seriously inter-ested to do the trick.'[7]

Joe hovered in the gallery and courted his audience. Men who'd been in the trenches came and said he'd got it just right, that there was nothing to match it, but this swell of good feeling didn't translate into the sales and money he so needed. He was beginning to feel the rub. 'I will not do anything unreal or false,' he said. 'My experience is that people want straight stuff. The problem of course is a difficult one, to combine artistic expression with the expression of historic and topographical truth.'[8]

It was a problem indeed. This was 1922 and there were now so many versions of the war in circulation. It was as if reality had splintered into fragments. Joe saw it with his own eyes, in every other gallery on Bond Street and beyond. The fractured and twisted forms of Modernism apparently made sense after the carnage of the battlefield. All the critics said so. A brutal, mechanised war required a sharp-edged language of expression, something that was neither literal nor subjective. Wyndham Lewis, Paul Nash, Christopher Nevinson: these were the artists who stole the headlines and caused such excitement.

Joe mistrusted Modernism: how it distorted and disguised reality. He considered it a craze, a worthless fad. The war, what he'd been through, the friends that he'd lost, had to be properly represented. 'A picture may be really fine from the point of view of abstract aesthetic expression and of no value as a war record.'[9] But he was always defending his position, which was a sure enough sign that it was under threat.

The dazzling future so hoped for, and so hard fought for, didn't look how anyone thought it would. When Joe returned to Broughty Ferry he was deeply unsettled by the picture before him, but he put on a good face for the sake of his family. And it wasn't all bad. There were still some commissions trickling in, and he turned some of his paintings into etchings to make more regular money. Prints were cheaper and easier to sell, and etching itself was enjoying quite a revival.

Etching had a particular appeal, of that there was no doubt. In etching, the artist draws with a needle onto a metal plate that is covered with a waxy ground. The plate is then immersed in acid, and the bare metal, exposed by the lines of the drawing, is eroded. The depth of the etch is controlled by the amount of time the acid is allowed to bite the metal. The longer in acid, the deeper the line and the darker the print, but each impression can vary greatly, and the effects are a wonderfully rich, painterly chiaroscuro of tone.

Joe loved the etching process, the focus on line and tone, and he looked for inspiration outside, taking sketching trips along the Tay and hiking far into the Highlands in all kinds of weather. The war had given him his best subjects, but just recently the war had kept him indoors. It did his lungs good to get out in the open, and although he walked with a stick, it was more from habit than necessity. It was time to find fresh drama and Joe hoped to find it in the landscapes of his home: wild Highland views, serene and empty lochs, craggy ancient coasts.

Nancy wondered where her husband disappeared to. He was often gone from dawn until dusk, looking for both an answer and escape. He returned with endless sketches that formed the basis of new plates. By looking down on the world, Joe Gray felt he might still control it. Certainly, he could etch it. He was back in the landscape, the observer hard at work.

Nothing changed quickly. There was no lightning bolt or earthquake, no watershed moment. Joe was obstinate and blinkered, as artists often are. He reassured himself that his work was still popular: his etchings sold well, allowing him to buy his own printing press, and his battle paintings remained a focal point in local galleries. Ernest Blaikley, the curator of the Imperial War Museum, assured him *A Ration Party* was still one of the 'most appreciated in the collection'.[10]

Yes. Ernest Blaikley. The connections are there to be made. The man who had once trained snipers under Hesketh-Prichard was now a well-regarded member of the London art establishment. Joe had corresponded with Blaikley for some time, spurred on by a desire for accuracy in his war work. What started as an innocent request ('Mr. Blaikley, may I ask please if it would be possible for me to borrow a few details of German equipment?'[11]) became a protracted correspondence. ('Do you have such objects as field cooking kitchens and field guns in the museum? . . . Do you think . . . that it would be possible to borrow for a month or two a set of leather infantry equipment, such as was worn by the Scottish Divisions at Loos? . . . I would not ask for anything else, and I would not say where I got it.'[12]) Blaikley deflected Joe's enquiries with humour and tact, making arrangements instead for him to sketch the items in the museum store. It was how they first met, and would continue to meet.

The two men had plenty in common. Blaikley was himself an etcher, a devotee of drawing and direct observation, and a founding member of the Society of Graphic Art. A stickler for accuracy, Blaikley's time teaching map-reading to snipers served him well, since his first task on joining the Imperial War Museum had been to catalogue all the trench maps and intelligence summaries collected from the Western Front. His second had been to index the thousands of aerial photographs taken by British servicemen of that exact same area. Solomon J. Solomon had said it took the eyes of an artist to understand aerial photography, and Blaikley bore that theory out. He created an unparalleled resource, a precise record of one war that would ultimately be used in another.

Step in close to see the details, and then pull back and patterns start to emerge. A landscape seen in monochrome might seem so very simple, yet the grainy lines, the minuscule variations of light or shade, a particular tone or texture, contains any number of possibilities.

'The worker in black and white, although working in an art which is simpler, is allowed the freest range.' So spoke Sir John Findlay, the owner of the *Scotsman*, as he welcomed the crowds to another exhibition at the Victoria Gallery, this time a group show of the Dundee Art Society. To the agreement of all present, Findlay expressed the view that the graphic arts still had a direct and wide appeal.

'Although it might be heresy to say it, there is a definite need on the part of modern artists to consider the public a little more than many do. There is still room in the world for a good deal of descriptive art.'[13]

Joe stood at the front and applauded that sentiment. He wore the same dark suit and cravat that he'd worn for his last opening, but his hair was now dishevelled, his eyes a little tired, and his fingers stained with ink. Still, he was excited to be exhibiting his new etchings. There was a strong market for his expressive Highland views, heather-covered banks and wild and lonely lochs. He etched a world untouched by war and barely touched by man, landscapes borne out of deep contemplation. A return to something simple, personal, hand-crafted.

If anybody asked, he eagerly explained how he carried out his own experiments and prepared each plate personally. Much as he loved the fluidity of the hand-drawn line, he built up tone not just through fine and dense strokes, but by repeatedly inking and wiping the plate, thereby creating wonderfully different atmospheric effects. He would spend hours moderating shadows, balancing every nuance of light and shade, making his subject more or less visible.

Joseph Gray didn't want to be a war artist any more; he wanted instead to be an etcher of landscapes. He hadn't yet seen how the two might come together.

D *is Deception, which plainly implies*
You've got to tell Jerry some credible lies

The colours aren't what I expected – the pale green sinking into sulphurous yellow – and I'm disappointed to find that it is smaller than all the other canvases crowded on the rack. I lean further forward, focusing entirely on this painting, on the ghostly, ragged outlines and the murky ground they're sunk in.

'It's nothing like the photographs,' I say, turning to the curator who has brought me here to see it.

She nods quickly. 'But the light isn't very good. I mean, this is not the ideal place to view it.'

We are standing in the basement storeroom of the Imperial War Museum, hemmed in by metal racks that stretch from floor to ceiling. There is no natural light, of course, and the air is cold and still. These wire racks before me are lined with paintings of every description and it's both amazing and depressing to see how much is hidden. I stare off into the shadows to other doors, conscious that my great-grandfather made similar trips, not to this exact store but to one surely like it, all those years ago. Back then, he came to the museum in search of artefacts. Now he has become one.

I've come back to *A Ration Party*, Joe's first war painting. It was once very popular with the public, according to Ernest Blaikley, who singled it out for special mention. That Blaikley admired it means something, but it hasn't been on display here for years. 'An incident in a famous battle'[1] is lost amidst hundreds of other such incidents. Looking at it now, I can understand why. It is a vivid depiction of a true event, combining factual detail with drama and action, but perhaps it is *too* naturalistic. This war, the First World War, shattered old certainties and traditions, and afterwards nothing would look the same again. A break was needed. Younger artists like Paul Nash and Christopher Nevinson responded with a bold and brutal language of hard edges and Cubist forms that resonate to this day. They provide the narrative thread in the galleries upstairs.

Joe simply didn't shock enough.

It is the abiding paradox of camouflage: that it is as much about standing out as blending in. But why do I mention camouflage? Because I see it in *A Ration Party*, how every form is blended and layered, how brushstrokes merge and mingle. I see it in all Joe's paintings and drawings from the time, and I can read about it, too, in his archive, sealed away in another part of this museum.

It's as if Joe left a trail of breadcrumbs for me to follow him back through time, but still he is elusive. How to distinguish between art and camouflage, and should I even try? As I make my way upstairs into daylight, I linger for a moment in the crowded ground-floor galleries, and now I'm thinking about camouflage, of course, I can see it everywhere. There are Spitfires hanging, trucks abandoned, artillery everywhere, all decked out in wildly disruptive patterns. It is hard to imagine any of them blending into a background, yet *this* is what most people know to be camouflage: fractal greens, browns and greys arranged in a seemingly chaotic pattern.

'I very well remember at the beginning of the war being with Picasso on the boulevard Raspail when the first camouflaged truck passed. It was at night, we had heard of camouflage but we had not yet seen it and Picasso amazed looked at it and then cried out yes it is we who have made it, that is cubism.'[2]

These words, written by the poet Gertrude Stein, have done much to contribute to the popular idea that Cubism gave birth to camouflage. But appearances can be deceptive. From what I've read and seen, it was the traditional artists who shaped this story, which became Joe's story. Take, for example, Solomon J. Solomon: he was a Royal Academician, a history painter and portraitist whose approach to camouflage was firmly realist. Solomon stressed that only the artist skilled at modelling could understand camouflage. More than that, Solomon was working from the theories of another renowned portrait and landscape painter, the American Abbott Handerson Thayer.

Thayer has been called the 'father of camouflage'. He is best known for his paintings of idealised beauty – ethereal women and children – but he sought the same purity and beauty in nature, and it was his close observation of the natural world that led him to deduce two theories of what he called 'Concealing Colouration'. Thayer saw how many birds and animals were darkly coloured on the back – where they received the most sunlight – and paler on the shadowy regions of their underside, which afforded them greater protection. He also noticed how the disruptive markings of certain animals, such as spots and stripes, helped to disguise their contours. Such ideas were clearly in Solomon's mind when he wrote to *The Times* on the subject of uniforms and colour, and there's evidence that both the French and the British referred to Thayer's book, *Concealing Coloration in the Animal Kingdom*, published in 1909.

Thayer was eager to assist the military after the First World War broke out and travelled to England in 1915, having persuaded his old friend and respected painter John Singer Sargent to fix a meeting at the British War Office. However, Thayer was a nervous type who buckled when confronted with any kind of criticism. After touring the country he left Sargent to attend in his place, equipped with a suitcase containing a decrepit hunting jacket, to which he'd attached painted rags, fabric swatches and his wife's stockings. It was not a million miles away from the 'Ghillie suit' of the Lovat Scouts, but to Sargent, it was an obscenity. ('A bundle of rags!' he later fumed. 'I wouldn't have touched it with my *stick!*'[3])

Thayer's interest in visual representation – his knowledge of light and shade and the tricks of preception – could have made him receptive to Cubism and its fractured forms, but when he first encountered it at the Armory Show of 1913 he was outraged. Like Solomon, and like Joe, Thayer saw it as an affront to all that he valued.

Solomon had made his name with history paintings, and when that fell out of fashion had turned to portraiture. He was fifty-four when the war broke out and the energy he devoted to camouflage could be seen as a defence against changing tastes in art. This, after all, is a man who regularly lambasted the silly rebellions of the avant-garde and made it perfectly clear his deciphering of German camouflage 'was a triumph of classical perspective over *modern* deception'.[4]

It's interesting, then, to consider camouflage not as a by-product of Cubism but a refusal or rebuttal of it. The head of the French 'service de camouflage', Guirand de Scévola, was himself a trad-itional painter. True, he recruited all schools of artists into his unit, from Impressionists (whose interest in changing atmospheric effects undoubtedly served them well) to Cubists, such as Jacques Villon and André Mare. But it was Guirand de Scévola who took the credit for a patterning technique applied to artillery that became known as 'zébrage' and bore a likeness to Cubism, and he insisted that his invention was by no means a homage. Cubism fractured and flattened the figure to reveal its every facet, whereas camouflage did the opposite: 'To deform totally the appearance of an object,' he wrote, 'I had employed the means by which the Cubists used to represent it.'[5]

Yet if camouflage blurred the line between traditional and avant-garde, then it's the example of dazzle painting that is the most compelling. Dazzle painting was the brainchild of Norman Wilkinson, a professional marine painter who, like Joe, had worked as a popular illustrator and whose work was regularly published in the *Illustrated London News* before the start of the war. Whilst Joe went into the Army, Wilkinson had joined the Navy. Having worked on submarine patrols in the Dardanelles, Gallipoli and Gibraltar, Wilkinson had taken charge of a mine-sweeping launch in Devonport in 1917.

Knowing how effective submarines could be at tracking targets, he hit upon a novel idea for ship camouflage: 'since it was impossible to paint a ship so that she could not be seen by a submarine, the extreme opposite was the answer – in other words to paint her, not for low visibility, but in such a way to break up her form and thus confuse a submarine officer as to the course on which she was taking.'[6]

The proposed method, named dazzle painting, obliterated the contours of the ship by applying irregular blocks of strongly contrasting colours, 'consequently making it a matter of difficulty for a submarine to decide on the exact course of the vessel to be attacked'.[7]

It was striking in theory and in practice, and Wilkinson was, thankfully, very practical. Like Guirand de Scévola, he was already inside the military machine when he hit upon his plan, and after securing the approval of the Admiralty he was able to use studios at the Royal Academy schools and enlist the help of fellow artists. By the start of 1918, some 4,400 vessels had been painted with dazzle camouflage. These eye-catching designs with their energetic zigzags and repeated diagonals shared a likeness to both Cubism and the style of the Vorticists – the British answer to Italy's Futurists – and Wilkinson had been quick to recruit the prominent Vorticist Edward Wadsworth to his project.

The effectiveness of dazzle camouflage (or 'Razzle Dazzle' as some called it) wasn't easy to prove, but it was adopted by the Americans with enthusiasm and swiftly secured a place in the popular imagination. In 1919 the Chelsea Arts Club even held a 'Great Dazzle Ball' in its honour, where much was made of the unlikely combination of art, fashion and the military. 'Four British naval officers, distinguished for their success at camouflage, had charge of designing the dresses, and the ballroom looked like the Grand Fleet with all its warpaint on, ready for action. Who could have thought a dozen years ago, when the Secessionists began to secede and the Cubists began to cube, that soon all governments would be subsidizing this new form of art to the extent of millions a year?'[8]

Was camouflage really a 'new form of art'? Solomon and Guirand de Scévola emerged from the war with their traditional aesthetic intact, as indeed did Wilkinson. He'd go back to painting maritime subjects in an entirely realist vein, and looking at his works in the Imperial War Museum, there's no discernible break in style.

Perhaps then, camouflage made a neutral space where the academic and avant-garde could meet and try to make sense of each other. It allowed for temporary connections and collaborations. It cut across styles and and started conversations.

Norman Wilkinson did not yet know Joseph Gray, but their paintings were on display at the museum for a long time after Armistice, and Blaikley rated both. He viewed them as artists who had taken their direct experience of the war and created powerful records of the time.

Such records were still needed. As late as 1931 Blaikley was still fielding requests from artists, begging to have their work accessioned into the collection. He also offered advice to those seeking to commission new work. One morning he gave a gallery tour to a group of officers from the Sherwood Foresters. They had come to him to discuss their hopes for a series of paintings that would depict their regiment's involvement in different theatres of the war. As they paused for some time before *A Ration Party*, Blaikley suggested Joseph Gray would be a good fit for a Neuve Chapelle work. Norman Wilkinson, meanwhile, could paint the Dardanelles campaign.

Both artists were commissioned at the exact same time by the exact same regiment. This would be Joe's last war picture, his last faithful recreation of a battle now long past. But if the painting itself wasn't important, the connections it made were crucial.

Perhaps I am trying too hard to find the origins and explanations for the path Joe would soon take, but it was a small world, this art world and if Joe was beginning to wonder what use a traditional, representational war artist might be in this fast-changing world, he only had to look over his shoulder to see.

Or put another way: you don't neccesarily have to be a radical artist to have a radical idea.

E is for Enemy: keep him in doubt
  When you must make a mess what that mess
                                      is about

Dear Blaikley,

    It was nice of you to think of me when the painting
proposition was suggested to you, and it so happens that
at this moment I am again in touch with military folk and
I should be glad to undertake any commissions of this
description. In a few weeks I shall be taking a studio near
Kensington. I hope to meet you personally then and could
discuss the matter with you and with the army officers.[1]

The year was 1932; so many years had passed but it was still
the war, the war, the war.

Joseph Gray, once considered 'the Black Watch artist',[2] recognised by others now as an 'eminent etcher',[3] was trying to be both
and more, and he was moving to London to do it. A fresh start. A
clean state. Only it wasn't and couldn't be.

He had immersed himself in landscape and built up a decent
reputation as 'an etcher of the hills and sea',[4] travelling widely to
find fresh inpsiration. He had become a master of mood, of a
storm brewing or a dawn breaking. Blaikley had seen them reproduced in the various art magazines, where they had drawn much
praise. This, in fact, made him cautious. He wasn't sure how Joe

felt about returning to war subjects: 'It occurred to me that perhaps you might not feel inclined to execute this work. I know you have been doing work of a rather different nature lately?'[5] Yet Blaikley also knew that times were hard. Print-making had offered only the shortest-lived livelihood; the Crash of 1929 had seen to that.

Joe was trying his best to ride over the crisis, or at least give that impression. His reply to Blaikley was buoyant: 'I have recently once more turned to portraiture. At portraiture, particularly portraits of men, I have always been very successful, and it is primarily as a portrait painter that I am "setting up" in London.'[6]

Blaikley was surprised but then reasoned that it wasn't such a leap. Joe's war paintings had always contained portraits, after all – and very good ones at that. So there it was: Joseph Gray: Black Watch artist, eminent etcher, and now portrait painter.

A man forging his own destiny, or a slave to changing tastes in art? He was both, he was more and he was doing it with style. Joe had rented a studio at 33 Tite Street, Chelsea, an address he advertised proudly. It had the richest kind of history, the most glamorous associations that he hardly had to hint at. This was the building previously occupied by John Singer Sargent, one-time friend of Abbott Thayer. Sargent had been a great realist painter and renowned portraitist, the man responsible for the vast and iconic *Gassed*, a stand-out masterpiece of the last war.

No wonder Joe looked pleased when he greeted Blaikley and Lieutenant Colonel Wilkinson from the Sherwood Foresters. The three men stood together, admiring the pilaster-lined walls and high ceilings, the fall of a cold October light through the vast arched window. The bite in the air didn't matter, since the past encircled them, glittering and warm. A decade ago all manner of the great and good had come here in search of immortality, to have their portraits painted by Mr Sargent. Joe just needed a fraction of his success. He paced the room and spoke confidently and easily, showing off various examples of his work and describing the rigours of his process. He listed recent commissions and name-dropped indiscriminately.

'That was a £750 picture but of course I can do anything from £10 upwards.'

Did that sound a little desperate? One had to be careful not to sound *too* eager. They quickly turned to the subject of Neuve Chapelle. Joe furrowed his brow, nodding thoughtfully as he listened to the brief. He was clearly the right man for the job.

The war, the war, the war – how it now encircled them. John Shann Wilkinson had enjoyed an illustrious career with the Sherwood Foresters, serving in India, Africa, Ireland, and latterly the War Office. He'd be back there soon enough, in fact, and promoted to brigadier. It felt somewhat disconcerting to be arranging depictions of a war long past when another looked increasingly likely. Disarmament was constantly being redefined, and the inferior state of Britain's air defences was now called 'Britain's Air Peril'. In just one month's time Stanley Baldwin would raise the matter in Parliament: 'I think it is well also for the man in the street to realise that there is no power on earth that can protect him from being bombed. Whatever people may tell him, the bomber will always get through.'[7]

Joe's elegant sales patter did at least acknowledge current difficulties: 'The higher priced etching market is now under a cloud – particularly in America. My agents in Bond Street advise limitation of additions and plates so as to maintain prices.'[8]

This was what he told people but it wasn't strictly true. Harold Dickens, his so-called Bond Street agent, had cut him off in 1928 and would scrupulously record his own version of events: 'Gray's market had passed the boom – large stocks were coming into auction,' and, 'I told him I had not committed myself in any way – I had studiously avoided making any fuss of him when he was in London.'[9]

Joe glossed over such difficulties, as was now his way. 'I considered it advisable to change my publisher'[10] was all he ever said. As far as he could tell, everyone was lying to everyone else, pretending they had prospects when really there were none. Private patronage was dying out, the commerical galleries were closing, but an artist had to make his own opportunities. Joe would paint the Thames, he would paint Neuve Chapelle, he would paint any lord or general or bishop who knocked on his door. He clung to the world he recognised just when everyone else seemed to be shifting towards extremes.

Modernism had taunted Joe, Nazism terrified him. The war, the war, the war, it hadn't ever ended. It was only getting worse.

The year was 1934. Two more years of shrinking prospects. Nancy Gray, the artist's wife, was no longer acting a part. Unhappiness hung around her, a mix of bitterness and regret. She mostly blamed her husband for their current situation. She hadn't minded leaving her parents – London had offered better prospects than Dundee, a small town teetering on the brink of ruin – but Dundee now seemed safer, a world she knew. When Joe had convinced her to move south she'd been full of excitement. Until all their savings were gone. London had meant to offer fresh opportunities, new contacts, untold adventures. It hadn't come good on any of its promises and neither had her husband.

Tite Street had been an ideal, but the reality of living lay else-where. The Sutherland Hotel, a converted Edwardian town house near Paddington Station, had become their 'temporary lodgings' for the last two years. Nancy would never adjust but Joe tried not to notice. He kept piling on the promises, and she would pace back and forth in their ground-floor room like a tigress in a cage. Joe reasoned it was not such an unpleasant sort of place but Nancy assured him it could never feel like home, and having recently been 'men only', there had been audible mutterings over whether it was an appropriate setting to bring up a child.

Nobody knew what to do with young Maureen. Nobody knew what to do at all.

It wasn't the memories of the war that so haunted Nancy but this lingering and disappointing aftermath. She knew they weren't starving, but here they were with no prospects and no security. Joe had managed to secure a few portrait commissions, but the last one, *Lord Brocket in His Garter Robes*, was never paid for in full. Brocket had died suddenly, leaving a Nazi sympathiser son who wouldn't honour his father's commitments. How Joe fumed. The world was going to ruin.

'You must give up Tite Street.'

Nancy wasn't trying to be cruel – she merely wanted Joe to see the world for what it was. She wanted him to accept there was no more room for dreaming. For once Joe did as he was told, but as he crammed his easels and canvases into the room they shared, it only seemed to enforce the sense of homelessness. Joseph Gray, the indefatigable optimist, was slowly losing his faith. He had fought hard against fashion and now, when he looked in the galleries on

Bond Street, he saw nothing he recognised. The Surrealists and Abstractionists were busy making waves with an elite group of collectors to support them. What did they understand of the real world?

'War means Air War and that Air War means inescapable and horrible death to hundreds and thousands, or millions.'[11]

Rarely a day went by when he didn't read it somewhere. Nancy felt he was becoming obsessed by it, but debating the world situation distracted him from his personal problems, and at least she didn't have to endure it. She had taken on the role of breadwinner, having been lucky to find work with a barrister at Lincoln's Inn. Of course, returning home each evening, she never felt lucky. She began to avoid Joe. If Maureen had been there it might have been different, but Maureen had gone.

It had seemed like a sensible plan: one of the residents of the Sutherland knew a family in Herne Bay who were willing to take another child. Nancy and Joe considered it a better environment for their daughter.

'They have a young girl the same age as you, and there is a very good school nearby. You could be sisters.'

Maureen was a shy child held back by a quite considerable deafness. Joe blamed himself for that – he had always been a little deaf, and the war had only made him more so.

'You must not let that stop you or slow you down,' he assured her. 'Just like me, you will make good friends.'

They went together to inspect this new home, a new possible family and school.

Maureen held tight to her father's hand, but she rather liked the idea of having a sibling and she was made to feel very welcome.

Joe knew it was safer, better. For a small weekly sum his little girl could be taken care of. She'd have security and stability – two things her parents couldn't give her. Herne Bay was certainly a pleasant place, with clear sea air and a beach and esplanade. Joe loved Maureen so much it made him ache, but he was sure it was the right decision. They walked to the clock tower, then on to the pier.

'I will visit at weekends or you will come to us. I will write and send you postcards. Mind you do the same.'

Staring out at the flat, grey sea, Joe promised Maureen that everything would come right. He still believed it would. Nancy, back at the Sutherland, wasn't as sure.

Maureen didn't realise then but something very precious was coming to an end.

'We would never live together as a family again.'

Poor Joe. Denial means many things: it is a refusal to admit the truth, the blocking out of difficult facts, and it is also a form of protection. For Joe, denial was essential to his survival. He *had* to believe his luck would change. He knocked on doors and telephoned magazines, hoping to find commercial work. He didn't give up, although the sad fact was he had lost his daughter. Did he realise he was losing his wife as well? To anyone who looked long enough, the signs were already there: it was in the tilt of her head as she turned away, it was in every word she didn't say aloud.

Poor Nancy. She had fallen in love with Joe because he was passionate, exciting and, yes, a bit of a dreamer. Now, the very things that had drawn her to him made their lives so impossible. It was hard not to feel duped, a little betrayed, by her own desires as much as his. She was facing facts even if he couldn't. She knew Joe loved her, but it wasn't enough. Love, in fact, seemed to complicate everything.

They were as stubborn as each other, and as unhappy, and so they avoided talking about it. What could that possibly achieve? No. Instead they needed distractions, to escape their unhappiness with the world and each other, and so they stayed together but grew apart. Each night followed the same pattern now there wasn't a child to tend to: they'd sit at different ends of the residents' lounge. Joe passed the hours reading and rereading the newspapers. Nancy channelled her energy into a new-found love of bridge.

Bridge is a complicated game of memory and skill, it requires practice and focus, and it has one defining trait – the hand you are dealt does not automatically decree how successful you will be. Nancy played constantly and ruthlessly, but her success was not singular. Bridge, after all, is also a game of pairs. She found herself an equally talented partner.

Dick Orr-Ewing was another long-term resident of the Sutherland Hotel. He was charming and clever, with just a dash of the exotic mixed with the heroic. He was born in Jamalpur and christened Arthur George Ewing, had served in the King Edward's Horse, been made a lieutenant and awarded an MBE for his sevice in Iraq. After the war, Dick had gone to Cambridge and trained as an engineer, which is when he'd dropped in the 'Orr-' to his name, perhaps hoping to be confused with or mistaken for a baronet. Dick could out-bluff even Joe – he was full of tall tales from distant places, a bit of a self-created colonial fantasy, if you will – but his professional qualifications were true enough. He'd spent much of the last decade in Calcutta building dams and bridges and roads. He could speak several languages, and was regarded as quite the expert on the uses of reinforced concrete. But now, like everybody else, Dick was out of work and stranded at the Sutherland.

He had been one of the first residents Joe met and they'd formed a solid friendship, recognising in each other that shared survivor's spirit. And there was another connection: Joe had studied engineering before going to art school, the plan always being that he'd work as a ship's engineer and go to sea like his father. Unfortunately, Joseph Gray Senior had proved no kind of role model: a violent drunk who had crashed and sunk at least two ships, and had in fact died at sea. Joe became an artist to make himself anew. Did he regret his choices now? Perhaps. He saw something in Dick, a fragment of a self he might have been. The two men shared newspapers and discussed the inevitable, impending conflict. They knew it would be devastating. Dick had seen first-hand the impact of aerial bombing in Iraq. They talked and talked.

'Well, if there is another war, at least Dick will be employable. Everyone needs *engineers*.'

Nancy only had to say it once.

Joe measured out his reply.

'I have a plan,' he said.

And he did, he truly did.

The year was 1935. Not a good year for starting a new business, but they went ahead regardless. Joe and Nancy were now in partnership with Dick Orr-Ewing, producing greetings cards, of all things. It had been Joe's idea – and yes, it *was* part of his plan. Dick had put in a bit of money at the start, whilst Joe made the designs and used his contacts to have them printed. All three would then sell them door to door.

Maureen, a fleeting weekend visitor to the Sutherland, was baffled by the new enterprise. Because of her deafness there was plenty she didn't hear, and living apart from her parents, there was still more she didn't see. There were now so many gaps in the puzzle they had become, but she loved them all the more for it, and she imagined them quite without flaws or imperfections. Her mother seemed especially lively now – smiling and vivacious.

Clearly Dick Orr-Ewing brought out the best in people. It was important, Maureen felt sure, to band together when times were so difficult. She admired these three adults for not giving up, for finding a way through, and it was even better when they tried to include her. Dick had suggested she make her own little design to be sent to the printers, and she had sketched a cat, a small cat asleep in front of a fireplace. A nice domestic image.

Yet something wasn't right about this picture.

Their business, Ray's Prints, wasn't going to make anyone rich. Joe had thought it a good plan, but it wasn't *the* plan. No. If anything, this new venture was a stop-gap, a cover story. Joe could sketch out a few card designs in five minutes. What truly occupied him took up a lot more time.

'No attempt is made in these pages to consider every aspect of the subject, but the writer has endeavoured to indicate the more important aspects of it, and to discover those possible lines of advance most promising of results in view of modern aerial developments.'

When Maureen first read the notes she didn't understand them.

'The writer is, he believes, the only British artist closely identified with military circles since 1918. He has maintained his study of military matters and has been particularly interested in the increasing power of the aerial offensive.'[12]

Maureen read on. 'The writer makes no claim to specialised military knowledge beyond that acquired as a temporary soldier, and subsequently as a civilian student of military matters, but he has also had a practical training, as before adopting art as a profession, he studied engineering for three years.'[13]

Maureen pulled away. Her father had studied engineering? She never even knew. She wanted to ask him, but he wasn't there. Joe was becoming very good at disappearing. One minute he'd be hunched over his old typewriter and then he'd be off doing 'research' at some secret location. It was all very mysterious, and it was also quite annoying.

Maureen watched the clock in the hotel lounge; she watched it and she waited. She wanted to see her father. Nancy and Dick didn't seem to mind his long absences, but she did. She was going to ask him what he was doing; what was taking up so much of his time and taking him away from her.

When he finally appeared in the lobby, laden down with papers, he looked thoroughly exhausted. His expression only brightened when his daughter ran towards him.

'Ah! There you are!'

She loved that his mood lifted so swiftly.

'But I have to go soon,' she warned.

He nodded as if he knew, as if there was already a secret between them. 'Let's walk.'

Joe loved to walk, to be outside, but Maureen was conscious of the time ticking by, and the train that would take her back to Herne Bay. Her father seemed to understand and was already propelling her out of the door.

'Let's take a turn around the square, shall we?'

He glanced behind him for a second, as if to check something.

'How nice to have some time together, just you and I.'

Norfolk Square is not a square, in fact, but a long and elegant rectangle bordered with tall plane trees. Joe walked quickly, rapping his old stick on the railings as they went.

Maureen walked by his side, looking and feeling serious. There were questions she wanted to ask him, but she wasn't sure exactly how. These were times when so much went unspoken, when nobody wanted to give voice to their worst fears.

Still, she quickened her pace and made her confession.

'I read some of your notes, Dad. I hope you don't mind.'

Joe cast his eyes downwards.

'So you know my secret.'

But she didn't, not really, not then.

'Will there be another war?' she asked.

Her father stopped in his tracks. He nodded. 'There is a real danger, yes. I'm sure you have heard that already. But we can do things, we can find ways to protect ourselves. There are different ways to fight . . .'

Maureen nodded like she understood.

'Your notes . . . what are you going to do with them?'

Joe opened his eyes wide. 'Well, I am writing a book. I am going to send it to the War Office as soon as I can.'

Maureen blinked. A book? The War Office?

Joe was walking ahead of her. 'I happen to know a chap there.'

Maureen nodded to herself and took a deep breath.

The square looked glorious in the dying sun, the trees casting the most spindly, haunting shadows. Maureen stared at her father's back. He lifted his head and looked skywards like he always did.

He usually had some little observation, he'd notice some small detail and point it out to her. But now he stayed silent, lost in his own world.

Then he turned. 'Tell me, what do you think of Orr-Ewing?'

Maureen found she had to think for a minute before she replied. 'I like him very much. Why?'

Joe nodded, sniffed. 'No reason.' He turned back to the path and they carried on walking.

'Touch of the tar-brush, I reckon.'

Maureen wanted to ask what he meant by that. It was a strange thing to say. But her father was gazing up at the trees. A gentle breeze lifted their leaves and he had stopped, narrowing his eyes to study this small movement.

Maureen walked around him, opened her mouth to speak, but he raised a hand to shush her. She followed his eyes and waited for him to tell her what it was he'd spotted. He didn't. He stayed entirely silent.

Not for the first or last time, Maureen wondered what it was that her father saw so clearly, that she herself couldn't see.

F *is for False Work, which will serve to distract*
The enemy's eye from the genuine fact

Camouflage and Air Defence exists in several forms. Its ageing, crumpled sheets escape out of the cardboard folder that holds it. It looks fragile to the touch, with some pages creased and folded. There are typing mistakes and handwritten annotations in pencil and red ink, exclamation marks and underlinings. The two copies held in the Imperial War Museum are not identical. 'Copy No. 4' has this written across it: 'not published at request of Brigadier J. S. Wilkinson, on behalf of General Staff. 1936'.

John Shann Wilkinson. The connections are there to be made. The last man to commission Joe as a war artist was the first man to consider him a future camoufleur.

Camouflage and Air Defence a draft for a proposed book by Major (then Mr.) Joseph Gray, was submitted to General Staff, War Office by the author through me towards the end of 1935. I was then Deputy Director of Movements and Quartering and interested in Passive Defence. Mr. Gray's work was an exhaustive study of the possible utilisation of Camouflage as defence against modern air attack. The author particularly stressed the necessity of developing big scale static camouflage and decoy operations.[1]

Wilkinson was impressed and circulated the manuscript to other members of the War Office, and to the Committee of Imperial Defence, the Home Office and the Air Ministry.

Joe had been writing it in earnest for several months and researching it for even longer, and he had been doing so right here, in the Imperial War Museum. Maureen had wondered where her father was always disappearing to and now I am able to offer an explanation. He had a secret love, a new obsession – and her name was camouflage.

It had been over a decade since Joe had been given his first tour of the museum stores by Ernest Blaikley. Back then his sole objective was to make his paintings more authentic, to have every detail real and right. But now he was looking for every instance where reality had been made to lie.

'I told Blaikley I was making a study of camouflage and thus asked to see all the related objects; from the netting and painted screens, to the observation posts and sniper's capes. I knew that much had been salvaged from the Front and not just from the British side.'[2] Joe wanted first to acquire a broad sweep of knowledge, because after that he would dive into the detail. He asked to see books, pamphlets, reports, and most important of all, all those aerial photographs that Blaikley himself had catalogued after Armistice. 'Although I had done no flying I was very familiar with the landscape viewed from heights as I climbed regularly in Scotland, and had spent time in the Pyrenees.'[3] Joe wanted to look again at the world from above and try to understand it.

If Blaikley was initially surprised by Joe's new project, he was quick to lend his support. By 1935 most people accepted that another war was coming. Throughout the 1930s the theory of a 'knock-out blow' had taken hold, with writers predicting an air assault of enemy bombers. There would be none of the atrophying siege-style battles of the last war, fought on some distant land over the water. It would happen quickly, striking at major cities, disabling the industrial areas and docklands. Of course London was the obvious target: the greatest city in the world but also the most vulnerable, containing one fifth of the British population. So what could be done? There was a clamour for more air power as a counter force, and the RAF was being expanded, but Joe wasn't alone in arguing that the best defence wasn't simply offence.

It wasn't too late to start hiding things, even very large things. In the last war Joe had shown himself adept at personal camouflage. Hiding one man was very different to hiding a factory or even a city. Nonetheless, he was going to try.

He began writing *Camouflage and Air Defence* as a call to arms, but not in the conventional sense. Britain couldn't match Germany in fighting forces – the expansion of the Luftwaffe was becoming the stuff of legend – but he hoped to show that there were other ways to fight. Camouflage could be a powerful defensive weapon. It could surprise the enemy, offer greater secrecy to troop movements at home and in the field, and 'aid the protection of the civilian population and maintain their morale under strain'.[4]

This latter part was crucial. Joe was thinking about urban centres, docks and factories, our vital resources. He was thinking about home and civil defence. Camouflage in the last war had had a very different focus. Now, with the 'increasing power of the aerial offensive and mechanisation of modern armies',[5] it was vital to develop new strategies *and* materials. He admitted to be looking into 'a new type of camouflage prepared as a permanent feature of the building . . . an accessory ready for immediate fixture'.[6] He wanted to create fake landscapes to hide the real ones. It had to be bold, ambitious and different, since all previous methods were known to the enemy and therefore redundant, or only possibly useful as decoys: 'old methods should be used in a subtle manner to mislead and decoy'.[7] Yes, right from the start, 'development of false areas and decoy vital points' would be key to drawing enemy fire. 'An enemy bombing fleet confronted with three possible objectives where one was anticipated must attack all if there is to be any assurance of success.'[8] It wasn't just about hiding, but creating doubt and diffusing every threat.

Camouflage and Air Defence opens with an explanation of the principles and practicalities of creating good structural covers, with chapters 1 and 2 dealing with, first, shadows (and how to lose them) and then colour. A lesson in 'the Perspective of Shadows' is clearly indebted to Solomon J. Solomon. Joe states any man-made structure is betrayed by the shadows it makes. 'The object of constructive camouflage, therefore, is to mislead the enemy by concealing the true shape and position of a vital point, losing it in its surroundings.'[9] The camoufleur must focus on toning down and blending in, to avoid 'false' or 'betraying shadow'. Joe reminds us time and again: 'there are no actual lines in nature – only tones'[10] and in any scheme, the camoufleur must consider not just 'the bombing airman' but 'a skilled aerial photograph reader of the enemy Intelligence'.[11]

Chapter 2 addresses the problem of colour – and it *is* a problem. Joe warns about past camouflage methods and in particular the use of paint. 'Nothing could be more helpful to the diving bomber than obviously false colour values or the use of some variations of the old striped or daubed roof camouflage painting.'[12] He makes the point that old camouflage patterns could only work 'for guns in the field as they are moved from place to place',[13] but are largely useless when considering static sites. He also shows examples of German camouflage, pointing out that the 'Germans wisely never depended on painted design alone unless the object was movable such as a gun'.[14]

How then to hide? Chapter 3 is devoted exclusively to the smokescreen. Joe thought smokescreens had huge potential (as indeed would Winston Churchill). Smokescreens could be summoned quickly to obscure large areas – ideal for cities or industrial areas. (There was also a precedent as the French had used smokescreens over Paris in the last war to good effect). Time and again, Joe stresses that complete cover isn't essential: 'The ideal camouflage system for concealing vital points and misleading the enemy would be a combination of constructive camouflage and *slight* smoke screen.'[15]

He wants to make it clear that concealment is not everything, and placing *too* great an emphasis on hiding things misses another opportunity: that is 'misdirection'.

Chapter 4 tackles this in more detail, looking at the creation of 'false areas' or decoys, and also 'the camouflage of natural features'. Joe considers various ways to throw an enemy pilot off course. If, for example, the pilot was working off a map and looking for a particular river or area of woodland to guide him towards his target, it might be easier and cheaper to obscure *that* feature than the actual target. The message comes across loud and clear: much could be done to 'blind' and 'mislead' enemy planes. It might not prevent an attack altogether, but it could cause vital delays and wastage of bombs. He examines specific examples, such as aerodromes and military depots, discusses methods of changing orientation, hiding roads and creating 'false woods', making fake roads out of canvas, or altering the course of a railroad with a dummy junction and false tracks.

It's understandable that Joe devotes so much time to civil or home defence as this is where he saw an urgent need, but he also looks further. In another chapter he addresses the problems with the Army in the field, that is artillery, kit and even uniform. His advice is grounded in his own battle experience. 'The writer suggests that the present infantry pack is too regular and the flat top, being almost horizontal, catches the light.'[16] He reminds everyone that 'mathematical accuracy' could be 'very conspicuous', which is a clear lesson learned from the trenches.

There is more – so much more. *Camouflage and Air Defence* starts off as a call to arms but becomes an exhaustive study, complete with photographs and diagrams, references to past examples and future predictions. Joe is brimming over with ideas, yet concedes that his research is incomplete. He submits the manuscript as a matter of urgency, and doesn't draw any positive conclusions. He makes it clear that there has been a long period of apathy, and whatever sophisticated methods the British now devise, the Germans will be doing the same, or possibly more and better.

'The German painter has never been distinguished in the history of the fine arts as a creative artist, but he was always outstanding for attention to technical details, painstaking research, the earnest study of visual laws and the scientific aspects of this craft. These are the qualities most necessary to the military designer.'[17]

Britain *has* to raise her game, before it is too late.

Wilkinson took notice, and when he circulated *Camouflage and Air Defence* the response was positive. Brigadier Arthur Sayer, president of the Royal Engineers and Signals Board, was uncharacteristically enthusiastic. He judged much of the book 'sound and valuable',[18] as did Colonel John Turner, director of Works and Buildings at the Air Ministry. As the man responsible for Britain's expanding airfields, Turner was already agitating for a national camouflage scheme, so Joe's suggestions were music to his ears.

In July 1935 the Home Office had issued its first set of proposals for Air Raid Precautions and it was agreed that camouflage could be used passively. Yet there was no unified policy. Joe felt his ideas were right on target, and they were, only this was now a problem.

Wilkinson summoned Joe to his offices on Horse Guards Avenue and asked him outright about his plans for this manuscript. Joe explained that he was busy revising and finessing it in order to send it to publishers. He believed that *Camouflage and Air Defence* would make 'a successful if controversial book',[19] and could even be serialised in the newspapers.

Wilkinson was aghast.

'But you simply cannot publish. A great many of your ideas may be used. What if it fell into enemy hands?'

Joe didn't have an answer. Had he naively imagined that he could serve the national interest, find a new audience *and* make some money? Wilkinson immediately made it clear that this would not be the case. The copies in circulation would remain confidential, to be used only by approved personnel.

Wilkinson consoled Joe with the assurance he had done them all a great service, and that there was no doubt many of his ideas would be used.

This gave Joe the opportunity he needed.

'Well then, if my ideas on camouflage are going to prove so useful, might I suggest that I myself could also be useful?'

It was what he'd hoped for. *Camouflage and Air Defence* was a thorough study and a call to action, but it was also a job application.

Nothing happened as quickly as he hoped. In the summer of 1936 the Committee of Imperial Defence approved the installation of a defensive barrage of 450 balloons across London's skyline. Such singular initiatives highlighted the desperate need to take action elsewhere. How to defend cities and vital sites against the threat of bombing, and what would be done by whom, would soon become critical questions. It wasn't until October 1936 that a Camouflage Sub-Committee was established, its aim to develop new methods for 'passive defence'.[20] It would be another year before the newly formed Camouflage Research Establishment (CRE) came into being. It was only then that Joe was finally called for interview.

Based at Farnborough in Hampshire and headed by Francis Wyatt, now a lieutenant colonel, the CRE was tasked with hiding factories and the like – what became known as 'static camouflage'. Having been director of Camouflage in the last war, Wyatt had a practical outlook and 'was not obsessed with the idea that camouflage can be indiscriminately applied to every building'.[21] Whatever his memories of Solomon J. Solomon, he accepted that artists were invaluable in developing good strategies. The good camoufleur needed 'a trained facility for painting and drawing' and had to be adept at 'translating and memorizing that appearance of ground as seen from the air in terms of colour, tone and texture'. Furthermore, a bit of 'imagination and ingenuity' were essential for creating designs that were practical and economical.[22]

Wyatt was impressed by Joe on paper and in person: here was a man who possessed the right skills and knowledge and had war experience, but when called back a second time before a panel, Joe's deafness let him down. The room had a terrible echo and he couldn't hear the questions.

Rejection was frustrating, but it wasn't the end. After all, you don't *hear* camouflage. Joe was determined to find another way in.

In the early months of 1938 he was summoned to the Royal Engineers and Signals Board (RESB) in Melbourne House in London's Aldwych. Here he found an eccentric collection of characters and departments, headed by Brigadier Sayer, a famously austere figure who never wore an overcoat, even on the coldest of days. Sayer's staff were both devoted to and terrified of him, and amongst their number was a Scot named Charles Le Breton-Simmons. Simmons had served in Egypt, Gallipoli and France and was now in charge of the new Camouflage Section. (He was, in fact, its only member.) He was also as deaf as Joe, so it's difficult to imagine how the interview began, but it concluded with Simmons appointing Joe as his 'camouflage draughtsman' on a salary of £288 per annum.

Nancy was relieved to learn her husband was finally employed, but for Joe it wasn't enough. He found himself making detailed copies of old camouflage sketches, writing up notes on 'how to garnish nets' and replicating camouflage patterns to be applied to bits of artillery. There was much repetition and no innovation – exactly the thing he had warned against in *Camouflage and Air Defence*. He clashed with Le Breton-Simmons over this, but Simmons reminded Joe that they could only work within their resources. It was time, Joe decided, to push all of their 'resources'.

And time was drawing on. There was an ever-growing list of 'vulnerable' and 'vital' sites in need of attention, everything from factories and commercial oil installations, to wireless and cable systems. As 1938 advanced, Hitler's ambitions grew: Austria was annexed, triggering the Sudetenland Crisis. Chamberlain's attempts at appeasement did little to allay a growing sense of anxiety. CRE began testing out different camouflage patterns and types of paint, which only demonstrated the wide range of problems: the varying quality of paint, issues of shine and glare. In the meantime, Joe's small department was overwhelmed with work.

The Air Ministry established its own civil camouflage department at Adastral House – opposite Joe's workplace on Aldwych. The building contained a large studio and viewing room where Britain's key industrial sites could be painted and looked at from different angles. Artist Lancelot Glasson was appointed as head. Glasson had served as one of Wyatt's camoufleurs in the last war and lost a leg at Ypres. He began recruiting fellow artists, favouring those who had experience of flying, amongst them Gilbert Solomon, a former pilot in the Royal Flying Corps and nephew of Solomon J. Solomon.

At RESB Joe and Simmons also began seeking out artists with past military experience. Freddie Beddington was one of the first. The dapper and debonaire Beddington was now in his forties and working in the City, but he had been a sharpshooter on the Western Front and after Armistice studied under Henry Tonks at the Slade. On top of this he had excellent connections. His brother, the equally suave Jack Beddington, was the publicity manager of Shell, which had, throughout the 1930s, saved many struggling artists from penury by giving them design work. He now set out to save more by suggesting them to his brother as potential camoufleurs.

Connections were there to be used. Jack Sayer, a commerical artist and cousin of the brigadier, and Johnny Churchill, a muralist and the nephew of the soon-to-be prime minister, were also brought in to RESB, although the latter's appointment was pure serendipity:

> The War Office had thought it a good idea to open a department for studying camouflage. They called in Major Simmons, a regular soldier who was deaf. Then they summoned Joseph Gray, an artist who had been in the war as a private in the Black Watch and had written a remarkable account of the strategic possibilities of the subject . . . he was deaf too. I happened to be extraordinarily lucky when applying for work in this department because in walked a very important gentleman from Ordnance who wanted advice about concealing his factory. He was deaf as well, and his deaf-aid machine would not work. Thus my first unofficial military job was shouting out and then writing down secret information about his factory while Simmons and Gray 'Whatted?' their heads off.[23]

Recruitment sped up once Captain Richard Buckley joined the panel, though his interview methods left much to be desired. The wildly mercurial Buckley had experience of camouflage from the last war and saw it as a visual art, yet when confronted with well-known artists he preferred to bark out less obvious questions – enquiring, for instance, whether they had done any hunting, shooting or fishing. Film-maker Geoffrey Barkas, put forward by Jack Beddington, was only accepted because he had seen active service. The Surrealist painter Julian Trevelyan had already started designing camouflage schemes as a civilian to earn some money, but found it was his love of sailing that swung it for Buckley. A keen sailor, Buckley's frown finally lifted.

It was a crazy world, this world of camouflage, and it was fast filling up with unusual characters. Joe fitted right in – how could he not? He was one of the first and so he helped to shape it. But there was still so much to do. Camouflage had thrown him a life-line and now it was to be his creed and his cause. It could even be his muse and his mistress.

Except. Except.

He already had one.

Because camouflage didn't just give Joe a fresh lease of life.

It allowed him to make a new one.

G *is for Garnishing, this should be wound*
To copy the texture and tone of the ground

'There are not many materials suitable for constructional camouflage purposes, light enough in weight to be portable, close enough
in texture to conceal . . .'

Maureen had stared at the torn scrap of paper, the muddle of
words. It made no sense. Then her father had lifted it from her
hands and turned it over.

'Look here.'

There was a name and address.

'Miss Mary Meade,

The Needlewoman,

18 Henrietta Street.'

'Go and talk to this Miss Meade,' he had said. 'She needs an
office girl. She is expecting you.'

Maureen had memorised the address, folding the scrap of paper
into her coat pocket, and presented herself for interview. How
quickly she'd grown up. Now seventeen, she was old enough to
earn her keep, a terrifying but liberating prospect. Nancy had
found her a room in a house in Raynes Park, and Joe had found
her this job. They wanted her to be independent, but Maureen was
still cripplingly shy. It was difficult to imagine how she might
negotiate her way in any London office.

How lucky then that Joe knew somebody. Joe always seemed to

know somebody. Maureen supposed her father had contacts in every office in the country. She didn't think to ask quite how he knew anyone at a woman's magazine, but her father was full of surprises.

'Are you interested in art? Do you visit exhibitions?'

The question came out of nowhere. Miss Meade ('Oh please, do call me Mary') was leaning over a large table, wielding a large pair of scissors and examining a new dress pattern. She peered across the office at Maureen, fine eyebrows arched.

'I just saw a most interesting exhibition at Shell Mex House. You should see it. Do you like art?'

Maureen sat rigid before her typewriter. She had been there a matter of weeks and this Miss Meade, *Mary*, was always asking questions. It was a little off-putting, but Mary was rather a bohemian sort, and Maureen knew it was rude not to answer. Did she like art? She thought of her various attempts at drawing at the Sutherland, of her father always scraping around for money, the years of frustration and uncertainty.

'It is a simple question.'

Mary straightened up, cradling the scissors in her long and elegant hands. She was tall and thin, with roughened brown hair framing a pale face more handsome than beautiful.

'I was thinking, because of your family. Your father is an artist, after all. That must be interesting.'

Maureen pressed her fingers on the edge of the desk. It seemed important that she summon a decent response.

She took a breath.

'I don't think artists should have families.'

It was a shocking comment now that she heard it out loud. She had surprised herself, and apparently everyone else. The whole office had fallen silent.

Mary released the scissors.

'My dear. What *do* you mean?'

Maureen could feel herself blushing, but she had to carry on.

'I *mean*, artists should not marry and have families . . . since they simply never have the means to support them.'

'Ah!' Mary nodded lightly. 'I see.' She sucked in her lips. 'It isn't an easy life, I agree.'

Maureen noticed a strange look pass between her colleagues. She felt so very mortified. What a thing to blurt out. With burning cheeks she ducked her head and carried on typing, reminding herself to hold her tongue in future.

Yet the evidence lay just a few yards away, recorded in a slim appointments diary, a dark ox-blood leather, now tattered and bruised and resting in my palm. Joe had taken Mary to that exhibition she'd just mentioned.

Mary Meade, or rather *Katherine* Mary Meade, was a careful keeper of diaries. She had made detailed entries of all her goings-on ever since she was a girl. Since working at *The Needlewoman* she had favoured preferred smaller journals adorned with pithy proverbs:

'*Let the shipwrecks of others be your sea marks.*'

'*Get a move on, procrastination causes loss.*'

She never did heed them. From January 1937 the word 'Gray' hovers on every other page, swiftly reduced to a 'G'. He is marked at least once during the week and always at the weekends. There is often an 'X' beside it, but nothing more, which is unusual since Mary generally wrote detailed entries for everything and everyone. And so already it's a secret, recorded by the most minimal of means. 'X' marks the spot, where the treasure was buried. Joe and Mary. They were always together; they couldn't bear to be apart.

Neither would ever reveal where or when they first met – most likely it was in Chelsea through artist friends. Joe hadn't been looking to fall in love, but he fell heavily and quickly, and it overlapped conveniently with his new area of research, his new preoccupation.

One form of camouflage had inspired another, or did both arise from a single impulse?

Joe was, at least, consistent.

Mary Meade, Miss Mary Meade. It's entirely understandable why she caught his artist's eye. She had the sort of face he liked to draw: a broad forehead and good cheekbones, a bold nose. All good angles. Everything about Mary felt original. She didn't follow fashion but made her own. Clever and cultured, she thought hard about things and formed her own opinions. She asked questions when other people stayed silent, and she wasn't afraid to show her feelings. She also loved art with a passion. Perhaps it was inevitable she would fall in love with an artist.

That she loved Joe is clear. She loved how he looked at the world; she loved his disarming sense of humour and his singularity, how he had survived so much without losing his head or his hope. They quickly developed their own little rhythm, meeting at private views in Chelsea galleries or the pubs on the Fulham Road – anywhere with a distinct or offbeat flavour – and established a network of mutual friends: open-minded, creative types such as the artists Charles McCall and James Proudfoot, the novelist Harold Freeman and his costume-designer wife Elisabeth Bödecker. They'd gather for dinner or have drinks at Mary's flat in Vale Court, which became their secluded haven.

Mary could be completely herself with Joe, and Joe, for his part, felt ten years younger. That there existed a fifteen-year age gap didn't seem to matter. In fact, it matched that between Mary's own parents. She was the eldest daughter of Charles Hippsley Meade, a deeply religious man with a lively intellect but no fixed occupation, and his beloved Kitty. They were a devoted couple, producing three children: first Mary, then James (already a respected economist), and finally Diana. The Meades lived in somewhat dilapidated grandeur at Lansdown Crescent, one of Bath's glorious stretches of Georgiana. This highly conservative and rather stifling atmosphere, overflowing with retired colonels, was something Mary and her brother James had been all too eager to escape.

Mary was her father's favourite; she could do no wrong in his eyes, and when he died in 1938 Joe was already there to comfort her. Was Joe a father figure? A little, perhaps. Mary was very distinctly a different generation to Joe. She'd been a child when the First World War broke out and she'd grown up in a nation mutilated by loss – but that loss was all she knew. There was no before and after; there was only now. Those poor dead young men had left a space in which she was free to move. The 1921 census put it into cold figures: there were nearly 2 million more women than men in Britain. Mary wasn't entirely sure what she wanted, but she had accepted that a husband and children were not guaranteed. For Joe, that must have been a relief.

Mary was a free spirit. As soon as she was old enough she had taken off to Paris to study dressmaking, and then returned to London to attend the Royal College of Needlework. After qualifying as a teacher she had worked for a time at *The Embroideress* magazine, before travelling to America to take up a post at the Women's Educational and Industrial Union of Boston, where she taught needlecraft as part of the programme to foster the 'educational, industrial, and social advancement' of women.

Mary was deadly serious about her craft. At *The Embroideress* she'd implore her readers to educate themselves with visits to the National Gallery. ('Luini paints a scalloped edge to a chemise, Moretto da Brescia a smocked one, and Raphael one in outline stitch. All embroiderers would do well to look at paintings as often as possible, since good technique is nothing without understanding the importance of colour and design.'[1]) Fresh back from America she had taken up her post at the *The Needlewoman*, where she involved herself in all aspects of the magazine production: from writing comment pieces to devising patterns for both high-fashion clothing and home decorations – everything from monogrammed bathing suits to cushion covers based on Persian tapestries. Mary liked to challenge her readers. With Maureen's help, she also replied to their enquiries. Letters poured in each week: questions about knitting patterns or where to get the best corsets or how to clean aluminium saucepans. You could ask 'Miss Meade' anything and be sure of a reply. To her readers she must have seemed the epitome of the thirties woman: resourceful and practical, rising above the economic crises of the time and urging her readers to do the same. ('Depressions sociological or meteorological cannot depress the woman who has just discovered an extremely daring combination of colours'![2])

Everyone was impressed by her. If Joe had grown used to seeing a world in black and white, then Mary was glorious technicolour. She was a terrific idealist with huge reserves of passion, and she was also in possession of the most jaw-dropping temper. He would draw cartoons of a tall, thin woman with fists clenched, smoke coming out of her ears, sending everyone running for cover.

But Mary had every right to blow off steam now and then. After all when she first met Joe she didn't know he was married.

'At the beginning I thought you knew all about me,' he wrote. 'All our mutual friends did. I was horrified when I found out you didn't. Of course I would have left you immediately then – but did you want me to? – or would you have let me? You know perfectly well you did not – and would not.'

Joe would argue that he never lied to Mary, he just didn't tell her the whole truth. If Mary was shocked by the discovery, she accepted it quickly, just as she accepted his daughter as her office girl. That was a daring move on Joe's part, to get Maureen a job working for the woman who was his mistress, but there was a logic to it. His camouflage commitments were keeping him very busy, and increasingly he was being called out of London. Mary could keep an eye on Maureen on his behalf, and Joe was comforted by the thought of these two women together. He hoped they'd find a bit of common ground without him.

Spectacularly naive or an ingenious double bluff? It was a bit of both. Joe was more than aware of the need for secrecy, and he certainly never gave Maureen any reason to suspect. And Nancy was also watching. She remained at the Sutherland but saw Maureen every week. More than that, she had arranged for her daughter to lodge at a doctor's residence where Susan Henry, their former maid from Broughty Ferry, was now housekeeper. Susan had Nancy's confidence, always.

Joe had to be very careful. He wrote to Mary constantly – rushed notes full of abbreviations and code words wherever possible. He called Mary 'P.F.', he called himself 'P.C.'. (I still don't know what 'P.F.' means: Perfect Fool? Pie Face?) 'P.C.' meant 'Popcorn' (I have no idea why). Later, Gray becomes 'Grumble';

pennies become 'pumbles', drinking is 'drumbling' and the war a 'wumble'. It made things sound amusing and rather silly when they weren't, and this Joe admitted: 'I am afraid I have an unfortunate gift of appearing unsympathetic . . . I just simply can't say things, and I think use understatement as a sort of camouflage.'

He often uses that word, declaring, 'I cannot camouflage what I feel,' and yet he does. He is always now in camouflage and he begs Mary to keep their secrets.

'You had better be careful with these letters. Do you lock them up? Nobody must read our letters but us!' For the longest time nobody did.

By 1938 Joe had his own keys to Vale Court and could come and go as he pleased, athough he scrupulously avoided the cleaning lady and never stayed all night. He'd linger with Mary as long as he could, then wander back to Paddington in the early hours of the morning, pausing for a hot Oxo drink at the stall outside the station. He was still returning to Nancy at the Sutherland, even if his heart was now elsewhere.

Maureen had no inkling, and apparently neither did Nancy. They assumed Joe was always working, and a moving target is harder to track. Every day he was either inspecting sites or devising plans or testing new materials. No one ever seemed to know where he was, and by the time they found him, he had moved on again.

Mary coped with Joe and his chaos well, since she herself was always busy. Maureen, meanwhile, was enjoying working life and the freedom it brought. But commuting each day to Charing Cross, she wondered how much longer this unsteady peace would last. It had been a long and anxious summer. Mr Chamberlain had signed the Munich Agreement, promising 'Peace for our Time', but all this really did was give Britain more time to prepare. That's what Joe was doing, after all.

Even the air felt heavy with threat, and the changing weather set everyone's nerves on edge. Joe would go wherever he was needed, but what about the women? Mary had started considering jobs outside of the capital – Joe's persistent talk of bombing raids was making her very edgy. But Maureen had decided she wouldn't go anywhere. For the first time in a long time she felt settled, and she had other reasons for staying that she wasn't yet ready to admit.

It was the end of another long week. Everyone seemed so eager to race to their homes, but Maureen couldn't face the stuffy train yet. Instead, she walked across town to the Sutherland, people-watching and window-shopping as she went. She hadn't heard from her father in a while and although this wasn't unusual, she was worried it might become too much the pattern. Maureen still needed Joe and if war was declared then she'd need him even more.

For once she found him sitting still. Her parents now occupied a large room on the ground floor of what was called 'the annexe'. Maureen assumed her father needed more space for his work, and he seemed to be working now. The door was ajar but through the crack she saw him sitting, hunched at his desk, cigarette smoke drifting upwards. The curtains were half drawn; there were papers scattered all over the floor – writings and crossings out and strange little diagrams.

'Hello Dad.'

Maureen pushed the door further open and stepped inside.

Joe didn't look up or turn around. As usual, he hadn't heard.

She tiptoed around the clutter of papers, and craned her neck to see what it was he was doing. Then she stopped. Joe appeared to be engaged in some kind of tug-of-war. He was methodically pulling at and teasing out a bundle of metal fibres. Stray narrow tentacles had already sprung free and crept like ivy across the desk surface. Maureen's first thought was that her father had broken something. He stopped and flicked his cigarette onto the small ashtray.

She took another step towards him, but still he didn't look up. He carried on unravelling the fibres.

After a minute she went to stand right beside him.

'Dad.' She touched his shoulder. 'What *are* you doing?'

Joe looked up finally and his eyes refocused.

'Oh, hello!' He was surprised, then he grinned. 'Look at this, isn't it marvellous?' He held up the bundle of twinkling fibres to give her a better view. 'I jolly well think this is it. This time . . . I *really* think this is it!'

Maureen pushed her lips into a smile but felt utterly bemused and a little concerned. After all, her father was holding up what was nothing more than a loose pad of domestic steel wool, the kind of thing used for scouring pots and pans.

Her wide eyes held his.

'Sorry, Dad, you've lost me.'

'It's what I've been looking for!' Joe beamed.

Maureen looked at it again. Steel wool. Really? How could that possibly be anything other than what it was?

H *is for Hiding, so please keep it dark,*
And remember to go in the shade when
you park

All the time that he had been writing *Camouflage and Air Defence* Joe knew something was missing. Camouflage in the First World War meant hand-garnished nets and painted canvas, but neither could work in the long term or on a large scale. Nets had to be generously and carefully garnished with local vegetation, which swiftly wilted in bad weather. Painted canvas, when rolled up, became highly inflammable because the linseed oil (which was used as a primer) fermented.[1] Aerial photography also showed that it could be reflective. Joe had spent enough time studying them to recognise the pitfalls.

As the departments for camouflage expanded and diversified, the materials and ideas didn't. Disruptive paint patterns and garnished nets were the order of the day, which was precisely what Joe had warned against in his book. To make matters worse, the quality of both was unregulated and often abysmal.

Joe wanted something better, something standardised. It had to be tougher but still easy to handle, straightforward to maintain and manufacture. A modern, mechanised army needed a modern machine-made camouflage.

And if he couldn't find it, he'd invent it.

Almost every day he was travelling to inspect new sites,

recording their every aspect, considering their profiles, their corners and shadows, and then working out how to alter them. For the moment his plans had to be quick and simple. The Committee of Imperial Defence had decreed that the aim of static camouflage was to defeat the bombing airman, *not* the aerial photographer. This meant that visual concealment by day from a range of four or five miles at a height of 3,000 to 5,000 feet was enough. The aim was to confuse the enemy pilot and put him off his target, thereby giving the anti-aircraft guns more time to respond. Camouflage for this purpose could just be painted, although attention was being given to devising paints with gritty textures to reduce any glare.

The persistent problem, however, was that the preferred building style in the last decade had been stark and pale, with industrial buildings hastily built out of cheap materials – galvanised iron, concrete, asbestos sheeting – all of them conspicuously light and shiny. Another problem was the easily recognisable 'soup plate' shape of oil tanks and gasometers. These were sitting ducks for the Luftwaffe, so it was crucial 'to secure a measure of concealment as soon as possible, while more elaborate preparations are being made'.[2]

But what might the 'more elaborate preparations' entail? The year 1938 saw crises on many fronts, and Lieutenant Colonel Wyatt voiced his concerns over the inconsistencies in camouflage policy and procedure. He warned: 'Numerous instances have come to my notice of paint manufacturers and painting contractors being asked by managers of large factories to camouflage their premises. There is no doubt that industry is becoming camouflage conscious and this fact is being exploited by the paint trade. The evil of this is only too obvious, and unless it is stopped at once, it will get beyond control.'³ Wyatt saw how much money and time could be wasted on schemes that were ultimately futile, and how paint alone couldn't do the job.

Joe wanted to find an alternative. A pile of yellowed typewritten notes reveal his work in progress. 'There are not many materials suitable for constructional camouflage purposes, light enough in weight to be portable, close enough in texture to conceal yet open enough to give ventilation when used in positions which require ventilation.'⁴

He had no facilities at RESB to experiment, nor was it in his job description. But it didn't stop him. Finding 'the perfect cover' would make his work so much easier, which meant it *was* part of his job even if it wasn't recognised as such. He began experimenting with different natural materials – straw mats, wood fibres, chipboard, sandpaper – anything with a good texture. He laid out samples on the floor of his room in the Sutherland, shining lights down from different angles to consider their effects.

He knew what he was looking for. Aerial photographs had shown it was all about texture – a soft mid-tone with some depth, a good bit of 'contained shadow' was ideal.

It was all about trial and error, and Norfolk Square was soon his laboratory. Just as Solomon J. Solomon had experimented in his back garden, so Joe grappled with the finer points of camouflage in a public square at night. It was far from glamorous, it was verging on the ridiculous. His straw mats might have worked had it not been for their fragility – they couldn't withstand a wintry night outdoors – Joe was quite revolted by the sodden mess that awaited him the next morning. Straw and sandpaper combinations were ruled out for the same reason, though a thicker coir fibre fared better. It was relatively waterproof and sturdy, but it had a tendency to absorb water and then became too heavy for its purpose. There was no point creating a good lightweight cover that sagged after a downfall. It was all so frustrating. He knew exactly what he wanted his material to do; he just couldn't think how to make it. He consulted his colleagues and tried to combine different materials together; he went back to read and reread his old notes. He tried, he tested, he failed, and he tried again. Nothing was quite right.

Although now a camoufleur, Joe still thought like an artist. This was part of the problem, especially since he was an artist whose speciality had been precise observation. In the spare moments between his camouflage inspections he sketched different kinds of vegetation from the train or car – he looked at wheat, woodland, hedges and moss – trying to think up ways to lift them off the page and into three dimensions. He went back to RESB, wandering between departments, picking the brain of any interested engineer.

Of course he was being too literal. Ever the realist, slavishly trying to recreate reality was going to be his hurdle. He stared long and hard at the landscape, but he couldn't see the wood for the trees.

'Utilizing techniques of film producers, sculptors and modellers, workers in metal, and even the technique of artificial flower manufacture, complete realism might be achieved in the duplication of natural features, but not as a practical proposition on a scale demanded and not without enormous expenditure.'[5]

'How to get away from representation?' Joe scribbled angrily over one typescript. '*How?*'

But he didn't have to get away from representation; he just had to think of it differently. The answer came to him late at night when he was leafing through one of his art books. 'One conveys the idea of the true by means of the false.' It was a quote lifted from Degas, an artist whose paintings had the look of spontaneity but were actually the opposite. Joe typed it out. 'One conveys the idea of the true by means of the false.' His mistrust of modern art was unchanged – Cubism, Futurism, Surrealism – he couldn't marry the form with the content. However, Impressionism was different. The Impressionists responded to natural light and built up texture, daubing and dashing their paint. It was easy to recognise the features in an Impressionist landscape and yet it looked almost abstract up close.

'It is not possible except at close range to note individual blades of grass or individual leaves of trees. In painting a field or trees the brush is swept broadly across the canvas – no attempt is made to express detail in a literal photographic manner.'

Joe picked up his oil paints for the first time in over a year and layered some thickly on his palette. 'Heavy ridged paint applied with a coarse, stiff brush, the fibres of which "plough" the oil paint, so it is furrowed. Each small ridge of paint casts its own shadow, while its upper surfaces reflect the light in varying degrees . . .' Pulling away from the surface, with the paint still glistening and fresh, something was becoming clear. 'Natural effects are freely translated into paint without literal description of natural facts.' That was it. With the loosening of each brushstroke there began a rich play of light and shadow. 'IMPASTO. The whole idea of imitating nature in a literal manner was impracticable. An abstract scheme must be evolved . . . in other words, nature's texturing quality and principles must be interpreted in a purely formal manner.'

He didn't find the answer, though – not through painting. It was all in his etching plates. Etchers scrape lines in their plates to create not just images but actual effects. Deeper lines quickly fill with ink, creating richer, velvety textures. Etchers can 'use a medley of lines to express vibration of tonal values', and through a dense cross-hatching of lines they create 'intensely realistic effects'. They can thus summon 'all kinds of natural textures – trees, grass, moorland etc. and even broken water'[6] by simply the curve and crossing of lines.

Now this was something. Joe bought some steel wire, the kind used for fencing. Wire had had a supporting role in the camouflage covers of the last war, but what if it could be knitted or bound into a mesh on its own? He used the thinnest kind in a criss-cross pattern, folded and 'knitted', then added clustered rosettes or 'cabbages' on top. It wasn't quite dense enough, but here was a seed. 'I considered a number of schemes comprising springs and metal strips', which is how he summarised the hours of frustration, the nights of lost sleep, and the cuts to all his fingers.

In the end he didn't find the answer – it found him. When browsing the stock of a local hardware store looking for thinner wire he came across the strangest twinkling bundle, tucked away unobtrusively near the cloths and dusters.

'I picked up a pad of domestic steel wool, examined it, and realised it was made of metal fibres inexpensively produced . . .'[7]

With pounding heart Joe grabbed seven more. His excitement seemed wildly out of proportion to the objects in question but then, he was not a man familiar with household chores. Steel wool, traditionally used for the scouring of pots and pans, was the closest thing yet to his new camouflage cover. Of course it was too dense and the wrong colour, but Joe sensed how it could be altered. Dashing back to the Sutherland, he set to work dissecting the skeins, a task far more complex than unwinding a normal ball of wool. It completely absorbed him until Maureen arrived.

As he held up a tangled abstract bundle to show her, he tugged at it hard.

'Skeins found to be composed of closely intermingled and, in places, matted very fine fibres. Strands . . . fragile, but assembled in such great quantity and so closely tangled, that skein as such is strong and difficult to break.'[8]

Joe gave some to Maureen to handle. She turned the fibres over, frowning hard, trying to imagine how this could be important. Undeterred, Joe hurried out to purchase more, clearing out the stocks of several local retailers.

'I can knit them together and make a sort of mat,' he explained. And that is what he did for several nights. The finished product was then painted with a deep forest green. Joe was so certain that this was it, he rushed to share his invention with Le Breton-Simmons and Brigadier Sayer.

He first held it up, peering at them through it.

'You can see and fire a gun through it,' he explained. 'And it's fireproof.'

Then he laid it on the floor. It bristled and buckled like something alive.

Simmons shook his head. 'It is the oddest thing I have ever seen.'

Joe smiled. 'Not from a distance.'

Brigadier Sayer stood with arms folded, saying nothing. Joe knew it was his opinion that mattered. Their president had a sharp, appraising eye and was quick to see the faults in things. But he nodded slowly.

'Yes, this could be something.'

Sayer later called it 'a new material that approached the ideal for Camouflage'.[9] He told Joe to make contact with the British Steel Wool Company, then based in Kent, and ask them to either manufacture or locate some larger, coarser samples to be tested out in the open.

Joe set to work making enquiries and soon learned that in order to create a coarser variety of his steel wool, a 'Band' machine was needed, something that originated in Germany. Fortunately, there were some operating at several factories in England. They were in business.

The brigadier was already in the process of organising trials of different camouflage materials on a group of oil tanks near Bristol. He decided steel wool should be put to the test as soon as possible. Joe jumped at the opportunity and had more samples made, then he drove to Bristol to inspect the site. There was neither the time nor the money to cover the tanks entirely so he devised rectangular frames upon which the steel wool was fixed. The plan was to spread the material across the round top of the tanks, fixed with rabbit wire and bituminous tape, and then use these small frames between them to break up their telltale shape and reduce shadows. Hitching a lift in RAF reconnaissance aircraft, they flew over the area and recorded the results. It was flawless, a revelation in what it didn't show.

Joe was convinced his new material was essential. As the threat of war grew, so did the need for camouflage, more sophisticated and comprehensive schemes. Chamberlain's policy of appeasement had completely failed. In March 1939 Hitler invaded Czechoslovakia. The government pledged 8 per cent of its £25 million Civil Defence budget to 'obscuration of glare, and camouflage', and the Civil Defence Bill gave the government the power to insist that factories and public utilities be camouflaged. To support this initiative the Camouflage Sub-Committee produced the *Air Raid Precautions Handbook No. 11*, which aimed to 'place the art of camouflage on a common sense basis and so prevent waste of labour and materials on ignorantly conceived or unnecessary schemes'.[10] It was a desperate attempt to regulate and consolidate camouflage knowledge, but it was also (still) all about paint. There was a selection of fourteen 'Standard Camouflage Colours' and basic guidelines on how to apply it.

As if already anticipating the problems of how these ideas might be interpreted, the Handbook warned that 'those entrusted with the preparation of schemes need an appreciation of colour values and drawing, an experience of flying; a scientific or engineering training is a valuable asset'. It further stressed: 'Schemes should not be lightly undertaken without the advice of those experienced in the art.'[11]

Inevitably, however, plenty of unskilled eyes set to work devising schemes. Factory owners acted on their own initiative with disastrous results. Writing in the *Observer*, Jan Gordon noted the proliferation of 'camouflage curiosities', pointing out that 'Buildings elaborately and expensively camouflaged stand elbow to elbow with even larger buildings of staring white. Some look as if the abstract or jigsaw artist had come into his own with intent to advertise his work rather than conceal it . . . So far, perhaps, the prize for ineptitude should go to a large gasometer on which has been painted a huge tree some three times as large as any possible tree in the district.'[12]

Joe and his colleagues often found themselves correcting the mess created by amateurs. When Jack Sayer was dispatched to advise on a hutted camp sited on the cliffs of Dover, he was horrified by what he found. The commandant had received peremptory orders to camouflage every building, and, 'in the absence of any detailed instructions and perhaps with some hazy memory of the "dazzle painting"', had created something that 'was probably visible from Calais with the naked eye'.[13]

Such problems only enhanced the appeal of a 'standardised' camouflage material. Back at RESB, Brigadier Sayer hurriedly sought to push the testing and production of 'steel wool camouflage' up the agenda and brought it to the attention of Colonel John Turner and Norman Wilkinson (now Air Commodore Wilkinson, an adviser to the Air Ministry). Further tests were carried out on oil tanks at Llandarcy in South Wales during the spring and summer of 1939. Steel wool was pitted against other texturing materals, including asbestos wool, cork and coir screening. Once again, air reconnaissance showed that steel wool was the best.

On 28 July 1939, a meeting of camouflage officers was held at RESB with representatives from both the Air Ministry and the Admiralty. Mr Moulton, a representative of the British Steel Wool Company, attended and was asked to give estimates for the production of this new form of steel wool camouflage, and also to advise on the situation regarding rust retarding, which would be crucial if the material went into large-scale production.

Two men who would become key players in the story were also present. Peregrine Churchill was an engineer working as a civilian adviser to the Air Ministry, and Johnny's younger brother. Peregrine was the polar opposite to Johnny – quiet to the point of withdrawn and, thankfully for Joe, an absolute stickler for detail. Once he heard Sayer's presentation, Peregrine was excited by the possibilities of this steel wool camouflage. He sketched out a rough design for a gun cover on the spot, and promised to finesse it and forward it to Joe.

The second person now becoming involved was Cecil Schofield. Schofield was a businessman whose firm M&E Equipment had already done some contract work for the Air Ministry. Schofield had recently joined forces with the designer Eugene Mollo, who had become known for renovating cinema and theatre interiors across the south-east of England.

The coming war brought about some unlikely partnerships and the alliance of Schofield and Mollo was surely one of them. Schofield, an enthusiastic founder of companies and registerer of patents, was eager to explore any new market. He wore pinstripe suits, rented extravagant offices on Park Lane, and drove a Bentley very fast. By contrast, the reticent Russian-born Mollo had trained at the Royal College of Art, and firmly favoured the creative over the lucrative.

M&E Equipment had a factory in Kennington which had already begun developing new techniques for camouflage, and had recently acquired its own parkerising plant. Parkerising[14] was a process that protected steel from corrosion by the application of an electrochemical phosphate conversion coating, and was now being used in the manufacture of firearms. It quickly became apparent that this same process could easily be used to rust-proof steel wool. Within weeks Schofield had excitedly applied for a patent and declared Joseph Gray a visionary.

There is a surviving sample of steel wool at the Imperial War

Museum. It's hard to know how to describe it. One officer noted its 'fuzzy-wuzzy texture',[15] another likened it to a 'magnified but sparse door mat.'[16] The steel threads are thin, flat and prickly to touch, woven in a loose kind of mesh. They look very brittle in their box but then, they are sixty years old. Without the supporting chicken wire they curl and bristle. It's not hard to picture how they'd look on a larger scale – how they might conjure a curtain of undergrowth – and I've seen it for myself in the photographs Joe kept. There's one that is taken from beneath a cover, showing a man walking over it, balancing on the long supporting wires, arms outstretched. Close up, you could see and fire through steel wool, but from a distance it vibrates with shadows, resembling an innocuous bit of grassland.

There's no doubt about it, steel wool was the perfect cover. It also worked well as a decoy. Because if you are too busy hiding things, the chances are you will not always see what is being hidden from you.

I *is for Invention, consider the new*
Ways to conceal our secrets from view

> My dearest M,
>   I cannot wait until we are married.

But the M wasn't Mary. It was Maureen.

As 1939 progressed, London prepared for the worst – pavements were piled high with sandbags, paper was pinned onto every window, and barrage balloons blotted out blue sky. Young men, eager to enlist, seized the moment and proposed marriage. Young women, fearful of the future, threw caution to the wind and accepted.

Maureen didn't think her actions particularly rash. After all, she had agreed to marry the man she loved, the man she'd been seeing for almost as long as she had been in London. Yes, Maureen had her own blossoming romance and had kept it expertly hidden, as was fast becoming a family trait.

It had started in December 1937, at a Christmas party at the Sutherland Hotel. Maureen didn't know it but she'd become rather stunning: white camellia skin, dark, wide-set eyes and thick auburn hair just like her father. Her natural reserve only made her more intriguing. She had come to the party with Nancy, who was accompanied by Dick. Only Joe was missing, busy preparing for his interview with Francis Wyatt at Farnborough. Or perhaps he was with Mary. Either way, he would miss the sight of his only daughter being reluctantly drawn into an innocent parlour game.

All the young women present were asked to throw a hat in turn, the idea being that whichever gentleman caught the hat could partner them for a dance. It was a harmless way of breaking the ice and eliminating would-be wallflowers, but Maureen, self-conscious about her deafness and clumsy because of it, hated the attention. When given the hat she threw it quickly, keeping her eyes firmly shut. There was quite a scuffle but one young man – a keen rugby player – had a particularly tenacious grip. As the crowd dispersed there he stood: blond and bespectacled with a wide, toothy grin.

The name of this young man was Harold Barclay, but I must not call him Harold, because my grandfather always preferred people to call him by his second name, which was John. John Barclay, then, was also a Scot, born in Paisley. He was twenty-six and a trainee accountant, having followed his older brother David down to London to take his articles at Price Waterhouse.

David was also at the party, a rather domineering character who had lost his wife suddenly and tragically and become an alcoholic because of it. But David had been saved by and newly engaged to the dashing Betty Nuthall, a tennis star whose family owned a string of hotels including the Sutherland. John Barclay had no such colourful or complicated history, professing only to a deep terror of women. 'They were people, they could express opinions, they could make you feel terribly inferior or terribly superior, although the latter was something I never experienced.'[1]

For the longest time John Barclay avoided all women. Until he met Maureen.

'I don't know how I caught the hat,' he told her. 'I have the most frightful eyesight.'

Maureen had to laugh.

'Well, I'm badly deaf, so we shall make a fine pair.'

And they did. They truly did.

John and Maureen were seeing each other throughout 1938. In fact, John had moved closer to Maureen's lodgings in Raynes Park so that he might see her more. All the time Joe was working at RESB, developing his secret material and his secret life with Mary. Had he not been spreading his attention across so many subjects he might have noticed how silent and self-contained his daughter had become. Equally, if Maureen hadn't been so wrapped up in her glorious romance with John, she might've had time to speculate further on her father's activities. The subterfuge deepened on both sides. Maureen had considered telling her father. She had gone to the Sutherland that Friday evening, and it would have been perfect, catching Joe alone with his work, but he'd thrown her off with this odd business about steel wool scrubbing pads.

So she had carried on lying. When John proposed marriage she accepted without hesitation, because there was no time to lose. In a world full of uncertainty she had no doubts about him. They were meant for each other, and for the rest of her life, wherever she went, Maureen would keep close a small framed photograph of the two of them, strolling arm in arm along the Strand. John and Maureen in their Sunday best. They look so very young and carefree, light as air. They are laughing with happiness. Because their secret hadn't yet been discovered.

As Maureen planned her new life, Joe was doing the same. The coming war was a terrible prospect, but he had imagined it for so long the certainty came like a release. The irony was not lost on him – having spent years feeling relegated and redundant, he was suddenly in demand. Returning to uniform signalled something powerful, and a part of him wished he'd never left. He felt himself walking taller, looking younger, thinking clearly. At last there was an eager audience for his work, people hungry for his opinions.

But Mary Meade was not in that number. Joe sketched her cramming her belongings into a van and vacating Vale Court in a panic. Mary was too scared to stay in London and, true to her word, she had fixed herself a temporary job organising summer courses for the Crafts Council outside the capital. She was then going to retreat to her mother's in Bath. Joe was glad for it, since he had seen how nervy she'd become. His letters chased her all around the country, reassuring her: 'The position in London is very fine. The people generally are ready for anything and afraid of nothing.'

Mary hated being parted from Joe and felt quite uprooted, though for him life was much the same. 'Honestly P.F. time and distance are nothing at all. And we are as near now as at 17 Vale Court. Remember that!'

Maureen and John, Joe and Mary – the ground beneath them was shifting. But whilst Mary was consumed by worry, Joe thrived on it. He even imagined he might be sent abroad. Whatever was afoot, he hastily collected his artwork from Vale Court and the Sutherland, intending to send it down to Mary for safekeeping. It was rather therapeutic, bringing his etchings and paintings into the office.

Beddington said today are those drawings in the parcel? So I showed them to him. To cut a long story short he went off the deep end and is dying to show them to his Shell Mex brother. I think he would buy them and his brother, too. If we survive the War he says he will form a syndicate and back me financially so I can get down to it. Actually he really meant it and of course they are all frightfully wealthy and genuinely crazy about modern pictures. Well, I sure would like a syndicate!

Was it wrong to feel excited? He was facing another war – it was a terrible prospect – but at least he was doing something, and camouflage was a world where the unlikely did seem possible. Joe revelled in the fast-formed friendships, how men of wildly varying backgrounds were banding together. 'The plutos' (as he called them) were slumming it, welcoming him into their comfortable houses, ringing up endless bar bills at the Ritz. It felt like every door was swinging open. But he didn't for a minute imagine it could last.

The announcement came on 3 September. Britain was finally and officially at war with Germany. The changearound was instant. Simmons was dispatched to France with the Expeditionary Forces, and Freddie Beddington followed hot on his heels as corps camouflage officer. RESB was to be reorganised and Joe was promoted to major and acting director. It was quite a leap, to go from private in one war to major in another, but rapid promotions were the order of the day.

'As you can imagine the work is incredible. Practically every night till 11 or 12. I am now doing all [Simmons's] work in addition to my own and trying to train new people too.' Joe was involved in everything – making site visits and planning schemes, overseeing trials of steel wool, the recruitment and training of new camouflage officers. 'We are swamped by applicants. I have put up a notice "No Camouflage Applicants for Commissions can be seen without

Appointment. Gentlemen offering their services must write or phone." Really this is a great country. Poor old Hitler!'

Each morning he was greeted by the same spectacle: groups of eager young men wielding letters of recommendation, mostly ex-students from the Slade and the Royal College, hoping to get 'fixed up'. Joe was now meeting plenty of artists better off and more successful than he had ever been, and yet *he* was the one with influence. The penniless artist was now a major, in charge of a department, an expert in static camouflage. Who could have predicted it?

But then who could have predicted the telephone call that suddenly meant the floorboards seemed to open and swallow him? It was the only time Nancy had ever tried to get hold of him at the Board. Something terrible had happened.

Maureen was surprised by the sight of her father in his uniform – the peaked cap and major's crowns looked most impressive – but it was strange to see him here, arriving unannounced at her place of work. This clearly wasn't a social call, although it would have been lovely to pretend even for a few seconds that it was. Maureen had often hoped that her father might come to inspect her premises; she had wanted to take him to the Lyons tea house where they could people-watch and talk of trivial things. She had done this with John just the other week.

John, her fiancé.

> My dearest M,
> I cannot wait until we are married.

If only Susan hadn't discovered the note, wrapped around an engagement ring. If only Susan hadn't then called Nancy, who'd then called Joe. Susan had known Maureen since she was a baby, but she'd known Nancy longer and her loyalties were set in stone.

As if one declaration of war wasn't enough.

Maureen hadn't told her parents because she'd guessed how they would react. Everyone considered her naive and it was true she lacked confidence and had seen little of the world. The news of her engagement caused exactly the kind of fuss she had so wanted to avoid. Nancy was furious, quite inconsolable, and vented her fury on Joe.

She had summoned him back to the Sutherland and scolded him bitterly.

'This is your fault!' she said. 'Maureen needed your guidance and you failed her.'

Did she? Had he?

It wasn't the time to remind Nancy of where and when John and Maureen had first met – at the Sutherland, and right under her nose. Nancy ranted and raved at her husband. She saw him as a man who had neglected his family – who cared only for his work – but if she wanted a fight she'd be sorely disappointed. Joe didn't argue back or defend himself, because he felt he *was* guilty. He listened quietly and then promised his wife he would put a stop to this nonsense. Even then, he wasn't sure he could. Maureen was his creation, an only child who had learned long ago to keep her own counsel. There were times she didn't hear but plenty more times she simply didn't *listen*. Wasn't that just like him?

Joe hung his head for shame. The present situation was his fault. He had neglected Maureen, assuming everything was fine, and that she was safely watched over by other people. He felt confused and angry, and by the time he reached the magazine offices he had fairly worn himself out.

Maureen noticed the slight stoop, the hand twitching at his side.

'I think we should take a walk,' he suggested curtly, turning on his heel back towards the door.

She dutifully collected her coat and bag, and followed her father downstairs. No word passed between then as they left the building. She knew, without asking, that they were heading down to the Embankment. Joe veered towards water whenever he needed to calm his nerves.

Father and daughter walked slowly towards the Thames, a chill wind cutting through their clothes. Everyone they passed was also walking with purpose, preoccupied by war and what it meant. Maureen turned her head once to check her father's profile. She remembered their long walks along the Tay, when she'd been so small. They'd walk and talk for hours, with him eventually lifting her onto his shoulders, and he'd point out every incident in the landscape, keeping her eyes open long past her bedtime.

She stole another glance his way.

'You look jolly impressive.'

Joe nodded gruffly and steered her through the gateway into the Embankment Gardens.

'Sit down.' He gestured to a bench.

Maureen did as she was told, perching neatly on her hands, like a schoolgirl before a teacher.

'Well, young lady.' Joe kicked at the gravel under his feet. 'Perhaps you know what this is about. Your alleged *engagement?*'

Maureen held her breath. 'Oh! So you know.'

He was gripping his hands behind his back.

'Never have I heard of a more nonsensical and irresponsible notion. To get married *now*!'

Maureen tried to smile. Wasn't it just what everyone was doing?

'If two people love each other they *should* be together.'

Joe lifted his cap and scratched at his head, struggling to process this small declaration. He didn't know how to reply. Yes, people who loved each other should be together, but hasty marriages in the shadow of war were simply wrong. Was this what had agitated Nancy – the idea of her daughter repeating her own mistake? He stood very still, struggling with a strange mixture of emotions and memories. Then he gathered himself up.

'There are any number of reasons why this idea of marriage is madness, but firstly let me point out you are far too young. This John Barclay is much older than you!' (The age gap between Maureen and John was in fact half that between Joe and Mary.)

'Secondly, this John is a mere bank clerk – not even a qualified accountant.' (Was that really so much worse than being an artist?)

'Next there is the issue of where and how you shall live. John will volunteer. I assume he already has and that's the reason for your rush. But he could be sent God knows where.'

Maureen stopped him there. 'Well, that won't happen, in fact. John has already tried to enlist and been turned down, twice. He's very upset but he's got the most terrible eyesight . . .' There was an awkward hesitation. 'And he's also rather crestfallen, as the last time they told him he was colour-blind.'

Joe stifled a small gasp. A colour-blind bank clerk. His daughter was rejecting him in so many ways. But what he hated most of all was the now familiar feeling that the world was changing and he couldn't keep up.

Maureen was still talking: 'We shall live in Wimbledon. I shall be a fire warden at the office and John has volunteered for the ARP.'[2]

They had planned it all out.

Joe took a long breath in, suddenly self-conscious about his new uniform.

'Well, that is all very well. But neither of you young people know what this war will be like.'

'We shall find out together,' Maureen replied. 'I need to be twenty-one to get the licence, so I'll need your permisson.'

Joe shook his head. 'I cannot. You know what your mother thinks about all this. I agree with her. Absolutely.'

(But did he really?)

'John will look after me.'

'*I* can look after you.'

Maureen stood up and faced him. She knew she was supposed to bow her head and defer to her father's judgement.

'I am terribly sorry, Dad, but I'm going to do it anyway.'

It was quite a blow. Major Joseph Gray was able to convince brigadiers of the vast potential of static cover, he had a score of new recruits eating from his hand, but he couldn't convince his daughter of the dangers of marrying young.

He took a step back. 'I am very disappointed.'

Maureen kept her head up and said nothing.

It was an impasse.

But the worst was still to come.

Nancy. Joe would have to deliver this news back to his wife. He had promised her he would put things right. He had failed. It was damnable. Impossible. No, he simply couldn't face her. He had other things to attend to, after all.

He kissed his daughter lightly on the forehead and walked briskly away.

Then he did what he did best – he disappeared.

J *is the Job which has got to be done:*
The Camoufleur knows it and so does the Hun

Joe didn't simply run *away*, although that's how it appeared. He ran *to*.

After the outbreak of war the newly created Ministry of Home Security took charge of civil camouflage. Joe was now deputy assistant director of the new operational research section, known as RE8. RE8 was responsible for camouflage of all 'Military Establishments, Fixed Permanent Defences, Royal Ordnance Factories (excluding Agency factories run by civil firms) [and] Ministry of Supply Establishments'.[1]

There was a huge amount to organise. The disappointments and difficulties in his personal life only made Joe more determined to prove himself in other ways. He had to get his newly patented, rust-proofed steel wool accepted by the War Office. Steel wool was the answer. It had to be put into large-scale production before the year was out. That became his singular obsession.

So Joe ran from a situation he felt he couldn't change and focused on something he might. He saw steel wool to be crucial. Screening a few oil tanks had only ever been just the start. In his mind's eye, he envisaged acres of bristling threads, stretched out over frames, moulded into hedgerows and hayricks, suspended on poles to make fake trees.

Self-portrait, 1953,
charcoal on paper.

Ration Party of the 4th Black Watch at the Battle Of Neuve Chapelle, 1915, 1919, oil on
canvas.

*Above: After Neuve Chapelle
(10 March 1915)*, 1922,
oil on canvas.

Left: John Dye, Maureen and Joe Gray
(*right*) in the garden at Broughty Ferry,
c. 1921.

Opposite page: Joseph Gray at work
on *After Neuve Chapelle*

After Neuve Chapelle,
13 March 1915:
a Private of the Black
Watch, after the battle,
1917, pen and ink
on paper.

Joseph Gray, *c.* 1916

Scottish landscape, drypoint etching, *c.* 1928.

Agnes (Nancy) Gray,
c. 1922.

Sample of steel wool material (*centre*) compared to scrim (*above*) and photograph of steel wool in use at Cobham (*bottom*).

John Churchill, *The Retreat to Dunkirk, May 1940, The Beaches*, reproduction of pen and ink drawing first published in *Illustrated London News*.

Group photograph of 'Recruits of 1st and 2nd Camouflage Training Course, Larkhill, June 1940'.

Maureen Gray and John
Barclay, the Strand,
October 1939.

Snow-covered steel-wool cover
at Cobham, January 1940.

He gave a copy of *Camouflage and Air Defence* to Eugene Mollo, drawing his attention to the parts where he discusses the need for large-scale covers. They talked about Solomon J. Solomon and his theories about German camouflage schemes. Joe sensed they understood each other, that Mollo saw, as he did, that more needed to be done.

'I am very worried,' Joe admitted. Even though steel wool had made an impact, things weren't progressing as he'd hoped. He felt both Simmons and Brigadier Sayer had recognised its potential but didn't quite know how to apply it. He felt steel wool was being 'played with'.[2] With Simmons off in France Joe feared the momentum might vanish. Old-style netting was still the mainstay material, with a woefully inadequate amount of coloured hessian woven into it. Joe predicted that now war was declared, the Army would stick with what it knew, even if netting was far from the magic cover everyone assumed.

He had to get the War Office on side and there was only one way to do it. Ever the artist, he proposed an exhibition. Firing off memos left and right, he spread the word about steel wool, emphasising its versatility and how quickly it might now be mass-produced. To prove the point he asked that M&E produce a dozen rolls, twenty-five yards long, and persuaded Peregrine Churchill to design some more ambitious covers. They had to strike a balance between making straighforward builds – so that unskilled labour could be used – but equally they had to impress, amaze and of course conceal. Joe wanted everyone to see that steel wool wasn't some 'niche' material, and could do far more than paint or netting combined.

One thing now counting in Joe's favour was that by mid-November the supply of hessian-garnished nets was running into problems – raw materials were not coming forward. He seized the moment; in a memorandum dated 20 November 1939, he wrote:

> In view of the present urgent need for standardised camouflage materials I venture to submit that consideration might be given to the use of this material in the field. When hemp netting and scrim were standardised and ordered in large quantities it was presumed that a fireproofing treatment had been evolved. But actually such a treatment had not ... As the conditions in France are static or semi-static the use of wire-netting appears to deserve consideration.[3]

Brigadier Sayer felt nervous about the expense and recommended that trials be kept to a modest scale, focusing on pillboxes – those concrete guard posts that were springing up all over the landscape. '[Steel Wool] should be tried practically in the field as soon as possible,' he wrote. 'It would appear particularly suitable for Pill Boxes, Anti-Tank and M.G. gun emplacements and perhaps also for certain obstacles in the defensive positions now under preparation.'[4]

Having secured some green space at Cobham, a short distance out of London, Mollo and his men began work on covers to conceal cars and guns. They conducted various trials into December to see how the material weathered, and experimented with different textures. ('Coarse is better and slightly more like grass in appearance although the difference between the two is indistinguishable from the air.'[5]) The preparation of steel wool needed care, but end results proved its value. 'In its final processed form it had plenty of contained shadow and when viewed from the air or from a distance provided a perfect screen, even though from the underside it seemed absurdly sparse.'[6]

Joe was pleased with his 'babies' but was soon needed elsewhere. Richard Buckley had organised the very first camouflage training course at Netheravon and summoned Joe there to lecture. The course was designed primarily to deal with camouflage for troops going on active service. Johnny Churchill attended before being dispatched to France, as did portrait painter Tom Van Oss, Surrealists Julian Trevelyan and Roland Penrose, and a renowned zoologist by the name of Hugh B. Cott ('mostly artists . . . a few scientists, film experts and other queer birds,'[7] noted Van Oss in a letter home). Although Buckley was in charge he was swiftly overwhelmed and lost his voice,[8] which meant Joe had to step into the breach. 'Just got a minute before another lecture!' he told Mary. 'We are having a terrific time and go at it again after dinner every night.'

Joe improvised lectures on different aspects of camouflage – 'a matter of common sense and good discipline'[9] – and discussed individual and then collective concealment, and the basics of aerial photography. He also listed the various materials for camouflage and how to use them: from canvas (cut into strips to garnish nets), to scrim (absorbs light, can be used to cover guns), to coir (good for dark tones) and netting (for general static cover). But it was too good a chance not to publicise his new material as well. When Buckley recovered he was both grateful and receptive to Joe's descriptions of steel wool. He agreed to inspect the camouflage trials and offer his opinion.

December was a bitterly cold month, but steel wool withstood heavy rain and snow, freezing temperatures and gale force winds.

Even if a cover was damaged it made no difference 'because natural fields are full of patches and variations and incidents of different kinds'.[10] M&E grew more and more confident in their hand-
ling of it and they even covered a small stretch of water. The
exhibits generated 'first-class' results.[11] Jack Sayer was one of a
steady stream of visitors at the time. There is a photograph of him
standing with Joe and Schofield and various men in suits. They all
look to Joe, their faces tense and serious, and he stoops pensively
with hands clasped behind his back, head bowed, a cigarette dang-
ling from his mouth. He doesn't look happy. Why doesn't he look
happy? Why?

Two days before Christmas Joe had to take leave to return to
London, although he only went as far as Raynes Park. Maureen
was expecting him, immaculate in her best jacket and skirt. Not a
wedding dress because she couldn't afford one, and she didn't
think it right.

'You look lovely,' Joe told her.

She was relieved that he had come.

He smiled, then stopped himself. 'But you know, it's not too
late.'

Maureen clasped her hands together.

'Don't try to dissuade me, Dad. I am marrying John today.'

She said it very firmly, as if she were now the adult talking to a
child.

Joe sighed and held out his hand.

'Well, let's get a move on, then.'

He had hired a taxi to take them to Richmond register office,
where John would be waiting. Nancy had decided not to come to
the wedding. She would instead preside over a 'celebration' lunch,

which was to be held at the nearby Stuart Hotel. Everything was deferred, however, because, in a strange twist on tradition, the groom was running late. There was a dense and icy fog that delayed all the trains to Richmond, and this meant John missed the time allotted for the service. Furious to be kept waiting, Joe bundled Maureen back into the taxi.

They drove in circles around Richmond Park. Staring out at the frozen landscape, Joe still tried his best to change his daughter's mind. Didn't she see what a dreadful mistake this was? A hasty marriage in the shadow of war was bound to fail. What would she do about work? She would be better off leaving London and becoming a land girl.

'I could find you something. I am sure I could. Let me have a few days to call people.'

Maureen began to wonder if Joe had arranged the fog especially, but she didn't dare make it into a joke. Joe was too deadly serious.

'You have no idea what this war will be like.'

'Which is why I want to be married,' she replied.

The war only clarified Maureen's choices: it made the world in black and white. For Joe there were too many shades of grey. He talked on, his words echoing round the taxi as it completed its second circuit. Nothing worked. Maureen was her father's daughter, and her mind was quite made up.

After an hour and a half John finally materialised. By now Joe was worn out, and he was at least more convinced of the depth of Maureen's feelings. The sight of John beaming broadly on the steps of the register office even gave him some relief. They clearly loved each other, there was no denying or mistaking it.

Perhaps, just perhaps, they would prove everyone wrong.

John and Maureen joined a long and winding queue of people waiting to be married, and after the shortest of ceremonies, they retired to the Stuart Hotel, where Nancy waited with a few other guests, tight-lipped and po-faced and thoroughly disapproving.

There are no surviving photographs of the happy occasion. Not a single one. The story was they didn't come out 'because of the bad weather'. This seems very odd, especially when there are endless black-and-white photographs dated from the weeks that followed. All of them show an empty, snow-filled landscape. (Proof, at least, of the bad weather.) Of course, those snowy hills are less than half the story.

Joe had taken a day off to see his only daughter married, and then refused all Christmas leave and returned directly to Cobham. An idea was forming in his mind. M&E were satisfied with their work but he wanted more. He wanted something bigger and bolder.

'Gray had revolutionary ideas,' recalled Cecil Schofield, with more than a note of unease. There was a modest-sized quarry next to their test site, and Joe declared with some flourish that this was the spot. He proposed that M&E cover the quarry with steel wool so that it would blend in with the surrounding hillside. It would be a grand set piece and definitive proof of steel wool's potential.

Even a showman like Schofield baulked. He was rightly worrying about the cost. 'I must confess we were reluctant to undertake this work, as Camouflage on this scale did not appear to be a practicable proposition and Major Gray wanted it done without payment.'[12]

But Joe had that glint in his eye. He argued that camouflage on such a scale was possible and would soon be necessary. He said the Germans were probably already doing it, and he produced his manuscript and insisted Schofield read it. Still Schofield hesitated. He liked Joe, theirs had been a friendship oiled by good whisky and late nights, but he had to think of it from the business point of view.

In the end, it wasn't Joe who convinced him, it was Mollo.

'I regarded the proposition from a very different angle,' Mollo reflected. 'I believed great things may be done in Army camouflage . . . Gray said he did not intend material to imitate only grass, but it could be cut and twisted and spray painted to make trees and even small woods, hedges, haystacks, bushes and practically anything.'[13]

The threat of Nazi invasion was now very real, and Mollo had first-hand experience of what this could mean. He had been thirteen years old when the Russian Revolution broke out, and had served in the White Russian River Fleet before being captured by the Red Army. Perhaps because of this, and because of his own artistic background, Mollo was keen to keep on with the experiments. He told Schofield they should do it, that it was worth the investment of time and men and money. After all, if the cover was a success, they'd soon be reimbursed.

Camouflage could be business, after all.

John Mollo, Eugene's son, visited Cobham a number of times with his father and watched the project take shape. To a child it was a wondrous sight: a giant frame rather like a circus tent being lifted into place. Tubular steel posts had to be erected around the edge of the quarry, dropped into sockets of concrete. They were then joined by steel fencing strand wire, stretched and tied, creating a giant cat's cradle. In some parts these wires were strong enough for men to balance on. Steel wool, spray painted to match the surrounding grassland, was then rolled out and secured to the wires.

The overall effect was amazing, worryingly so.

'The quarry vanished and in its place appeared undulating grass slopes with bushes and saplings here and there. It was so effective even at the closest range, that it was dangerous to approach as one could not see where the grass ended and the cover began. It was necessary to wire it in to prevent accidents,' noted Cecil Schofield. 'This cover was inspected and approved in my presence by representatives of General Staff War Office, Air Ministry, Admiralty, Home Office and French Army. It was, I submit, "the pathfinder" and the prototype for all that followed.'[14]

Word spread fast and towards the end of January 1940 Freddie Beddington flew back from France for a special viewing. He met Buckley at Cobham so they could compare notes. An officer present reported that both men flew over all of 'the exhibits' separately at different times of the day. They were astonished by what they saw, or rather what they didn't see. It was unanimously agreed that Joe's cover provided 100 per cent concealment. It was also noted that out of four different-coloured rolls also laid out for inspection, none could be seen except when circling at a few hundred feet. Ground reconaissance proved equally challenging and in fact 'very dangerous'[15] since nobody knew where reality ended and artifice began.

Beddington felt both 'enthusiasm and relief' at what he found. 'The position,' he wrote, 'was critical. Camouflage materials were in terribly short supply, there was no material specially designed for static purposes in existence ... In pressing Gray from France to give priority to this material I had written "I hope to God your material comes forward in time" – I meant it.'[16]

Knowing he would be heading back over the Channel at any moment, Beddington asked that an order be made for 10,000 square yards of steel wool to take back with him, coloured the beet clay colour of north-east France.

The war was just beginning but one small battle had been won.

K is the Knowledge of how to combine Doing the job with leaving no sign

Good cover was the first rule of camouflage. With steel wool approved and Maureen married, Joe was now able to focus on what else needed to be hidden.

Nancy Gray moved in to a flat in Wimbledon with Maureen and John. Joe rarely mentioned her to Mary. If he did, he only ever referred to her as 'A.G.' He was very glad to quit the Sutherland and leave one life behind. But it was the beginning of a strangely itinerant existence. He rented a small room near Marlborough Gate, but used it rarely. He had keys to Mary's flat, but he hated to be there without her. In the end, the place he preferred was the office.

It didn't matter that he wasn't meant to sleep there, since Major Gray was getting used to breaking rules. Joe either pretended he didn't *hear* the orders telling him what not to do, or he was deaf to the reprisals. After taking over Buckley's camouflage course in Netheravon he had been 'given a tremendous dressing down, for exceeding his orders, absenting himself, doing another man's work and so on.'[1] Did it bother him? Not at all.

'I say, I've had the most fearful rocket from your cousin,' he grinned to Jack Sayer. 'It must have been for staying on to help old Buckles . . . What a good thing I'm deaf! I never heard half of what he said but I knew he was wild by the way he kept hitting his desk!'[2]

And so Joe made his weakness a strength, insulating himself against army protocol and all its notions of order. He was determined to do things in his own way, and when Francis Wyatt came out of retirement to head the department he was 'rather fascinated' to find himself in command of 'a sort of crazy gang'.[3] Fortunately 'he was an easy-going chief with a strong sense of humour. He at once recognised that his Major Gray was a wayward genius, who would never be methodical or punctual, but who was nevertheless dedicated to his job.'[4]

Joe got away with it because he was so good. He was, in fact, *uncannily* good. Jack Sayer considered Joe the backbone of RE8, a man with a shrewd eye and 'uncanny resource and ingenuity'.[5] But Sayer never understood how someone so outwardly haphazard in his habits could be so thoroughly effective.

Joe tried to show him exactly how it was done, whisking him down to Dover in the early months of 1940. There they were tasked with devising a camouflage treatment for one of the many gun sites now appearing along the coastline. In this instance, it was an old naval gun brought out of retirement from the last war and mounted on a railway chassis.

There was no time for an aerial reconaissance as the job had to be done the next day, so they met with a Mr Ellis, the representative from ICI, who had a team of painters standing by. Ellis was desperate to know what colours to order, what Joe had in mind, but for now he'd have to wait.

They spent a long time inspecting the site and its surrounding area, with Joe pointing out features of interest, surveying the gun from every angle through the changing light. Ellis had found them a small hotel near Deal to stay at overnight and joined them there with a set of scale drawings, expecting them to set to work immediately on the toning down and blending in that would be required.

They did not. Instead Joe set about ordering a large meal. He then made a detailed assessment of the drinks menu. The poorly stocked bar was no deterrent.

'Let's not worry about work just yet,' he said, smiling enigmatically.

Ellis, although anxious to get the job done, gave in rather quickly, and so three men spent a most convivial evening and discussed just about everything except the matter in hand.

It was only as Ellis rose unsteadily to his feet that he remembered.

'What about hiding this great gun?'

Joe was suddenly and miraculously sober, as if the last few hours of drinking had not happened at all.

'You have my solemn promise the plans will be ready by morning,' he said.

Sayer watched as Ellis staggered upstairs and wondered how on earth that would be possible. Then he turned back to find Joe purchasing a small bottle of Drambuie – 'about the only thing left in the bar'.[6]

'Come along,' Joe smiled to his younger colleague. 'Let's get to work.'

They retired to Joe's room and there laid out the maps and drawings on the floor, and spent the rest of the night working out the best camouflage scheme – an intricate design of contrasting planes and paint colours with carefully netted edges. Sayer wasn't entirely sure if the alcohol helped or hindered, but the completed plans were gently nudged under Ellis's door by him once he was finally able to take to his bed.

'Ellis had vanished with them before we surfaced in the morning and we never saw the results of our efforts. But Ellis must have been much impressed by the success of our methods because whenever he had occasion to call at our office thereafter he always brought some Drambuie for us.'[7]

Joe's work on camouflage was itself neatly camouflaged: he'd confound and confuse, create a diversion and then surprise everyone by doing what he was meant to. Words like 'erratic' and 'chaotic' swirled around him, making their own smokescreen. Even Jack Sayer didn't know the whole truth. He mistakenly called Joe a Scot, born in Dundee, who between the wars had lived in Chelsea. He never knew of Joe being married or having a daughter, though remarked that his way of life was so 'casual and disorganised'[8] it was always a worry *where* he slept most nights.

Joe had the ability to be always there and yet never there. He'd work all hours and bed down in the office, then be ready for the next day before it began. Flying was the best way to see what needed to be hidden, but flights for camoufleurs were hard to secure. The No. 1 Camouflage Unit operating from Baginton had only six Stinsons – small and cramped American passenger planes that didn't fare well on a windy day – 'rather like flying in a paper bag'.[9] So Joe made friends in the RAF and hitched lifts on any number of unauthorised flights from various locations, improvising his own grand tour of the south coast. He generally resurfaced when he ran out of money and needed rescuing, putting in a call to Captain Ayscough, who was in charge of petty cash.

Here's a fine fiasco!
Send for Captain Ayscough!
Major Gray has 'phoned to say
He's lost his pistol – spent his pay –
Dropped his warrant down a drain –
Gone and missed his ruddy train –
Kindly send an aeroplane . . .
Thank you, Captain Ayscough![10]

J. P. Sayer

But Joe didn't just get away with it – he gloried in it. Jack Sayer sketched him taking flight from his desk with Francis Wyatt looking on. 'What a Will o' the Wisp you are, Gray!' ran the caption. Joe declared it quite marvellous and posted it to Mary. Soon he was sending her a cartoon every week, and photographs taken of him, and poems written about him. It was a clever way of making himself present, and what a presence he became. Mary wouldn't see him for weeks but she had these wonderful images instead: Joe grinning from the cockpit of an aeroplane, lounging on the grass at an aerodrome, peering out from under a camouflage canopy.

He made it look so easy – that didn't mean it was.

'The work is never-ending – I'm simply snowed under. Please come up, even for a day. I miss you terribly and have had an awful week of depression – never had anything like it before. I can't describe what I have gone through but I will tell you when I see you. I realise I must walk about in the open more, visit our old places and keep some perspective.'

One day of flying was exhausting, and the organising and reporting afterwards took longer. The reality was Joe worked too hard, drank too much, and fell asleep in his clothes. He loved the challenge and the camaraderie – finding himself in amongst 'an exceptionally first rate lot of chaps' – but his worries about the future shrouded everything. He was in the skies or looking up at them, expecting enemy aeroplanes. He wasn't sure the British could win this war, and he feared for his recruits and their young families. He was having a second chance at life when they had barely had a first. It didn't seem right.

He came to rely on alcohol, he couldn't help it – it felt necessary and it swiftly became part of the job. Before Johnny Churchill went to France with the British Expeditionary Force, Joe took him to one side and dispensed two bits of advice. The first was: 'Be natural, especially with generals, because we will be dealing with high-ranking officers.' The second was: 'Be able to hold your drink.'

He wasn't being frivolous.

'Our work will meet with opposition and indifference, and often the most difficult issues – the fixing of permission to do this and that – will be settled in the Mess.'[11]

Joe knew how to make an impression. If people wouldn't take camouflage seriously then why not make it funny: buy drinks and tell outrageous stories, put on a bit of a show. Camouflage was as much about standing out as blending in, and those first impressions mattered. Joe saw something of himself in Johnny – the black sheep of the family, the bon viveur, the occasional clown. Johnny's father had had a dim view of his son's artistic tendencies ('playing the ass in the gutter'[12]), but once he went off to France, he changed his tune completely. ('My Johnny is now a Captain and in France! He is doing Camouflage work and having a splendid time.'[13])

Camouflage made rebels and renegades acceptable. It turned opinions and expectations upside down. 'Camouflage violated a principle dear to the pipe-clay heart of every staff officer: it went against the military obsession with neatness, spit-and-polish, drill field regularity. Camouflage was considered careless and "undisciplined". It made a virtue of dispersion, irregularity, and improvisation.'[14] For men like Joe and Johnny, that left everything to play for.

But Johnny was soon in trouble not of his own making. The situation in France was crumbling, and he found himself under constant fire from German bombers along the Belgian border. 'A mood of alarm and hysteria was developing among the troops of the BEF.'[15] Freddie Beddington had not had the chance to test out Joe's steel wool. Instead, he'd found himself burning all his maps and schemes in a brewer's vat outside Boulogne. He returned to England to work with Richard Buckley in establishing the camouflage training courses, the second of which began in early May.

Jack Sayer was dispatched with two dozen other new recruits by train from Charing Cross. He was one of the few who wore a respectable suit; the rest had donned various interpretations of military attire and and resembled 'the chorus line of a First World War musical comedy'.[16] When Buckley met them on the platform at Shorncliffe he was understandably concerned. 'I cannot say, gentlemen, what effect you will produce on the enemy. But, by God, you terrify me!'[17]

In response they offered him every variant of salute, apart from the correct one. But what did Buckley expect? They were painters and illustrators, sculptors and set designers, art directors and film-makers. They were not soldiers. Not yet.

What awaited them was a mixture of the practical and the theoretical. 'Our days were filled with much strenuous outdoor work as well as lectures and a certain amount of flying.'[18] 'Buckles' would deliver what he called his 'set-pieces', lecturing on light and shade and texture, and the relative importance of colour and tone to the air camera. He taught the men about nets and how to garnish them, and he would make them dig pits and try to conceal them. He could also, quite suddenly, explode in anger, but he succeeded in infecting everyone with a passion for their subject. And it wasn't only hard work. Each evening they lounged in the Mess, smoking and drinking the finest Madeira. 'I have rarely enjoyed such excellent and lavish food as I did those four weeks,' recalled Sayer.[19]

Back at the Board, Joe was scheduled to travel up to Larkhill for three days' solid lecturing, but he was caught between too many commitments. He was finalising the production of steel wool and instructions on how to use it, answering endless requests for camouflage from up and down the country, worrying about the new camouflage officers coming out of training and the old ones still abroad. The surrender of France felt imminent and it filled him with despair.

'I am having the most frightful time,' he wrote to Mary. 'The work is never-ending and the news just gets worse. Some of our chaps unaccounted for. Still waiting. In London, things are definitely getting hotter and I would be very glad to feel you were in Bath during the coming period.'

Mary was safe in Bath, but what about everyone else? On 25

May the War Office made the decision to evacuate British forces. Even up at Larkhill, Barkas and Sayer saw evidence of the chaos of defeat.

'We got back to camp in time to meet a long, slow, straggling procession of men climbing with difficulty the gentle slope towards the mess. Ragged, grimy men, unshaven, caked with mud and dust . . . I saw none who spoke or smiled. They stumbled on like zombies – dead but walking. They were men from Dunkirk.'[20]

Sayer caught a train down to London that weekend, eager to see his young family. On the Sunday he stopped in at Melbourne House knowing that Joe would be at his desk, ploughing through paperwork with his usual flair.

They were sharing a sandwich, discussing the latest recruits, when the door of the office was suddenly flung open. There stood Johnny Churchill, clean-shaven but sodden.

'I say! *What a war!*'[21]

It was the wonderful bit of theatre – it would soon become a catchphrase.

'Good God,' Joe croaked. 'Where *have* you come from?'

Johnny flung himself down in a chair.

'Dunkirk, my dear man. *Fantastic.*'

Johnny hadn't come directly to the office, however. After reaching Dover he'd boarded the first train to London, stopping briefly at the Grosvenor Hotel to shave, before taking a taxi to the Admiralty and reporting to his uncle Winston, who had been prime minister for a matter of weeks.

'I have had the most dreadful time. They need more boats – smaller ones. I offered to go back. You have no idea. The scene on the beaches was amazing.'

Johnny then pulled some crumpled papers from his tunic pocket, scattering them loosely across the desk.

'Here, I made some sketches.'

Joe took up Johnny's sketches, scanning them quickly. Then it came like a reflex reaction – he abruptly cleared his desk and spread out two sheets of paper.

'Draw it, while it's still fresh.'

Johnny had sunk deeper into the chair, eyes already closing.

'Sorry, I don't think I can, old chap.'

Joe pretended not to hear, or perhaps he really didn't. He was reaching into one of his desk drawers, from which he produced a bottle of Kummel.

Kummel was a sweet, colourless liqueur flavoured with caraway seed, cumin and fennel. It was very popular before the war, and never recommended as a substitute for breakfast.

Johnny barely stirred.

'Perhaps a sandwich?' Sayer offered.

'Let me sleep for a couple of hours and I'll be all right.'

'Rot!' Joe took a roll of paper and, leaning over, whacked Johnny on the head. 'You will use your sketch notes and draw at once what you have seen before it goes from your mind.'

Johnny sighed but didn't move.

Bang went the roll of paper again.

'All right, all right.' Johnny pulled himself up.

'Your drawings will be a direct record. Think on that.'

Joe handed Johnny a glass of Kummel and then stood over him for the next two hours, regularly whacking him with a roll of paper to keep him awake.

June 1940

Dearest P.F.

I had been going to write a long letter this weekend but have to go off to Larkhill tomorrow for 3 days. I hope you are getting on fine. I have missed you more than somewhat! What a catastrophe in France but what a masterpiece getting so many away – Johnny arrived after having had a very stiff time. On Sunday while I was working he did two amazing drawings of the beach at Dunkirk, which he is going to try in the London Illustrated News. The beach was like Southend on a Bank Holiday. Thousands and thousands of men. Troops firing away and the German bombers cracking away at them with bombs and machine guns. Then all kinds of boats from fishing smacks up to large steamers. Tug boats as well, in fact anything that would float and scores of row boats all filling up with men or being sunk by the German dive bombers. They are exceptionally good drawings and realise the scene wonderfully.

Johnny's drawings were indeed published in the *Illustrated London News* on 8 June 1940. 'I think the two ink and wash sketches he produced that afternoon were probably the best things he had ever done,'[22] declared Sayer.

Joe kept a treasured copy. They are now rather tired and tattered but I can see Johnny's signature with the accompanying dedication – 'for Gray, with pleasant memories of the day they were drawn.'

L *is for Lay-out: the way that you face*
Is of vital importance so choose the right place

After Dunkirk the invasion of Britain was a real and present threat. Within forty-eight hours of the troops' evacuation from northern France, the Luftwaffe began sending sorties across the Channel. In the following weeks small daylight raids on coastal towns in the south and east began. The Luftwaffe engaged RAF fighters in aerial combat and from August started to destroy Britain's defences. There was much to hide and no time to lose.

At Larkhill, Joe's lectures in static camouflage brought the second course to a close. The men assembled for a group photograph along with officers from the first course who were recovering from their experiences in France. It was a glorious summer's day, their last all together. They still didn't look much like soldiers, but that seemed to be the point.

Richard Buckley and Freddie Beddington are seated centre front (Joe marked them out with crowns on the reverse). Buckley, arms crossed, frowns inscrutably, his bristling whiskers hiding most of his face. Beddington, sporting a more reserved moustache, sits beside him, debonair but as unreadable. Tom Van Oss, just back from France, sits cross-legged in front of them – tanned, handsome and grinning like a schoolboy. To his left is Peter Proud, an art director from Warner Brothers. The bespectacled Godfrey Baxter, a theatrical producer for Glyndebourne, is squinting at the back,

137

fourth from the right. He was at least trying to stand to attention, as is Charles McCall, a Scottish painter whom Joe had recommended for work in camouflage. Steven Sykes, a designer of stained glass, stands at the back on the far right; John Lewis, an illustrator, stands beside the film-maker Geoffrey Barkas, who keeps his cap at a jaunty angle.

All were in uniform apart from Jack Sayer, who smiles wryly in his pale suit, holding a lit cigarette.

Joe wasn't in the picture but he added the names afterwards, sending the photograph to Mary for safekeeping. It was a precious memory of the men he'd count as friends, brothers, some even his 'babies'. The affection was mostly reciprocated: Tom Van Oss called him a 'good fatherly angel' and sketched him as a wise old owl;[1] for Jack Sayer he was the 'father-confessor'[2] figure to many a camouflage officer. He was 'Grayowl', more often 'Grumble'. The only person seemingly impervious to Joe's charms was John Lewis. He dismissed that 'elderly *illustrator*' whose lectures he'd had to sit through. As far as Lewis was concerned, Joe's only 'claim to fame' came later, when he nearly burned down Farnham Castle after it became the Camouflage Development and Training Centre. The story went that after talking to the troops late one night, Joe fell asleep with a lit cigarette. He had to be saved first from potential incineration, and then from a court martial.[3]

It made a good story – one of so many. Joe would not be the first or last camouflage officer to risk a court martial, and whatever the men now thought of each other, there were more pressing matters demanding their attention.

Dispatched to different corners of Britain, camouflage officers had to teach the gospel of camouflage to regular troops, and apply themselves practically to hiding anything of value. Steven Sykes was posted to Newcastle, Geoffrey Barkas went with Michael Farrar Bell to Northern Ireland. Others, like Tom Van Oss, were sent to Anti-Aircraft (AA) Command in York, and Johnny Churchill to AA Command in Stanmore, Middlesex.

'I am afraid I cannot tell you what it is [I am doing],' wrote Van Oss to his family, 'but it is proving exceedingly interesting, full of variety, and sustaining, because the importance of the subject is *not* universally accepted.'[4]

Persuading everyone else in the Army that camouflage was neither 'a fashionable nuisance' nor 'a magic cloak'[5] took up a huge amount of time, but camouflage officers were endlessly inventive. They designed pamphlets, poems and cartoons to both amuse and indoctrinate. Similarly, the best lectures on camouflage were as diverting. Van Oss filled cinemas with audiences of up to a thousand at a time, and always found that a bit of blaring music put 'the mass of pink-faced, smoking, khaki-clad men in a good mood'.[6] Props and tricks were encouraged: jokes, anecdotes, and even naked ladies. Roland Penrose became camouflage instructor to the Home Guard and fired their interest in concealment by using slides of his lover, Lee Miller, covered in nothing more than camouflage cream, netting and strategically placed vegetation. Julian Trevelyan followed his friend's example, finding that a few X-rated slides slipped into his presentation always kept the troops alert. Godfrey Baxter, meanwhile, spent most of his time in the Mess sinking gin and delivering famously racy lectures: 'At every dance you have probably noticed the girl with the black velvet dress with a great hand-mark on her bottom where her partner has held her too tight. All he has done is to destroy the contained shadow on the velvet, as you are busy doing when you walk about in the grass around your gun-site.'[7]

But camouflage officers also had to practise what they preached, and now devoted hours to disguising the gun sites, bomb stores and hutted camps that were fast appearing. Every village had its 'strong post' to defend. Pillboxes, those 'awkward little pentagonal objects'[8] used for anti-aircraft guns, were a constant challenge. Joe had advised such features were best merged with existing structures – for example, barns, hedges or haystacks – but in the early days camoufleurs couldn't resist being more inventive. These depressing concrete blocks underwent ingenious transformations and were disguised as ruined forts, summer houses, fairground stalls, chicken coops and garages complete with petrol pumps. Of course, that in itself created issues, since too elaborate a design would attract attention and public comment. 'Our concealment must be so complete that even the fact that we are hiding something shall not be apparent,' reminded Penrose.[9]

Still, artists couldn't help themselves. Julian Trevelyan writing to Edward Seago, another well-known artist recruited into camouflage, detailed his painting of two anti-aircraft guns – one following a 'pointillist' design and another using a disruptive pattern of countershading. He explained that in order to paint the other guns of the battery along precisely the same lines, Seago had to authorise the purchase of six different camouflage shades, recommending a specific local paint manufacturer so that Trevelyan could be present and 'could supervise the mixing of the correct shades' personally.[10] While such attention to detail was laudable, it's vaguely reminiscent of a soldier's remarks on Solomon J. Solomon in the last war: 'I can see him now standing away from the tank with one eye closed and holding his brush at arm's length between the delicate touches that he painted on to her.'[11]

Many camoufleurs held tight to their pre-war artistic sensibil-
ities. Major Seago was often irritated by the question 'You were an
artist, weren't you, before the war?' 'I *am* an artist,' he would
haughtily protest.[12] But Joe chose a different tack. Rather than
talking up his art background, he referred back to his experience
as an observer in the trenches. He told men to *see* like an artist but
think like a soldier, and whatever his rumbustiousness, his schemes
were as efficient as they were economic. He constantly warned the
men of RE8 against any flights of fancy. Because of the constraints
of time and money and the sheer scale of the task at hand, schemes
had to be kept simple.

Joe was also responsible for a variety of different sites, from
very large Royal Ordinance factories to smaller gun sites, and War
Department depots. Each structure or structures presented new
challenges depending on their shape or surroundings, and so
needed care and attention, but the procedure itself followed similar lines. Joe always recommended a ground reconnaissance in the
first instance, where it was important to meet the manager or
person responsible for the site (the maintenance of camouflage was
often as challenging as making it). After a ground inspection, there
would ideally be an opportunity to fly over the buildings, taking
photographs from different angles. Most officers were taught
aerial photography and so multitasked, although Joe admitted
to Mary he found the camera too cumbersome: 'a huge affair
compared with ordinary cameras and needs both hands to do it'.
He preferred to fly with a photographer so that he could observe
and then refer back to the images afterwards.

The simplest camouflage schemes involved darkening in a single
colour, the basic blending in. Written instructions were enough for

that, and Joe found he spent a lot of time providing this kind of advice. Any schemes that involved patterning needed more detailed drawings and sketches, and very occasionally a model might be made.

Everything had to be worked out, from design and fitting through to construction, but whatever the excitement over steel wool, Joe accepted that paint was still the main form of camouflage available. It was the cheapest and easiest method. With prominent features such as chimneys, complete concealment was impossible. The only option was to aim at confusion and so create a broad disruptive pattern, for example, and garnished nets could be used to mask any hard edges and eliminate harsher shadows. Elsewhere, any shiny surfaces such as corrugated iron or glass skylights had to be sanded down or coated with 'gritty' substances. Dealing with the surrounding area was as important. Scarred earth showed up light and was therefore always dangerous, as were outbuildings and parked cars and trucks (which were preferably dispersed). Similarly, railways or shiny road surfaces could easily give the game away. Railway stations were most often covered in netting and train tracks could be painted to look like roads. Road surfaces also had to be darkened and given a 'grittier' textured effect to blend with vegetation, or covered by screens. On the ground 'a lasting pattern can be produced by sprayed bitumen raked into a rough textured surface with white, sharp river sand as the contrasting pattern.'[13]

Joe developed the ideas that had formed the basis of *Camouflage and Air Defence*, though there was much he still had to consider, not least the impact of blackout. Initially, all camouflage was designed to protect against daylight raids, but this soon changed as

German bombers came to favour cover of night. Blackout had been enforced two days before the war's outbreak – with all windows and doors tightly covered and street lights and headlamps switched off or hooded. Concealment was everybody's everyday responsibility, but that also drew attention to certain features that almost defied concealment.

'I find it fascinating to fly over blacked-out expanses of the countryside,' Joe wrote to Mary. 'You would be amazed at how much is still visible with a full moon . . . Fascinating and damned frustrating!'

Man-made features were easy to spot in moonlight – not just the reflective surfaces of modern buildings, but the plumes of steam and smoke they emitted, the hard edges of road junctions, the glittering sheen on a reservoir. White smoke at night had to be eliminated, so the fuel source was altered to produce a darker smoke. Concealing water was near impossible, though. Scrap metal, tin sheeting and drums were used to devise screening to at least break up the shape of any lake or river, and gritty substances were floated on the surface – but only with limited success.

And there was a whole other problem with landmarks, which might be used by the enemy bomber to guide him to his target. Most were impossible to hide, although Jack Sayer delighted in the discovery of some paperwork relating to the Cerne Abbas giant, that 'unashamed phallic figure' cut into the Dorset downs. What could possibly be done to conceal it? 'Major X noted that the affair had come up again. Colonel Y agreed it was shockingly conspicuous and recommended camouflage, and so it went on until Brigadier Sayer gave his opinion that cold water should be thrown over the whole thing.'[14]

Yes, there was still fun to be had, and it wasn't just the processes of camouflage that caused amusement, but the materials themselves. Reducing shine was a full-time occupation. A lot of time was spent trying to make paint gritty, and when that failed, substances like coke breeze or cork granules were used. But the best secret weapon was sludge. As unattractive as it sounds, sludge oil could be recovered from the bottoms of bunkers and oil-burning merchant vessels and proved extremely effective at reducing both colour and shine on brickwork. It prompted this jolly ditty, presumably by Sayer:

> Sludge! Sludge! Glorious Sludge!
> Scraped from the bottom of tanks;
> Lots you can do with it – have a shampoo with it –
> Rub the old back with it – paint the town black
>   with it –
> Charm away bunions – fertilize onions –
> Massage the cranium – good for the brainium!
> If you're rheumatic, a slave to sciatica,
> Wallow away in it – spend the whole day in it –
> Order a drum of it – give the cat some of it –
> Have a good dig at it – take a nice swig at it –
> Paint the Home Guard with it – bomb Hitler
>   hard with it –
> Polish the floor with it – win the whole war
>   with it –
> Give me a Peerage as thanks!
> (The Viscount of Sidcup and Sludge! –
> Glorious, glorious SLUDGE!)
>   *Camouflage Game*

With the good-humoured Colonel Wyatt now in charge at RE8, he was in need of a staff captain, and Joe happily secured Kenneth Dalgliesh, a peacetime architect who had lost an arm at Arras, and proved to be a connoisseur of both port and beer. Dalgliesh had a low tolerance of civil servants and red tape, but proved extremely capable on the material side of camouflage, becoming deeply involved in experimental work with cork granules, sludge oil 'and other strange matters',[15] spending days on end at a research facility, testing out various industrial by-products to create a perfect texture.

For the record, Dalgliesh found sludge worked best when it was applied and then 'blinded' with dry earth, so that a solid dull surface could be obtained.

But if concealment was so crucial to saving lives and vital resources, what about steel wool? Peregrine Churchill for one grew very extremely frustrated when its supply wasn't forthcoming. In June 1940 he brought the matter to the prime minister's attention. He made it clear that the War Office and the Air Ministry both wanted large quantities but the demand was not being met. Frustrated by the delays, he insisted on an enquiry.

The results of this enquiry remained as a closed file in the National Archives, right up until the time that I requested they be opened. Peregrine, writing to his aunt Clemmie in July, made very serious allegations of 'fifth column activity'[16] against the Ministry of Supply. He felt sure that officials were fixing contracts and the firms now producing steel wool were quite incapable and incompetent.

The problem arose due to the fact that, because of competitive tendering, M&E Equipment could understandably not have a monopoly to produce steel wool. A new supplier, Williams & Williams, had been approached but were apparently producing substandard material, as were another firm, Tinsley Wire Industries. The Air Ministry had declared that the latest batch of steel wool was far 'too stringy'.

Whereas the quiet and careful Peregrine wanted to follow correct protocol with an 'official investigation', Johnny, being Johnny, couldn't wait. Incensed by the red tape and wasted time, he stormed the Chester factory of Williams & Williams and created merry hell.

'He entered my office,' wrote a traumatised Mr Williams, 'and informed me that he was in charge of camouflage throughout the country and without waiting for me, entered into a tirade about the position of camouflage, stating that the whole position needed investigating, that it was scandalous the number of lives being lost due to non-delivery of camouflage material, and did I not agree with him.'

Williams reacted with dismay and disbelief. 'I stated that I was not in a position to express an opinion but that we had only recently known about the camouflage and that we were doing everything possible to boost up delivery and provided that we get some fitters, we could deliver 100,000 square yards a week and that I believed that if we obtained the wire wool in bulk, similar to the samples just received from America, there would, I thought, be no difficulty in getting an output from the Plant we were making, of 125,000 square yards per week.'

Johnny was still not satisfied. 'He said he wanted 500,000 square yards a month and I pointed out to him that 125,000 square yards a week was 500,000 square yards a month. He then said that he wanted 500,000 square yards *a week*.'

Things went from bad to worse. 'He asked me if I knew people in the Ministry of Supply. I stated only by having contacted them on the telephone. He asked if I considered they were *Fascists*. He said the orders had been placed in January and what had we been doing in the meantime?' Mr Williams promptly explained that they'd been making Nissen huts and other items for the war effort.

Johnny spluttered and stamped the floor.

'Another racket!' he exclaimed.

The meeting ended abruptly with Johnny making various threats. Poor Mr Williams consoled himself that Johnny's artistic temperament was to blame.

'I have since learned that Captain Churchill in civil life is an artist and interior decorator, and upon learning this, understood his attitude at the interview.'[17]

For the prime minister it was embarrassing, but the intensity of the debate shows how much camouflage had come to matter. The enquiry eventually concluded that any delay in manufacture was simply a matter of departments being stretched to their limits. As for Johnny, there was talk of a court martial. 'Johnny gets into and out of hot water,' Joe told Mary. 'He is really too undiplomatic. He will either be made a brigadier or will be shot!' Neither, in fact, occurred. But the spotlight on steel wool seemed to speed up production. By autumn, Tinsley Wire Industries were delivering 80,000 square yards a week, and Williams & Williams 20,000 square yards. Both firms were working double shifts.

The Air Ministry considered steel wool crucial, particularly for the camouflage of its aircraft factories, hangars and for aircraft dispersal, but there was still some way to go to have it widely accepted. After the declaration of war, the Ministry of Home Security had taken charge of civil camouflage and established the

Civil Defence Camouflage Establishment, based in the picturesque town of Leamington Spa, conveniently located in the almost exact centre of England. Wing Commander T. R. Cave-Brown-Cave, a professor of engineering at Southampton University, was the new director, with Captain Glasson named chief camouflage officer. Office headquarters were located in the elegant Regent Hotel, and an old ice rink was commandeered as a camouflage workshop. ('An old skating rink in Leamington is now filled with artists with hair of various lengths, painting camouflage schemes onto models of all the most important factories engaged in our war production.')[18] A revolving stage was constructed, complete with adjustable 'sun' and special viewing balcony. This, the men at RE8 thought rather extravagant: 'The Leamington experts, rather to our amusement, even went so far as to rig their own private solar system. The precious models when painted were set up on a turn table . . . a movable lighting was manipulated to simulate sunlight and moonlight at various times and seasons. Undoubtedly a fascinating *toy*.'[19]

But the Civil Defence Camouflage Establishment was supposed to be the place where new techniques and materials were developed, and Captain Glasson expressed reluctance to use steel wool. He thought it too expensive and 'only doubtfully fireproof'.[20] Several colleagues queried this, suggesting he 'was condemning something he knew little about'[21] and that it was in the national interest to support its production. The issue was debated because the Air Ministry had initially requested up to 10 million square yards of steel wool, and then responsibility for the camouflage of many of its sites was transferred to Home Security.

But Glasson's reluctance to support steel wool was coloured by his own interest in another screening material, one made out of seaweed. Dried seaweed contains a large percentage of alginic acid, which was extracted from it in the form of crude sodium alginate. This was then converted into calcium alginate, which was spun into a fibre. The final material was promptly codenamed 'BG' ('BG', stood for 'Bloody Good' – after so many other materials had been labelled 'NBG').

The battle between BG and steel wool was extensively documented. Glasson rightly argued that seaweed was cheaper and more readily available and therefore surely *better*; however, the means of transforming it into something hard-wearing proved costly and labour-intensive. In the end, after two years of trials, the appointment of two research chemists and the endless allocation of resources, BG was still neither strong enough nor sufficiently weatherproof to be used on anything like the scale of steel wool.

It is strangely satisfying to find John Lewis, the camoufleur who had been so unimpressed by Joe as a lecturer, being yet more dismayed by the material that was meant to rival his. In the spring of 1941 Lewis was inspecting some large guns near Tunbridge Wells. 'The actual guns, which were Big Bertha-like relics of the first war, were concealed under 18,000 square yards of netting and stuff that looked like grass. It was actually a kind of seaweed.' Yes, this was the famous 'BG', although, according to Lewis, 'It was not all that *BG*, for when the weather was damp it drooped in the manner of any proper seaweed and all its covering capabilities were lost. Sodium alginate found its proper level after the war in the manufacture of ice cream.'[22]

M is for Maintenance of the disguise
Leaving covers unchecked is always unwise

17 Vale Court
9 September 1940
Dearest M.,
I am adding a P.S. to my letter to let you know that a bomb landed in my bedroom last night.

But the M wasn't Mary. This was James Meade, Mary's brother, writing to his wife Margaret in Canada. James had been staying in Mary's flat in Vale Court. Only the flat was no more.

The Battle of Britain had begun in earnest in June 1940 and by August the Luftwaffe was moving inland, targeting London suburbs. The much-feared 'mighty blow'[1] came on Saturday 7 September. Six hundred bombers swarmed in tight formation up the Thames, and with a thundering, furious certainty they laid waste to east London, dropping their explosives on the power stations and docks. They returned the next night. The Strand was bombed, St Thomas's hospital and St Paul's, the West End, Buckingham Palace, Lambeth Palace, Piccadilly, the House of Commons. Chelsea was also badly hit because German planes would fly up the Thames in search of Battersea power station. The only landmark that stood out was the Water Tower on Campden Hill in Kensington, and as soon as the German pilots spotted it they knew they'd flown too far. They'd turn around and jettison spare bombs en route.

James Meade had only recently returned to England after a stint in Geneva, working at the League of Nations. He was back in London to take up a post as economic adviser in the War Cabinet. His plans to stay in Vale Court were brought to an abrupt end.

'Luckily, we had all taken refuge in the basement & no one was at all hurt. I am afraid that a good deal of Mary's things were destroyed, and I rather suspect that I have lost a lot of my clothes!' James tried hard to assure his wife it was really only a 'small fire' and 'London seems very normal again this morning. Now I am living at the office and sleeping on a "Lilo" in the deep air-raid shelter. So I am as safe and as comfortable as one can possibly be.'²

It was business as usual, that was the idea. But not for Mary. When she learned that Vale Court had been hit she was distraught. Her home and many of her belongings had been destroyed, and that private place where she and Joe could meet was gone for good. Joe had braced himself for such a violent shock and it almost came like a relief since it was what he'd been expecting.

'Why dear P.F. it seems practically impossible to realise that No. 17 has been smashed up in this frightful way but thank Heaven you were safely out of it. I spent that night with an A.A. Battery in Kent, who had lent us a couple of blankets, it being impossible to motor in the dark. I must say, the barrage over London made a fantastic sight!'

How typical of Joe to find the beauty in bombs dropping; his artist's eyes were drawn to the throbs of light, the warm glow of distant fires. Driving through the East End the next morning, he couldn't resist sketching the scenes he came across.

The firemen were still busy – on tops of ladders and roofs and so on hammering away and hosing tons of water – a most fantastic sight. The people are going about their morning work, these typical old women with their shopping bags and umbrellas – and scores of children of all ages still around – Nothing of military importance seemed to have been hit but I suppose they did get some of the docks and warehouses.

With London under attack, Joe's way of life would change and change again. It was a new kind of homelessness and a new extreme of sleeplessness. He would rarely get back to Marlborough Gate – 'it is practically impossible to get any means of conveyance after 9 or 10 o'clock. The Marlborough Gateites sleep – or try to – in the basement or ground floor but I think the Hyde Park guns keep most of them awake – Fortunately I don't hear the guns too much but even I hear the Hyde Park ones which are pretty 'ot!'

Mary had no choice but to remain at Lansdown Crescent with her mother, which proved difficult for both of them. Unlike Joe, Mary was unable to keep secrets – both her brother and her mother now knew about her 'complicated situation'. Mary assured them that Joe's marriage was long over, but this was small comfort to the recently widowed Kitty Meade. She thought her daughter impetuous and immature, and the uncertainty of these terrifying times had only made her vulnerable. War, like alcohol, could skew one's moral compass.

Fortunately, Joe was too busy to impose on them in Bath. He was himself a distant spectre, the will-o'-the-wisp of Sayer's cartoon. 'So sorry but working day and all night. Haven't a chance

to write. Hope to do so tomorrow though and you will understand!' Even when Mary came up to London to see the charred
ruins of Vale Court, they missed each other completely. 'This is just
a rushed note to tell you how sorry I am I didn't see you before
you went,' Joe scrawled on some scrap paper, before dashing off to
Dover again.

He was so caught up in the frenetic pace of work and the endless bombing raids he had little chance to reflect on what had been
lost. Mary tried to salvage a few bits of furniture and regain a
sense of perspective. Returning to Bath, she found herself a clerical
post at the Admiralty offices there. She wanted and needed to be
useful, to keep active, but she was fighting a terrible feeling she
might become now more stuck than ever before.

For the camoufleur, blackout was crucial, and for Joe it was also
an opportunity. Through the autumn and winter of 1940 he developed the dangerous habit of going out every evening under cover
of dark, with senses newly alert to each bombing raid. Oftentimes
the Churchill brothers joined him. More exhilarated than afraid,
Joe reported each adventure to Mary.

The night Bruton Street and Berkeley Square were bombed Johnny
Churchill and I were caught right in the middle of it and it was
terrific – but frightfully thrilling.

Another night Johnny and Peregrine and I went into a burning
house with the A.R.P. wardens – with pick axes and stump pumps
etc. We had all just got to the top floor when there was a shout –
'all out all out!' and like the Duke of York's men we all dashed out
again, thinking some huge bomb was about to go off – but it was
actually the fire brigade coming to the rescue. They had the ladders

up in no time and fairly blew the house to bits with the force of their water. What a marvellous picture it was from the street – wonderful! One of the incendiaries dropped only 10 yards from us. Very 'ot. Very 'ot. I find it very fascinating after the nightly bombardments start but must stop tempting fate too much.

He didn't – couldn't – stop, though. He just took up his pens and pencils and started sketching. Every night he would walk for hours, sharp-eyed, observing and then drawing some new spectacle, noting the demise of all his favourite Chelsea pubs. And he reported his endless close shaves and near misses to an increasingly horrified Mary. So used was Joe to living on his wits, he didn't consider how he amplified her anxieties. 'Present conditions are fantastic, I can't see how they will end – nor can I see how they can continue.'

But they did continue. His fellow camoufleurs tried to protect him – Tom Van Oss put him forward for membership of the Chelsea Arts Club, so at least he had another place at night – but Joe found it too depressing. Everyone went to the shelter, which he couldn't understand. What artist would want to miss 'a full moon and a terrific barrage'?

So he slipped back through the empty streets, deaf to the sirens and air raid warnings, visiting pubs and clubs along his route. He was like a cat with nine lives, insinuating himself into hotel lounges, having a drink and stealing the notepaper. Having survived one war, a few bombs couldn't scare him and the fact he couldn't hear them made him feel impervious.

But why tempt fate so much?

It was all about what he saw; his role was one of witness. London without electric light was transformed into something magical. The idea of all these magnificent buildings under threat only intensified his desire to see them one more time. The spectacle of an attack was too enthralling and apalling to miss. 'I say – what a war! Fantastic – what marvellous subjects for drawings – simply wonderful and horrific.'

The bombs, the air raids, the smoking ruins, revived such strong memories and with them came that heady fatalism. Joe had no death wish, but he had long accepted how life could be snatched away. His acceptance of this gave him back control, and control mattered greatly. He decided it was better to be killed doing what he loved rather than hiding in some cramped basement, trying and failing to get a good night's sleep. 'I lead a fantastic life when the blackout comes on. I have no real place to go so I sort of float around – seeing the most wonderful things in the barrage.'

He had slipped his moorings, reimagined himself. London offered a wild adventure and a secret escape, a release from the pressures of his work. On finding some fresh fire, his first instinct was to climb onto a roof and get the bird's eye view. Looking down on the world was still the best way to understand it. He was back in the role of observer, sketching new ruins on scraps of paper, summoning the outlines of buildings caressed by flames, the billowing contours of smoke clouds.

By 18 November Joe felt that he had 'started drawing seriously and got some rather good stuff under way'. He considered 'the right approach', and decided to transform his night-time sketches into a series of Blitz etchings, to be called 'The Battle of Britain'. Of course, he had no studio, and so he made his own. RE8 had moved offices across the road to Bush House and there, when only the fire-watchers were awake, Joe would sweep his reports aside and make space for 'etching needles, scrapers and brushes'.

Artist or camoufleur? He was both, and his already cluttered office became the site of a new industry. Sayer and Dalgliesh both had families waiting for them at home, but they stayed on, fascinated by the sight of Joe at his desk with a single screened lamp above his copper plate. There he'd stay, scratching and gouging, smearing on printer's ink at intervals and then wiping it so as to judge the effect, while his cigarette smoke drifted up through the light. So inspired were they by Joe's example that they soon joined him, and Joe conducted his own impromptu etching classes each night.

'They will be pretty fierce,' he told Mary, but if anything they were romantic, already suffused with a kind of nostalgia. These were views of fires half-seen, of passers-by in shadow, of dark clouds cloaking the city skyline. One image, *Incendiary*, shows a single building mostly in darkness but for the light in the upper window where a human figure waited. There is a fireman on the roof, his face lit up by the blaze, and two figures watching from street level. It could be a moment of terror and uncertainty, and surely it was or it had been, but now it is transformed into something strange and otherworldly.

In the last war Joe had laboured over every name and detail, but now he was more concerned with impressions and effects. He had learned from his study of camouflage that tone and texture mattered more. He was distilling the moment into a mood, a feeling, something more than simply seen.

The men of RE8 were not the only artists to find a certain magic in the buildings shattered by German bombs. A War Artists Advisory Committee had already been established, and would collect hundreds of images of air raids, but Joe's etchings would not be amongst them. He donated prints to regimental charities to raise money for veterans, and he promised them to his friends and colleagues – to James Meade, to Peregrine, to Jack Sayer; he even sold a set to his bank manager for some ready cash. He kept it personal and meaningful: that was what he wanted. Away in the future there was the possibility of making art full time and being with Mary, but not in this here and now. Joe wouldn't think of tomorrow until he got there. It was rather like he had fallen in love all over again.

So Joe was in love, but Mary was in Bath.

[H]ere's too the new phase of life, sweetheart. Am I writing too many love letters P.F.? Will you soon begin to take me for granted – as you used to say I took you (which I never did). Is it better to be ignored or adored? I do so adore you. Do you like being adored? X.

Mary lived for each letter but wrote back less and less. The contrast between their two lives could not have been more acute. Joe was ricocheting all over the country, always so much in demand, and Mary stayed in Bath, where every day was the same. He realised he had to make an effort to visit, and tried to arrange field inspections that incorporated a stopover. 'I have a job at Swindon which is not too far away and I hope to pop in for the night. So don't get excited if you receive a telegram – it will only be to say I am coming.' Of course he was careful, booking rooms at local pubs, paying his respects to Kitty Meade but never daring to impose as a guest.

The trouble was, whenever Joe materialised, it caused a 'disruption'. It was as if a bomb had dropped. He would be exhilarated from a long day's flying and Mary would feel sidelined, even jealous. Joe was aware of the disparity between their lives but his usual strategies of appeasement didn't work. Mary with her agile mind was easily agitated, and she felt under such scrutiny living back with her mother. She still loved Joe, with perhaps more intensity, and he felt entirely the same, yet they were slipping into a dreadful pattern – a brief encounter followed by an anguished parting. He always had to go back to his work, back to London, to the Board, to all his camouflage comrades. Mary felt she was fighting a whole other war with him, and not one she could win.

N *is for Nets which are simply a frame*
For the garnishing on them, so garnish
the same

Joe worked all through Christmas and into January 1941. He was
so busy writing and filing reports he barely had the energy for
etching. He spent more time with Sayer, Dalgliesh and Johnny and
Peregrine Churchill than he did with Mary. Then Wyatt ordered
him off on a tour of the north of England – Birmingham, York,
Darlington – then up to Scotland to see Le Breton-Simmons, who
was now heading up another camouflage training school in Edinburgh. Joe was an ambassador for the cause of camouflage, there
to convince everyone of its importance. It was freezing cold and
the bad weather limited his time flying, but in terms of his talks it
went well.

'The personal contact is worth a thousand files going back and
forwards and it means I meet all the Chief Engineers and Brigadiers and what not and explain where they go wrong and what we
want and so on and so forth.'

Camouflage was crucial, Joe said it over and over. It could save
lives, it could protect industry, it could hinder and limit the
Luftwaffe at every turn. By now his words were taking effect;
camouflage wasn't such a hard sell. After all, nobody wanted to
go to work in a brand new factory exposed from every angle.

Camouflage boosted morale and made people feel protected, and that had an impact on the war effort.

Joe returned to London late in February exhausted but elated, feeling that the trip had been 'a great success and must be repeated regularly'. And the good news kept trickling in: of steel wool hayricks and fir trees being used to disguise the King's own aerodrome,[1] of steel wool covers at Fighter Command HQ[2] and a whole landscape fabricated at Eynsham to hide a vast Air Ministry bomb store. Steel wool was proving useful, hard-wearing and endlessly versatile. It was creating large and small illusions just as he had hoped.

Peregrine Churchill remained the stalwart believer, and he was now consultant engineer at M&E Equipment, busily designing covers for the Air Ministry on priority sites up and down the country. Taking Joe's *Camouflage and Air Defence* as the basis for his ideas on structural camouflage, Peregrine drew up plans for trees, houses and hedges of steel wool and eagerly put them to use. Johnny at Stanmore had commandeered an old Anson bomber and was flying around the country examining and photographing anti-aircraft positions to see how much was visible from the air. For the first time these two very different brothers were united in a single enterprise.

Peregrine's ambitious project at Eynsham impressed Joe when he went to inspect it with Sayer. The magazines had been positioned in the hollow of a ridge, which allowed for a steel wool cover to be placed on top, on a frame, so that from the air it appeared like an innocent grassy slope. Peregrine had also added a few dummy hedges to enhance the overall effect. It was perfect, Joe thought, quite perfect.

'Looking down through the netting one could discern the

mounded magazines with their bombs and the system of service roads that led to them. The overhead cover extended right up until the point where the entry road left the public highway.'[3]

Steel wool was now available in two widths and two colours, but could be spray painted to merge with its environment. It could withstand gales and snow, it could be used as both a screen and for decoys – no wonder everyone was asking for it. But Joe knew the cost all too well and was quick to issue his own recommendations and 'notes on use'. He needed to emphasise that it was for priority sites, such as the entrances to aircraft hangars and secret wireless stations. He also advised that no *single* method of camouflage should ever be used – too much then depended on its success. It was always better to use a combination of good concealment and create 'false areas' and decoys.

Peregrine took his advice and when he came to camouflage a new large gun site in Dover, he produced a precise example of Joe's intentions – they used steel wool screens to shield the real gun positions but constructed decoys at a suitable distance, creating a fake railway line out of old and condemned track, making it run for about a mile beyond the real guns. Two decoy gun positions were then covered in less effective camouflage in the form of painted coir covers, about half a mile apart along this dummy track. As a finishing touch Peregrine constructed dummy cranes and concrete mixers around his dummies to give the impression of activity.

The plan was completed by March 1941 and Joe reckoned in the future it would take a month for completion of similar schemes. For this particular site no direct hits were recorded, and although both the real and dummy guns attracted the enemy's attention, there was enough uncertainty as to their exact location.

The problem with steel wool was that it was fast becoming so popular that camoufleurs had to be continually reminded not to use it wastefully: 'How often are we implored to issue twenty-five rolls of steel wool . . . only to find when we came round to see what has happened to it, that it has been spread in neat strips over a muddy mess that need never have been made at all! Or else it had been lavishly swathed around a pill box like bandages round a bad head wound.'[4]

A common misconception was that camouflage was some kind of 'concrete object which is applied to make things "invisible"',[5] and Joe worried steel wool was too good at hiding things, which might create a dangerous complacency. Bad habits were all too easy to fall into.

After three weeks of solid flying in March he felt he deserved a rest. He had missed Mary terribly and was desperate for time alone with her. But as he swept into Bath, expecting a warm welcome, he was quickly disppointed. James Meade was also visiting and the tension in the air was palpable. James found Joe's 'soldier back from the war' routine more than a little exasperating. Writing to Margaret, he complained: 'Mary is still carrying on with Gray (who as you know is married). Mother, of course, gets fearfully worried about this and Mary is so nervy that she bites your head off whatever you say. I am sorry for Mary, who is made all nervy both by the war and by being muddled up with Gray; but she really has become almost impossible to live with . . . This jolly atmosphere was all much heightened by the drone of German bombers at night!'[6]

Of course Joe sensed a storm was brewing. The War Office expert on spotting bad cover wasn't blind to the disruption that he himself created. But he wouldn't stop. Everybody now seemed to know about him and Mary, so there seemed no point hiding away. And camouflage was never just about concealment. He wondered if Johnny Churchill, such a dear friend, his best male friend, might now be useful as a decoy.

Johnny, despite his own enormous workload, had still found time to fall madly in love. The object of his affections was Mary Cookson, a stunningly pretty FANY[7] who was his driver at Stanmore. Having already been married and divorced, Johnny was more than happy to get engaged all over again. Joe invited the happy couple to Bath with him the following weekend. He thought they'd make a jolly party. Mary Cookson was terribly sweet and refreshingly prim, and Joe felt sure the two Marys would have great fun together. As for Kitty Meade, a visit from the nephew of the prime minister was a great prospect. Kitty was, after all, a bit of a snob.

'Is he *someone*?' she'd ask hopefully.

Well, Johnny really was. What could possibly go wrong?

Or put another way, what could possibly go *right*?

Joe, Johnny and Mary Cookson arrived in Bath in very high spirits, determined to bring a bit of the Blitz to Bath. Johnny liked to let off steam and was, by his own admission, the most terrible show-off. Back at Stanmore the AA Command had shared a vast Mess with Fighter Command, where the parties were often scandalous. Johnny launched himself on sleepy Bath with as much enthusiasm, insisting they start drinking immediately, first beer and then gin, stopping at several scenic bars before they reached the Crescent.

Mary Meade was fond of Johnny but they were already a little at war over Joe. She was also terribly worried what her mother would think. Kitty Meade, a paragon of politesse and gentility, was rather prone to migraines, and Mary was certain her mother would retreat to a darkened room at the first opportunity. But in fact Kitty was rather bowled over by Johnny. Yes, he was outrageous – he was a brilliant mimic and raconteur – but he was also very endearing. There was something about Johnny that brought out the maternal side in many women. Kitty was very flattered, if flustered, and then quickly excused Johnny some of his ebullience when she learned that he was celebrating his engagement.

How *that* now grated.

Joe didn't see it. He should have, but he didn't. He was too busy bubbling on the surface to see the undercurrents swirling round his feet. That evening Joe and Johnny, Mary Meade and 'Little Mary' (as she was now called) went to the Assembly Rooms, partly to dance and partly to marvel at its grand interior. Mary Meade had imagined this to be great fun: a pleasant way of mixing old friends with new, of showing her neighbours and colleagues dear Joe and his clever camouflage comrade. But Johnny, being Johnny, could not stop his antics and of course his drinking. Little Mary thought it tremendously funny – she was not much older than Maureen, so had at least youth as an excuse – and there was Joe playing the part of the genial major, good old 'Uncle Grumble'. Johnny shrieked and teased Mary Meade terribly, while Joe remained passive, exhausted and indulgent.

Perhaps the drink made her oversensitive, and perhaps Johnny enjoyed provoking her. She came to detest Johnny that evening and to see him as a genuine threat. She hated his closeness to Joe – and worse, so much worse, was Johnny's theatrical devotion to his new love, his fiancée. Little Mary was explaining to all and sundry how they were going to great lengths to have a church wedding, even though Johnny was divorced and her parents thoroughly disapproved of him. They were flushed and giddy with the inappropriateness of it all.

By the end of the evening Mary Meade felt she could barely breathe. She sat there like an unexploded bomb, inert but full of menace. Didn't Joe consider how this might hurt her? If someone as chaotic as Johnny had managed to extricate himself from an unhappy marriage and become engaged all over again, why on earth couldn't he? It was a perfectly reasonable question.

Joe sensed something had changed but was too drunk to fix it. The next morning Johnny took several photographs of them all, sunning themselves on the steps of Lansdown Cresent. Joe sat on the doorstep in his uniform, head bent over an open book. Mary Meade was propped to the side of the doorway on a stool, lighting a cigarette, her long and slender legs stretched out in front of her. Little Mary was perched neatly beside them, on the other side of the doorway, looking rather tired. Nobody was smiling for the camera, and nobody was talking.

14/5/41

Dear Mary

I am frightfully sorry I brought Johnny and little Mary down. Of course Johnny is very difficult to understand owing to his understatement of serious things and his overstatement on non-serious things. However, I must thank you and your mother for the splendid way in which you handled the business.

Both went away very happy and delighted, with no idea of the real position. Your remarks about making a fool out of you in public are quite incredible and impossible and I should say insane.

I frankly do not know what you are talking about. Johnny thinks a lot of you and so does Little Mary. You know what I think.

I object to the suggestion that Johnny and I are drunkards – if we were we could not do our work – and also we would look it. I agree we may have got rather tight now and then – about once every 6 months – but it has always been a sort of undergraduate or student affair and not the sort of thing you suggest – In any case I don't get dead drunk as you say – I go to sleep and wake up in an hour or so perfectly fit in every way.

If you had any realisation of my responsibilities and work with the army and the Ministry, or if you had any idea of Johnny's responsibilities with Fighter Command and the hundreds and sometimes thousands of miles he covers each week in car or aeroplane in addition to being responsible for enemy A.A. gun sites in the country – you might probably realise that it is not unnatural to rather overdo things in the rare occasions we have a few hours off duty and meet. He is my best man friend.

Also, of course, you don't know anything about a real Blitz! (sorry!) – and I don't want you to. Your remarks about rich friends and living in the Ritz and Claridges are nonsense.

Your remarks about A.G. are completely wide of the mark. A.G. has opened an account with my bank who pays in a proper sum each month. Maureen's husband is earning £10 a week and they require no financial assistance from me – Maureen had a first-class education and never lacked anything in her life but my guidance at one time. But she is very happy and as far as Maureen is concerned everything has turned out for the best.

It is very easy to say (and some people might say) 'get divorced and marry Mary Mumble'. If it was that easy I would have done it years ago. You have said at one time or another that I sit on the fence or am afraid to take a drastic step – but I cannot allow myself to be influenced by what you say in an emotional moment – I have got to think of what you will say in the future.

I hate being so far away from you and I hate this fantastic Blitz life of living in hotels or clubs or the office. I am sorry we didn't have time to talk about your job. The only reason I think Bath is best at the moment is that Bath is safest.

I am very sorry to hear that you had an argument with your mother but it is only natural that she should be worried at something which cuts so violently against her own traditions and experience – perhaps it is not fair that I should ever have come to Bath but you know that you always blamed me for not coming.

What do you want me to do?

P.C.

Joe didn't wait for a reply but rushed to see James in Whitehall to plead his cause. James wasn't sure what to think. 'The whole position is horribly tangled and involved,' he reported to Margaret. 'Gray, as you know, is married. He and Mary are very much in love. They have had a violent quarrel.'[8]

Mary had presented Joe with an ultimatum: he had to divorce Nancy and so be free to marry her. And Joe had refused, outright. At this moment, at this time, he felt it was impossible. He explained to James it was a matter of honour – he had married Nancy during one war and he would *not* abandon her in the midst of another. Joe was determined to do things in his own way. It was what he told everyone.

Mary was from a different class and time. She tried to understand but she couldn't, and Joe didn't know how to make her. What he felt towards Nancy was very complex. Guilt could be as strong an emotion as love, maybe even stronger. He would not, he could not, blow Nancy's world apart. His relationship to Mary was something different, already so 'disrupted', she could endure it for the moment.

He begged her for more time: 'How to find our way out I cannot think at the moment. But I am sure – at least I hope – you will understand.' There was a 'P.S.: This is what I saw tonight.' He included a hastily drawn sketch of a gutted church with two large bells strewn on the floor, an interior view of the still smoking ruins of St Clement Danes. Just a few nights earlier had seen one of the worst raids yet. The War Office, Westminster School, the British Museum, the Houses of Parliament – were all badly hit. The blaze at St Clement's had been really something, a furnace just minutes from Joe's office. As he'd inspected the charred ruins he knew it would make a beautiful etching.

James Meade almost felt sorry for Joe. He saw his worry and confusion. 'This doesn't seem to be a good time to try to seek a final solution of knotty personal problems,' he reflected. James was right, but it was probably the right time for a new tactic.

O *is Opacity over the gun*
You must garnish opaquely, but think of
the sun

The threat of an invasion of Britain seemed to have passed, but by
the spring of 1941 the news was never good. General Erwin
Rommel was thundering through North Africa, recapturing all
Cyrenaica except the vital port of Tobruk.

On the morning of 20 May 1941, German paratroopers of the
III Battalion of the 1st Air Landing Assault Regiment were
dropped south-east of Maleme airfield in Crete. Joe didn't hear the
news straightaway as he had taken a few hours off to attend Johnny's wedding to Little Mary. It took place in-between air raids at
St Ethelburga's in Bishopsgate, one of the few churches where
divorced persons were able to remarry. It was a beautiful setting
but the mood was sombre.

Joe had begged Mary to come: 'I may not have crossed out
some of the things which ought never to have been written. If that
is the case please forgive me and forget them. But you know you
always had a gift – when you got really started – of saying just the
sort of taunts and things which you know would hurt me most!'

Mary had not replied. For days she had left him hanging, too
angry to make up her mind. Then, at the very last minute she had
caught the train to London. Joe felt a huge relief to see her arrive
at the church, but the smile soon froze on his face. This wasn't his

Mary, she seemed quite different, cold and imperious and already thinner. As she took her place in the wooden pews, he sensed an invisible wall between them. She wouldn't look or speak to him.

Joe had made a fatal mistake. By bringing Johnny and Little Mary to Bath he had exposed a weakness – Nancy. He had pushed her to the edge of his mind, an unresolvable problem. For a long time now it had been easier for him to pretend she didn't exist, and that was what allowed him to carry on as he did. But she was still there, and they were still married. At the beginning Mary had been his secret, but somehow Nancy had taken her place. How complicated it made things.

Joe watched Johnny fidget as he waited for his bride. Only Johnny knew the whole story of Joe's marital woes, and even he didn't entirely understand. Joe supposed this was because Johnny was younger, he hadn't been through the last war or suffered the same hardships. True, Johnny had been divorced, but Johnny's first wife had left *him*, so that was entirely different. Joe couldn't, wouldn't, do any abandoning. This damnable war had caused so much chaos and he refused to make any more.

But if Joe now felt terribly vulnerable, it was a hundred times worse for Mary. Didn't he see? Mary Meade, Miss Mary Meade, unmarried and childless, a lowly clerk at the Admiralty, hopelessly embroiled in an affair with a married, much older man.

Joe gazed at her adoringly throughout the service. ('It was wonderful to see you again – but frightful not to be able to love you and tell you how much I love you.') Mary kept her eyes straight ahead. Just in front of them sat Peregrine with his aunt Clemmie. On the other side were a few members of Little Mary's family, though most had chosen not to come. The ceremony in this chilly, half-empty church had an air of unreality about it. Joe hoped it might show Mary how dreary a wartime wedding would be. He wanted so much more for her, couldn't she see? But it was too late for him to try to explain.

'I will be leaving directly after lunch,' she informed him.

So matter of fact. He felt crushed. As they gathered outside the church, Mary fixed a smile for the newlyweds and wished them all the best, but became rigid when Joe drew near. Lunch at the Savoy was brief and sober, and after Mary left for her train Joe couldn't wait to make his excuses and be away himself. He hurried back to the Board. Camouflage was a world he understood. It was now perhaps the only world in which *he* was understood. At least he had his brothers. 'It is quite true that all the camouflage chaps will do anything for me.' He was trying to reassure himself.

The war, the war, the war – its hard facts made sense to Joe. His job made sense. This was a critical period and camouflage still had much to do. It was more about the men going overseas and the ideas they took with them. He had been back and forth to Farnham these last months and the reports on different terrains showed how methods could change. It was important to adapt, to cope with new demands.

As the day drew to a close, he counted off his colleagues as they made up little groups to wend their way home in the blackout. Peregrine's words echoed in his ear, whispered over the clinking of glasses: 'Johnny won't stand a suburban villa life for more than six months.' Peregrine, with his dark eyes, a funny chap but a good one. He had a habit of always being right. Joe did so hope otherwise, since he felt his luck was very much tied up with Johnny's and in fact with every other chap here.

What to do? Nancy was still in Wimbledon and he sensed he should go and see her. But he wouldn't, he couldn't do the one thing Mary wanted. Of course he knew how it looked from the outside: that he was a coward. It wasn't that simple. He just couldn't explain it, not yet.

The fall of Crete came as a humiliating defeat. Brooding over Maleme, Winston Churchill wrote to the Commander-in-Chief of the Home Forces asking: 'How do we stand on the strategic and tactical camouflaging of defences against enemy attacks on airfields? What body is studying the lessons of Maleme and the batteries thereabouts?' It was noted that the anti-aircraft guns at Maleme had been laid out so as to give a full 360 degree arc, forfeiting concealment in the process. As a consequence, the guns were entirely exposed and easy to pick out by dive-bombers.

The prime minister suggested that 'the deceitful presentation of dummy guns' should surely be a priority. 'There might well be two or three dummy guns, or even more, for every real gun. The best of all camouflage is a confusing variety of options made in which no-one can tell the real from the sham.'[1] The words came back like an echo from *Camouflage and Air Defence*. In order for it to work effectively, camouflage had to combine concealment *with* deception.

Tom Van Oss was asked by Fighter Command to draft some 'Notes on Camouflage of Aerodrome Perimeter Defence' and consulted with Joe on his next visit. In his draft document he concluded that the concealing of aerodromes was impossible, but they could be made more difficult to find. Defences in Crete had been all too obvious, which meant they were swiftly overpowered. Tom stressed that certain very simple things might have been done to 'waste the enemy's time whilst relief is on its way'. Any light surfaces had to be darkened, any smooth surfaces roughened. This was common sense stuff – tracks and freshly dug earth easily draw

the eye – a bit of simple maintenance went a long way. Camouflage could create 'hesitation and doubt, wastage of bombs . . . loss
of time'.[2]

That same month, whether by chance or by design, Peregrine
took the opportunity to brief Lord Cherwell, the prime minister's
scientific adviser, on his latest schemes. Peregrine sent him a set of
photographs that showed, amongst other items, a camouflaged
Radio Direction Finding station and a vast hide concealing up to
twenty aircraft, both of which used steel wool and both of which
were invisible from the air. In his accompanying note Peregrine
listed the current problems with 'concealment' and went on to
propose a strategy 'for defence against tank and dive bombing
attack' where he stressed that deception was as important as concealment, and that dummy tanks and other obstacles should be
used to deflect an impending attack.

He went as far as to argue that 'where a permanent building
such as a Bomb Store or Wireless Station is to be built, a replica of
the existing landscape complete with dummy hedges etc., should
be reproduced at a convenient height above the ground BEFORE
the building is begun. The building should then be erected underneath.' Peregrine concluded: 'Concealment as a Strategic Weapon
can only be effective if full use is made of Dummies and Siting.'[3]

Camouflage wasn't a sticking plaster to be applied afterwards
but a strategy in itself – when would they see its potential?

The answer was soon, but it wouldn't happen on British soil. It
was in the North African desert, where several of Farnham's
'babies' had been posted early in 1941. Geoffrey Barkas, Peter
Proud, Steven Sykes, and even a stage magician, Jasper Maskelyne,
were confronted with the arid and inhospitable desert landscape, a
place where it was surely impossible to hide *anything*. But, of

course, the fact that hiding was so hard meant deception could be everything.

A brilliant chance to prove this came in April of 1941, when 36,000 Australians and other British Commonwealth troops were trapped in the port of Tobruk surrounded by German forces. Tobruk was the best port for hundreds of miles in North Africa. Rommel wouldn't attack across the Egyptian border as long as the Tobruk garrison threatened the lines of supply to his front-line units, and he retained almost complete air superiority. Everywhere was under constant surveillance and in danger of being attacked.

Before the war the charming and persuasive Peter Proud had become known for his ability to design lavish-looking film sets on deceptively modest budgets; now he breathed fresh life into every bit of desert debris. He used old scaffolding, canvas and battered petrol tins to make dummy soldiers, trucks, gun positions and even a decoy air strip. Every bit of scrap was used to distort the picture on the ground. To protect the vital port, Proud and his men strung a vast canvas depicting wreckage scenes and debris-littered netting between actual wrecked ships, thus creating a canopy under which undamaged ships might pass. They also concealed two Hurricane fighter planes in caves dug into a dry riverbed, and another was literally buried in a hole in the ground, covered with a trapdoor over which sand was spread.

But perhaps the most impressive set piece from the desert camoufleurs was the artful 'distressing' of Tobruk's water distillery plant. The plant was crucial but impossible to hide, and so, after a bombing raid, a paint and cement team went to work and what looked like a black and ragged hole was created in the roof and side of the main building. It was made to appear impressively deep by darkening the shadows with coal dust and waste oil. Rubber tyres were set alight so that by dawn it gave the impression that the building was still smouldering. It had exactly the desired effect. German reconaissance planes noted the distillery as destroyed, and so 'wasted' no more bombs on it.

Such ruses were scrupulously documented with a steady flow of reports, drawings and photographs filtering back to Farnham and beyond. The *Fortnightly D.O.*, a newsletter edited by Godfrey Baxter, would celebrate the desert camoufleurs and their ingenious recycling of unlikely materials. It had a brilliantly Heath Robinson appeal. After all, who would have thought that ten tonnes of condemned flour could be mixed with Worcester sauce and sand to make a paste that when applied to army vehicles blended them into the desert landscape? Or that battered petrol cans dusted with cement could be turned into rocks? It proved how the enemy could be defeated not by fire and man power, but guts and imagination.

Baxter concluded: 'The difference between Tobruk and this country is that out there camouflage is not a subject of after dinner speculation, but a matter of existence.'⁴

*

Telegram to KITTY MEADE 6/7/41
PLEASE CAN MARY LUNCH SATURDAY CONSTITUTIONAL
CLUB. OR DINNER AND PLAYERS THEATRE. JOHNNY AND
LITTLE MARY COMING. JAMES CONSULTED AND
APPROVES. MARY WILL STAY STANMORE SAT NIGHT. WELL
LOOKED AFTER. = GRAY

It was time for Joe to put on his own show. He was playing the part of the 'Good Victorian', providing suitable chaperones and married friends to make everything appear respectable. He would direct all his invitations to Kitty Meade first, for her approval. Yes, it was ridiculous. He and Mary were two educated adults 'with everything in the open', yet now they had to dance to someone else's tune. He had no other option. Mary had told Joe that she would not be coming to London as often, and she certainly wouldn't stay the night. She had made it very clear things could not go on as they had before. There would be no snatched intimacies or 'pretend hotel honeymoons'. Regardless of the fact that they had been physically intimate for years, Mary now believed that their situation was too exposed. They had to hold back. This was the right thing to do for the sake of her mother and her brother, and perhaps also for herself.

Joe pretended to accept it. 'I realised we have been asking too much of your mother. She has lived a sheltered and conventional life since she was a girl and can't understand that there can be any happiness – or safety – outside of those conventions.' But everybody now had an opinion on their relationship and Joe felt blisteringly uncomfortable. James, Kitty, Peregrine and even the newly respectable Johnny joined the debate. Johnny was fiercely possessive of Joe and said Mary didn't understand him. Mary, in turn, considered Johnny a thoroughly bad influence. They were both right, but what a tangle it was becoming. Joe wished, not for the first time, that they had kept the whole thing undercover. He wasn't sure he could bluff his way out.

Darling, over the past three years you and I, as fairly intelligent people, both with some experience of life, have done what we wanted to do, very frankly and honestly – for better or worse and with complete mutual understanding, knowing that we would never let each other down. Now the position is different, physically because we are parted, because other people have come into the picture. I don't care if I never sleep with you again so long as I know that you would if you could.

But he did care. He cared terribly. And he refused to accept conventional definitions. 'You and I cannot commit adultery, morally, even if the law can claim we have. The Dictionary says ADULTERY – "violation of the marriage bed".' Now, as no marriage bed was in existence, it could not possibly be violated.

But it wasn't enough. He could no longer turn up in Bath at a moment's notice or lure Mary away with a room at a hotel. He had to make everything seem proper.

And it worked. Mary came to London twice and Joe felt he was almost forgiven. He met James for dinner in town and for lunch at Whitehall, persistently reaffirming his sincerity. Camouflage was getting a better reputation, and Joe hoped it might rub off on him. He promised Mary he'd look after her and he genuinely felt he could. The tales of Tobruk delighted and enthralled him. He felt a direct connection. 'I am to a great extent responsible for the present organisation,' he wrote.

To a great extent I am still responsible – my 'babies' are doing first class work now wherever the army is in action. MI10 recently produced a captured German operations order which said that a recent German counter attack at Tobruk had been heavily defeated owing to the excellent camouflage of our tanks and guns and the Germans had no idea about them being there before they went into action. Please don't say anything about that because it suggests I am in the habit of disclosing information which I am actually not. Still, it was a bit of a feather in the camouflage cap and I thought you would like to know it, as it shows old Pop Corn looked ahead very well in 1935, now doesn't it? Everything will come right in the end, you will see.

ℙ *is for People moving around,*
Do so at night and merge with the ground

'It is incredible to me that Mrs Gray doesn't know or suspect the truth,' mused James Meade. 'Mrs Gray *must* know, surely.'[1] It was May 1941 and the lingering spectre of the mysterious and ever-absent Nancy Gray bothered his wife Margaret as well. The war was a test to any marriage, enforcing all kinds of difficult separations. Margaret wondered if their circumstances were really so different. But Joe had made it clear that Nancy Gray could not know the truth, that the very idea of divorce might 'drive her desperate'. This was rather disturbing. For James and Margaret, so happily married, it seemed terribly wrong and 'very immoral' to deceive someone. But Joe stood firm. He said Nancy must be left out of it – not forever, but for now.

Fortunately, every time the issue raised its head, the war got in the way. As 1941 progressed many people were convinced Hitler could not be defeated. All of continental Europe was controlled by Axis powers. The Blitz had pounded London. Having invaded Russia in June, the Germans had reached Moscow, and Rommel was driving across Africa.

On the Home Front, labour shortages were becoming serious and all women up to the age of forty would soon need to register for war work. Nancy chose this as her moment to vanish from London properly. She sent word to her husband, informing him that she had already volunteered her services to the YMCA.[2] She promised to let him know of her whereabouts once she was settled. Maureen was newly pregnant and moving to Paisley to stay with John's parents, so she too would also be out of the capital.

Joe hoped this would take the pressure off. He was praying that his problems might somehow solve themselves, and in the meantime he sought solace in the fact that he wasn't the only soldier being pulled in different directions. It was easy to blame the war – this damnable, interminable war. All around him people were coming together impulsively, getting divorced and having affairs, and why should anyone pass judgement? He saw it everywhere. At the Civil Defence Camouflage Establishment things were becoming terribly bohemian, with the most 'extraordinary rearrangements of . . . married couples: i.e. A + B became A – B but + D, and E + F became E – F but + G, etcetera.'[3]

It was no longer a matter of right or wrong, black or white – the world was altered and people acted accordingly. Even Johnny Churchill and Little Mary, who loved each other deeply, fought like cat and dog. Johnny still went out all night, which caused tremendous rows. Johnny blamed his star sign, which was Gemini. ('You have a dual nature,' announced his fortune teller. 'It is as if the twins Castor and Pollux were struggling against each other. You have tremendous vitality and yet you are lazy. You are faithful yet you can be unfaithful.'[4]) Joe shared the same star sign but never used it to explain away his behaviour.

Perhaps it was because he was an artist – artists were surely the worst.

'By an extraordinary coincidence I met Coldstream's friend Sonia tonight. He is to be in London he hopes Saturday and Sunday – so I will try to let him have the weekend (originally he

was to fly with me). I don't feel I can put up with this much longer
– not seeing you – and then not seeing you under proper circumstances. It is awful, dear, darling Mary.'

William Coldstream had become Johnny's staff captain at Stanmore. A well-known realist painter before the war, he was himself
caught between the demands of camouflage and his own emotional
entanglements. Like Joe, he was separated from the woman he
loved, and like Joe, the woman he loved was not his wife. Sonia
Brownwell was a gorgeous blonde many years younger, dubbed
the 'Euston Road Venus' by the men who'd painted her before the
war. Coldstream was quite besotted with her, though weighed
down by guilt from his children and failed marriage. Sonia herself
wasn't sure how much to commit.

Sonia and William, Johnny and Mary – sometimes people came
together and fitted perfectly, other times it felt accidental, temporary, and terribly uneven. James Meade couldn't understand these
ever-shifting states. Why wilfully make drama when there was so
much about already? Then came devastating news that rocked
them all. On 1 July, John Packham, the husband of James and
Mary's younger sister Diana, was killed when his ship, the HMS
Malvernian, was bombed in the Bay of Biscay. Diana was pregnant
with their first child and had only just made the happy announcement. The Meades gathered in Bath to process their grief and support one another. Joe repressed his first instinct to rush to Mary's
side. 'We must upset people as little as possible,' he wrote. 'Anything might happen in these days.'

How right he was. Mary tried to console Diana but she herself
was burdened by a confusing mixture of emotions. James found
the atmosphere unbearable. As far as he was concerned, John's
death had brought everything into focus. 'I don't know what is

going to happen. I think that Gray should either get a divorce or give up hanging about.'[5]

James chose to write to Joe. He thought it was the only way, since talking about delicate matters was difficult, and Joe's deafness made it more so. 'One cannot tell him anything of this kind by word of mouth without everybody else in the house (and many people outside) probably overhearing!'[6]

Putting pen to paper, James did not hold back. He told Joe that he was placing too much strain on the whole family by continuing with Mary. He also indicated that they should not have become involved in the first place, considering Joe's personal circumstances. James blamed Joe for pursuing Mary, even when his married state had become known. The decent thing, James believed, would have been for Joe to break off with Mary and then start afresh once he had arranged his divorce. Now the whole relationship was clouded by its unseemly beginning.

Joe tried to brush it off but felt bitterly misunderstood. What bothered him most was the persistent implication that he'd brought shame on Mary, that he'd deceived her into continuing their relationship. That wasn't how it had happened. 'Even if I had not loved you devotedly – which I did from the beginning, how could I possibly have left you?' he asked. 'The thing is unthinkable.'

But he accepted that he must now stay away from Bath, and he did so, promising to love Mary from afar in whatever way she'd allow. 'I will never leave you until I am sure that you want me to go. But I think you do love me as much as I love you – and even if you only love me half as much as I love you then nothing can ever part us.'

Mary accepted she had to make a break. She needed a new job, and she needed to get away from Bath and her family's scrutiny. Joe eagerly enlisted Sonia to help them, arranging to meet her at the Café Royal on Piccadilly – a place that was fast becoming a favourite haunt, not least because it was still functioning. Together they tried to concoct a plan of action. Sonia felt certain Mary could be useful at the Ministry of Information, where she was now working, but Joe seemed sceptical and the cocktails made him more so.

I'm not sure if you could produce enough camouflage and push – I mean cheek or bluff etc. to cover up lack of knowledge. You are a different type to Sonia – fortunately but no offence meant to S. She said she knew there was a new department to be formed called "anti-lies". That means reading all German and enemy propaganda and presumably bulletins, spotting the lies and putting in a general report. I am afraid lots of subtle German lies might be believed by the reader!

He suggested Mary come to London and discuss it. 'I don't think you need have any fear of spending a week or fortnight actually in London at present. The Germans are much too busy elsewhere to spare bombers for serious raids on London. The G's are realists whatever they are.'

Mary requested leave so that she could do as Joe suggested. She knew it was time to leave her 'passive' life in Bath behind, and the fact that Nancy had volunteered was a further incentive. Mary Churchill had gone to work in a munitions factory in Edgware. Maybe something like that would suit? Joe promised to make enquiries and use every contact he had. Then he wrote with a new idea: 'Sound City – very hush hush dare not mention – at any rate vital work with lots of women. I'll drop a line to Norman Loudon and make enquiries.' Sound City film studios based in Shepperton might have seemed an unlikely place for war work, but unlikely people and unlikely places now complemented each other rather well.

Q is the Question you cannot decide
But the Camouflage officer's there as a guide

'The film director today erects dummy structures on an enormous scale and when photographed, their detail is usually so exact that they cannot be distinguished from real solid buildings. If this work can be carried out by a film company, it can be carried out in the more serious business of war.'[1]

Joe had written these words in 1935, and it wouldn't be long before film studios and the military were pooling their resources.

In the First World War, fake airfields and flare paths had been used to divert bombing raids and exaggerate the number of aerodromes. To mimic a modern RAF station was going to be a far more complex affair – but it was possible. 'A Dummy landing ground could be laid down covering an appropriate area of smaller fields with canvas . . . a few dummy planes may be on the ground, but these must be moved regularly to different positions and vary in number.'[2]

Colonel John Turner was perhaps the third person to read *Camouflage and Air Defence*. He'd taken up the post of director of Works and Buildings at the Air Ministry in 1931, and had pointed out the need for a national camouflage scheme as early as 1935. But it was only as the Munich Crisis loomed that decoy airfields came into action.

Since he knew enough about real airfields, Turner was well

placed to implement their imitations, and he established his very own 'Department of Dummies' to this end. Its home? Sound City film studios in Shepperton.

Initially, real aircraft manufacturers had supplied dummy aeroplanes, but this quickly proved too costly and the film studios stepped in. Warner Brothers, British Gaumont and the London Film Company had all been invited to offer tenders for the manufacture of fake aircraft, and the best quote came in from Sound City.

Sound City was based at Littleton Park House, a stately mansion dating back to the seventeenth century, in a picturesque part of still rural Middlesex, some fifteen miles outside of London. Turner was impressed by the skill of its studio technicians (he would only ever speak of Sound City's craftsmen as 'engineers') and struck up a good understanding with the man in charge, Norman Loudon. By 1939 Loudon was a businessman of substance, having built his fortune managing Camerascopes, a company that manufactured flicker books for children. He had founded Sound City with the intention of creating the first British film studios purpose-built for talkies. Some in the trade dismissed Loudon's venture as a 'gaggle of dilettantes with a bit of money to waste',[3] but it was soon producing a film a fortnight, and the fact that five ex-naval commanders were on its staff possibly eased its assimilation into the war effort. 'It was not that different from what they had been doing since 1932. Now the audience for their fantasy world was to be the German armed forces.'[4]

Loudon worked and played hard, freely mixing business and pleasure. He had an appetite for glamour and high living, and a love of fishing that Joe shared. 'Loudon really is the supreme host and Sound City has the most expensive and best trout fishing in England.' When he wasn't trying to find Mary a job in one of the workshops, Joe begged her to join him there for the weekend instead. He imagined them squirrelled away at 'some fishy hotel'.

The work of RE8 was still primarily concealment, but by 1941 the trend towards deception was set. Joe sent Mary two photographs taken one after the other: the first shows him approaching a large anti-aircraft gun, in the second the barrel of the gun has slipped down and banged him on the head. He turns back to the camera, laughing. He is more embarrassed than hurt – of course the gun wasn't real. 'Sound City is a dangerous place. They all carry film cameras in their pockets!!'

The large sound stages were being used to manufacture bomber parts, whilst thousands of dummy aircraft, buildings, barges, tanks, people and guns were built in the scenery construction workshops. These were constructed as kits and sent far and wide to populate decoy airfields, factories or dock areas. ('The ideal dummy building would be collapsible and easily portable. So that it may be concealed until the last moment for erection.'⁵)

The aim was simple: to confuse the pilots of enemy aircraft. Whilst *real* airfields were disguised as farms with their aircraft dispersed to satellite sites or wooded areas, two types of dummy site were evolved: day dummies ('K' sites) and night dummies ('Q' sites). 'K' sites were built a few miles from the genuine airfield and needed a lot more work: ten dummy aircraft, worn tracks, disturbed areas made to look like bomb and petrol dumps, an air sock and machine gun post. These were manned by up to twenty men, part of whose job was to move the dummy aircraft to imitate activity. 'Q' sites were more successful, and simply used lighting effects devised by the studio technicians. This included red lamps to indicate high buildings and other obstructions, and a car head-lamp that could mimic a taxiing aircraft.

The success of the dummies was difficult to quantify but they became the stuff of legend. There were stories of 'Q' sites being so effective that RAF pilots actually tried to land on them, or ground staff erupted in panic when enemy bombers loomed.

'Sir, we are being attacked!' radioed one flight sergeant as the Luftwaffe strafed his site.

'Splendid, Sergeant, good show.'

'But Sir! We need fighter cover! They're wrecking my best decoys!'[6]

It sounds too good to be true, but that didn't matter. Dummies and decoys were an exercise in artistic licence.

'It is not necessary in creating a dummy town to erect a whole town,' Joe advised. 'The carefully considered use of smoke screen over a fairly large area with dummy houses and a few prominent buildings, showing deliberately in places, would give an excellent impression of a town in process of being camouflaged.'[7] Similarly, the lighting of a city or industrial centre could be recreated through simple techniques. Strobe lights could give the impression of welding (at a foundry) or recreate sparks coming off the tracks (as in areas where trams were used). A pool of water with a standard lamp hanging over it might be used to look like a reflection coming off a nearby river or lake.

RE8 had taken on a Captain Berry, who now made fakery his speciality: 'He would plan and set up various frameworks and lighting systems which would simulate faulty black-out, doors opening and shutting, the dim, hooded lights of a railway siding and other evidences of the situation of a large or important factory,' recalled Sayer. 'In actual fact, of course the real factory was three or four miles away and Berry's little contraptions were set up in the open country with, so I suppose, a couple of heroes sitting in a small, lonely hut ready to press the button that put the circuits in action if a raid was imminent, with the object of attracting all the bombs intended for the real target.'[8]

But decoys were no use once bombing had begun, and decoy fires were set to mislead bombers further. These were called 'Q' fires or 'SF' sites ('Special Fire'). 'Normally a "Q" fire should be about one mile from the installation and must be about 800 yards from any habitation . . . The decoy fire is lit after bombs have been dropped in or near the parent, whether or not fires are started, with the intention of drawing off further attack.'[9] The hope was that subsequent waves of bombers would be misled and drop their bombs on fires ignited several miles away. By 1941 the country was dotted with decoy sites. Cities, factories, oil terminals, ports and airfields all had their decoys.

The presence of film men in the North African desert un-doubtedly tightened the focus on deception. Barkas considered it a 'film production on a grand scale'[10], which made it sound almost glamorous.

'Very good work going on in Libya in the news,' Joe told Mary in November. 'We are greatly tickled by the references made to the value of concealment and camouflage. We have a good lot of chaps out there now. Can't say how it delights me to hear how the story unfolds.'

And what a story it was. The desert offered every possibility – a place where monotony might easily give way to mirage. General Archibald Wavell understood such tricks, and in April of 1941 came up with his own bit of wizardry. Attempting a quick sketch, he asked: 'Is it a wild idea that a tank could be camouflaged to look like a lorry from air by light canvas screens over top?'[11] It wasn't wild, it was brilliant. The note was handed to Jasper Maskelyne at the camouflage workshops and he set about making a collapsible tented structure from wood and canvas that could be used to disguise tanks. They became known as 'Sunshields' and would be one of the most useful deceptive devices of the desert war.

But Wavell's part in it was over. Churchill dismissed him in June and passed the initiative to Claude Auchinleck, a one-time painting companion of Edward Seago at Southern Command. The 'Auk' began planning Operation Crusader, an assault designed to relieve the siege of Tobruk. Yet even with this change of command the role of deception remained.

Crusader was scheduled for November 1941 but there were many months of build-up ahead of that, and Steven Sykes was selected by Barkas to camouflage a new railway line ending at Misheifa in Egypt that would be used to bring military supplies for the offensive. Sykes saw immediately that such a massive construction could never be hidden. Instead, he proposed to build a fake nine-mile extension to the existing track, ending in a dummy terminus that he hoped would sufficiently mislead enemy bombers. The decoy railhead had a double objective: it would provide a fresh target for enemy bombers, and the ongoing work would fool them into thinking that the British were planning to attack much later.

It was a clever scheme although as usual lacking resources, which meant it was built on a gradually shrinking scale. Sykes eventually found himself crafting rail track out of flattened petrol tins, bashed into shape and blackened – but aerial reconnaissance showed the effect was still convincing. The train itself was made out of various locomotive and car parts, and an army cookhouse stove was converted to burn 'black' to make smoke. To complement the picture Sykes also pitched tents, mocked up mess huts and used straw figures to man them, deploying old trucks and cars to add to the impression of activity. Then, as a finishing touch, he positioned cans containing waste petrol along the track that could be detonated electronically after a raid.

The fake railhead was bombed on 28 November and received hits in the following weeks, whilst in December a captured German map showed Sykes's extension to be real. This was 'campaign swaying'[12] publicity for camouflage. Back in England Colonel Buckley, a 'Concealment' man, felt the reverberations. He dispatched Julian Trevelyan to investigate. Trevelyan, when he eventually found Sykes's creation, reported: 'The dummy railhead looks very spectacular in the evening light. No living man is there; but dummy men are grubbing in dummy swill-troughs, and dummy lorries are unloading dummy tanks, while a dummy engine puffs dummy smoke in the eyes of a possible enemy.'[13]

The deception was so good – but how good? Sykes suspected Barkas exaggerated the number of bombs dropped on the railhead to further his cause,[14] and, according to Trevelyan, 'the planes have been over and shot at everything *except* the dummy railhead'. He also heard that 'they later paid it the compliment . . . of dropping a wooden bomb on it'.[15]

When everything had to be secret, there could be many versions of the truth. Jasper Maskelyne, the camoufleur who brought Wavell's 'Sunshields' to life, couldn't resist taking some liberties with reality. His ghostwritten memoir, *Magic – Top Secret*, and a later book, *The War Magician*, puts him centre stage in every conjuring act of camouflage in the desert, from creating an entire decoy port to divert bombers from Alexandria, and even making the Suez Canal disappear by means of dazzling searchlights. Such fictions were the perfect bait for Hollywood filmmakers and persist despite having been methodically debunked and disproved.[16]

Even now, when I mention Joe and his work in camouflage, people will ask: 'Oh, did he know that magician who made *a whole city* disappear?'

Camouflage layered fiction over fact, and told a good story at the expense of the truth. That is what made it so appealing. But there was always the danger that deception could turn into deceit, that the lies would take over. Joe thought he could play the game if he set the rules, but the fact remains that the greatest deception wasn't really his. It was Nancy's.

R *is for Regularity, huts in a row,*
Or guns equidistant are certain to show

By November 1941 Nancy Gray was harder to find than her husband.

She still is, in fact, all these years later. It is a frosty autumn morning and I am with my aunt Victoria in Bedfordshire, essentially going round in circles. We have driven past our destination several times, so poorly is it signposted. Eventually we stop and ask passers-by, who furrow their brows and claim to know vaguely but not exactly where it is we must go. I feel embarrassed to have dragged my aunt along with me.

We fall into uneasy silence that doesn't break even after we locate the nondescript layby where we'd been instructed to park. My relief now is laced with despair.

The sky is clear but a brisk wind makes me button up my coat. I try not to look across at Victoria as we walk for several minutes down a narrow footpath between flat and empty fields. I'm not even sure what we are walking towards. There is this single building in the distance, open at the sides. It is really just a barn.

At this point my aunt stops abruptly.

'Is that it?' She looks at me, eyebrows arched.

I stare back at the barn and shrug, and she turns away to answer her mobile phone, which has now started bleeping its own little distress signal.

Of course I'm disappointed, but as I approach this very ordinary structure I have what is now a familiar sinking feeling. I have written scores of letters that have remained unanswered, I have visited libraries and scoured public record offices and often come back empty-handed. I have spent months trying to find people who invariably tell me little, and so many characters in this story are now long dead. It's rare that I find what I am looking for. So, what *am* I looking for? I want to pin down my family members precisely, to know exactly what they were thinking and doing. I want to know the truth. It may seem impossible but still I must try.

It brings me here, to Gibraltar Barn Farm, and a clutch of laminated information sheets flapping in the breeze. I consider the now ageing poppy wreaths scattered about and look out across the fields. There is nobody else around, but I know Nancy was once here, blending into her own little background.

As we retrace our steps to the car I'm relieved that Maureen chose not to join us. I only realise later that she'd known all along.

'Not much to look at, is it?' she says, when I tell her what I found. 'But of course, that was the point.'

At first I do not understand.

'You knew?' I ask.

She nods. 'I *was* allowed there once, and I remember feeling distinctly underwhelmed. You would never guess they were dropping agents into France.'

No, you really wouldn't. But it feels somehow appropriate that Nancy Gray, a woman so fiercely private, would end up working at Britain's most secret air base. RAF Tempsford was operational from October 1941, and in 1942 became the base for two Special Duties Squadrons, No. 138 and No. 161, which dropped agents, arms and supplies into occupied Europe – under the auspices of the Special Operations Executive (SOE).

Since its activities were always secret, Tempsford had to look unexceptional. Gibraltar Barn was just that, with surrounding buildings made to look like animal houses. Such was the extent of the camouflage, a new pilot to the base thought it 'some elaborate leg-pull'. The whole place looked derelict.

> There was a huddle of buildings roughly the shape and size of Nissen huts but they looked like cowsheds. In fact, they *were* Nissen huts built within the walls of cowsheds, but I didn't know that until much later. They were grouped around a farm. That's another thing I didn't find out until later, that its name was Gibraltar Farm. Even if I had known, it wouldn't have meant anything. There were some hangars, so superbly camouflaged that it took me quite a while to realise that they *were* hangars. The whole place was odd, very odd.[1]

From this strange 'non-place' over a thousand agents were dropped, with 10,000 packages and 20,000 containers. The SOE had an entire unit dedicated to camouflaging anything in everything – microfilms and weapons in bicycle pumps and toothpaste tins.

Nancy was the manageress of a small canteen on the outskirts of the airfield. She had her own room to sleep in, though time to herself was rare. Most days she was up early, organising the kitchen and its rotas, and preparing food for the air crews. She was part of the 'official' side of things, fully aware there was a 'covert' side, with the cars coming in at the dead of night, and curtains always drawn. It rather suited Nancy. She had learned to compartmentalise her life and keep control. Putting out the flying rations each night, she didn't expect every plane to return. There were times when as many as twelve planes went out, and only two came back. That was hard, but everyone had to keep a brave face.

Nancy liked the military obsession with stiff upper lips and living by numbers, everything tidy and accounted for. She thought the war had brought out the best in her. At Tempsford she was proving to be an excellent manager, if rather strict, but this was in fact useful since it meant the men respected her. It also helped that she was still very striking, with piercing eyes and a haughty look. She made men work hard for a smile, but she also made that smile very dazzling.

Although addressed as 'Mrs Gray', Nancy never talked about her husband, nor did she feel the need to. The war saw so many couples separated – if it was liberating for Joe, it could be the same for his wife. Nancy was starting over. She had brushed aside unhappy memories of the Sutherland, and didn't think once about returning to Scotland. Her parents, after all, had excelled at disapproving and not allowing – so she would never have admitted the truth to them.

Nancy now refused to have regrets, just as she refused to acknowledge her husband's infidelity. Yes, she knew about Joe and Mary, but knowing and admitting were two quite different things. Nancy never confronted Joe – what would be the point? She found it simpler to ignore troubling facts or events, or even people. Wasn't this just what Joe was doing? Well, Nancy did it better. All three of her sisters had emigrated in their twenties and she had cut them off completely. Once they were gone, that was that. The fact was, if it looked likely anyone would leave Nancy Gray, she did her damnedest to leave them first.

Joe still paid money into her account but they had little other contact. Nancy had declared herself 'a most unsentimental type of person' – so even if Joe wrote to her, she would not keep his letters. She destroyed all of her personal correspondence, ripping it into microscopic shreds. That she'd had to sign the Official Secrets Act now served her very well.

Joe knew exactly what Nancy was like, which is why he never pushed her. 'Timing is of the essence,' he told Mary. 'Any man – especially a soldier – doesn't dare advance until he is sure of the ground.' It was a tactic from one war now applied to another. Joe had always been patient, and now he was waiting, biding his time for the right moment.

Perhaps it might come soon: one letter reached Nancy that she decided to keep. It was from Dick Orr-Ewing, writing from Scotland, and it had chased her down to Bedford. Dick, like Joe, had found himself eminently more employable once war broke out. By the end of 1939 he had been taken on by a reputable firm of civil engineers and had moved to Edinburgh to survey the proposed Forth Road Bridge. When this was delayed he joined the Home Guard and was appointed temporary civil engineer at a naval base in Orkney.

Joe and Dick had been good friends. They had lived under the same roof for years, even worked together. Joe liked Dick. Dick liked Joe. Dick *loved* Nancy. He had loved her from the start, and now he wrote and told her so.

Joe had constantly put Mary off, he had delayed and procrastinated, promising things would come right. He wasn't wrong.

One letter to Nancy could change everything. Dick knew she had separated from Joe and that it wasn't just the war that kept them apart. He had a very practical proposal. He suggested she get a divorce and marry him instead. He told her that he loved her and promised he could take care of her, and he offered the simplest reason why: 'Because if I am killed before the war is over, you will have my pension. You won't have to worry again.'

It wasn't romantic – it was really quite brutal – but Joe had already accepted he might die in an air raid and Dick shared that same fatalism. Here were two men who had already survived one war, and, perhaps more importantly, they had lived to see the misery and poverty of its aftermath. They were both thinking about what and who might survive them.

As long as Joe stayed married to Nancy, she would get his pension. It was the only thing he could offer. Mary had her own money. Nancy didn't. When Joe talked of his duty to Nancy, that's what he meant. He would not divorce her and leave her stranded in some desolate limbo. He had to see her taken care of. Dick's offer did that. It would relieve Joe of his responsibility. How handy that Nancy might actually love Dick, too.

Dick's proposal, as sincere as it was sensible, was a solution to a problem. He would take Joe's place, if Nancy wanted him.

Did she want him?

Only Nancy could say. She liked everything neat and tidy and under her control, and she did have control. She'd never deny that. From the moment she had moved with Joe to London she had felt disappointed and betrayed, and this was the role she'd play well – perhaps not so much the victim, but most certainly someone wronged. Joe was typecast as the errant husband – unreliable and chaotic – the counter to her steadfast resilience. Joe didn't fight it, because by then he was fighting other things. He left plenty of space for Dick to become the hero, Nancy's rescuer. It was all terribly convenient. As if it had been planned.

Joe had grown used to the idea of dying, but it was only when his plane crashed that he realised how much he wanted to live. He had been flying in one of the old Stinsons out of York, having just visited Tom Van Oss, when the plane suddenly lost power – one minute they were soaring over fields, the next they were hurtling back down to earth. They crash-landed, skidding through mud and grass, and Joe jumped out just before the whole thing burst into flames. Fortunately, everybody escaped unharmed, but the flames and the smoke left him very shaken.

'It was a good little plane.' He told Mary. 'It will always be a mystery what happened.'

How easy it was to die, and yet how hard it was to live. He returned to London in another man's uniform and found a letter waiting for him at the Board. Kitty Meade had decided to issue Joe with an ultimatum and, like James, she chose to put it all in writing. She said she would no longer tolerate his 'chaotic descents' into Bath and it was time for him to 'put his affairs in order'. Kitty didn't agree with divorce, but she saw no alternative. Like everyone in the family, she couldn't fathom why Joe insisted on staying married to a woman he barely saw and claimed to no longer love. It seemed bizarre to the point of suspicious. Kitty wasn't that much older than Joe, so she understood his talk of duty and tradition. But she felt it was time he acknowledged his duty to Mary.

This was all too embarrassing to talk about directly, but in black and white Kitty felt there was no ambiguity. She had been prompted by these whisperings about Mary taking another job outside of Bath. ('I am working hard on your behalf,' Joe had promised, 'all nice places 3/4 of an hour or so from London so P.C. could come home at night.') Kitty had been outraged. She did not trust Joe's motives in the slightest. Using his influence to 'fix things' was a ruse to get Mary out of the family home and living nearer him, so they might continue 'carrying on' in their unmarried state. Tired of the procrastinations and politeness, and no longer able to turn a blind eye, Mrs Meade demanded answers.

But Joe decided not to write back. He chose instead to speak with Kitty directly, improvising a handful of assurances over tea that weekend. He assured her that 'everything was under control' and 'everything would come right'. If it calmed Kitty temporarily, it had the opposite effect on Mary. She was incensed. It was bad enough when Joe patronised her, but to behave in such a way to her mother. She felt twice as foolish, and she raged at him on the station platform, practically pushing him onto a train back to London.

The moment he was back in the office he wrote to her. 'I really objected to your remarks about P.C. being weak. Very much the contrary I should say – or I would not have answered your mother's letter face to face – completely exposed to attack from any quarter. I have always insisted on working our problem out in my own way.'

But Mary had had enough of Joe doing things in his own way. She'd already decided she would *not* now take any job that would make it any easier for them to be together, rather she would take the job that best suited her skills and she didn't care where. She refused to let him control her.

As if he could. He knew he was trying and failing on all fronts. Nancy had called him twice at work and left messages, which perhaps meant something, but it was now impossible to get hold of her. He sat by the telephone and waited, trying not to feel too worried or too hopeful. He considered calling Johnny and getting the number of a friend who had recently been divorced. They had talked about it over lunch the other week. There were people who could help. But when the call came through it wasn't what he expected.

Tom Van Oss had been killed.

At first Joe couldn't believe it – nobody at the Board could. He stared at the reports from his last trip to York, the letter Tom had sent him. It was literally in front of him on the desk. He had written back, his reply now somewhere at the sorting office.

It couldn't be true, it made no sense. Tom had been inspecting coast defence batteries – 'praying for a calm sea inspection and a dropping of the N.E. wind'[2] – when his ship had struck a mine. Out of a crew of fifteen there were no survivors.

It was terrible. Tom had been one of Joe's very first recruits, a dear friend and a father to three young boys. If ever there was a reminder of how cruel war could be – this took Joe straight back to the trenches, to all his best friends dying. Death kept catching him by surprise.

'Darling P.F. I do love you frightfully,' he scrawled. 'We are very lucky really in spite of everything. When one thinks of what millions of people have to go through.' He was thinking of course of 'Poor Mrs Tommy Van Oss, I will write to her tomorrow. Tommy was really one of the most brilliant chaps we had . . . it is a great, great loss . . . They were at sea and the ship struck a mine. It is unlikely it was anything bigger than a destroyer. Probably one of those fast armed launches like the one I had.' Joe thought back to the ships he had travelled on, the inspections he had done. It could so easily have been him. Did he wish it had been? He'd survived the Blitz and a plane crash, and yet still there was a danger in making plans, in assuming there was a future to fight for. He sat in the same chair, in the same position, and at the same desk, as when he had interviewed Tommy on his first application. He remembered it vividly. He imagined Tommy right there in front of him. 'Then we were 4. Now we are 250 and more – and all very hot (– those that are left).' He felt blighted, weary, the old optimism gone. 'I hope my next plane will chose a[n] opportune moment for its disintegration – or if it doesn't perhaps the launch will oblige . . .' Yes. That would solve all his problems. Nancy could be a war widow and Mary would be free to do as she pleased. A future that didn't involve him.

'My dear Mary, my dear darling Mary . . .' He stared at the words and then crossed them out, unable to find the right expression. He couldn't write her the letter she so wanted and needed. The days had swept by in a blur. Mary had come to London to finalise the details of her new job, a job that might take her further from him. He was scared and confused.

How they had argued. How he was tired of it. And all because of the stupid telephone. Mary had been so desperate to get hold of Joe that she had made the operator interrupt him on a call. When she realised he had been speaking to Nancy, she had flown into a fury. It was ridiculous – a terrible misunderstanding – but Mary was still so very jealous. Joe assured her she had nothing to be jealous of. 'You are both divorced in my mind.' It was, of course, the wrong word to use. To Mary, this showed how Joe juggled his women. Joe for his part, could not abide Mary's lack of faith. All these people doubting him just because he waited.

I thought that you knew me implicitly and in every way and now I see you don't – I don't think you know anything about me at all. I see no dishonour in asking A.G. to divorce me. I see incredible dishonour in not acknowledging responsibility for her physical welfare. I have held certain principles about the behaviour of men and women all my life. I have stuck to them and I still hold them and have no intention of changing them. What sort of a man would you want me to be? If you don't agree with me then we should part at once and avoid inevitable disaster at a later date.

He read his words back over. All this scared him more than he'd dare admit, but he wouldn't cross any of it out. Mary needed to be reminded that she could still be free.

'I make you the following offer. (You know I love you – the point is do you love me or not?) I will ask Ag to divorce me so that I can marry you.'

There, he had said it: 'I will ask Ag to divorce me so that I can marry you.'

He stared long and hard at the words now fixed in thick black ink on the page.

It was the promise Mary needed.

Yes, he would marry her.

Though he still did not say when.

S stands for Siting, for Spoil or for Scrim
3 covers 2 but on 1 sink or swim

It would have made a fine painting. The Café Royal: bursting with
life and light on this freezing December evening. What a contrast
to the blacked-out streets. Every table was full. You could almost
forget there was a war going on, though uniforms were everywhere in evidence. Joe's eyes went straight to Mary, still *his* Mary,
sat between Johnny and James. She had come, as she had said she
would. Things were better now. How quickly storms could pass.
Four days in London, her new job all decided, and James had
organised this little party. 'James Meade of the War Office', as they
called him, or 'the Prof.' just for fun. He had brought along one of
his economist friends, Richard Stone. Both would end up with
Nobel Prizes, but right now, in this little party, economists and
artists were out to make merry. Johnny and Little Mary, Sonia and
Coldstream.

'I say! Grumble!' Johnny had spun round, glass lifted. 'What a
wumble!'

Johnny was on his usual form, vivacious and charming and
pouring drinks for everyone. Joe considered Johnny 'the best chap
I have ever met' except perhaps for James. It was marvellous, perfectly marvellous, an interlude of warmth and merriment in
amongst the horrors.

'Let's make the most of the moment,' was what everyone kept saying, and even Mary Meade agreed. She had sought Joe out at his office and read his last letter to her whilst sitting at his desk. She had seen all his papers, all his drawings and files. She understood a little better, or so he hoped.

Much was still uncertain, but then such was war. This moment, this evening, they were celebrating, raising toasts to Mary's new job. She had accepted a post as an occupational therapist. It was ideally suited to her skills and knowledge, and it would take her out of Bath, which now seemed essential. But she would be working in Basingstoke. This wasn't the posting Joe had hoped for, and it certainly wasn't going to facilitate, as Kitty Meade had feared, some freshly disreputable living arrangements for them.

Basingstoke wasn't a place Joe could easily get to, and James for one couldn't conceal his delight. He thought it a decent test of their commitment to one another. James was also glad Mary had made up her own mind, rather than hang around waiting for Joe to make up his. Joe naturally felt anxious but any lingering unease was dispelled by Johnny's laughter and his stories, and his continuing adoration of his own 'Little Mary'. The presence of William and Sonia further reassured Joe. Friends all together, and still alive. Things would be all right.

And for three nights they really were. Joe and Mary stayed at the Grosvenor in adjoining rooms. Everything was as glorious as it had ever been. 'Dear darling Mary, I am not going to try to say what I feel about the Grosvenor excepting that I regard it, and shall always regard it, as the most wonderful thing in the world.' Joe would forever call it their honeymoon, with Mary his 'Mrs Mumble'.

She told him he meant everything to her, and they declared it a whole new beginning. Unfortunately, it was, but not in the way anyone hoped.

On 7 December Japan bombed Pearl Harbor. 'Situation in the Pacific now very serious.' This meant America would join forces with Britain, but the war would not be over any time soon – 'No, the wumble is about to beginumble.' And camouflage still had a crucial part to play.

The threat of a Japanese attack on the western coast of America seemed very real in early 1942, and after Japanese submarines were tracked close to Santa Barbara, panic ensued. The Americans responded quickly and worked from the British example. Colonel John F. Ohmer had visited Britain in the late 1940s and seen first-hand the camouflage schemes implemented at air bases and factories during the Blitz. For months before Pearl Harbor he had argued relentlessly for the protective cover of American targets at home. Each time his proposals had been dismissed as too costly and of dubious value. Not any more.

Following Colonel Turner's example, Ohmer looked to the film studios for help. Hollywood's finest – MGM, Disney, Twentieth Century Fox – all became involved and their set designers and carpenters crafted ingenious covers in the national interest, creating acres of innocent hillside or quiet suburbia where once there had been air bases and factories. Photographs of the Lockheed Burbank aircraft plant show it hidden beneath an elaborate construction of 'chicken wire covered in chicken feathers and painted'; a vast canopy held up by telegraph poles, across which paid actors would sporadically traverse to give the impression of activity. There are fake shrubs, plywood buildings – it's the kind of land-

scape Joe had dreamed of. But what of his steel wool? Cecil Schofield had secured the American patent the previous year, and by
1942 it was making appearances in the press. *Life* magazine
reported that the Army was waking up to being at war. 'All U.S.
guns and trucks are being painted a dull olive drab. The Corps of
Engineers, in charge of camouflage, is conducting experiments in
foliage preservation, non-fading paint, steel wool as a garnishing
material, infra-red paint to deceive infra-red photography . . .'[1]
There were accompanying photographs of snipers adorned in steel
wool and hiding down a 'spider hole' – it looks like reliquary of
the last war, but what the newspapers reported was the smallest
tip of the iceberg.

Whilst camouflage stepped up in America it was being scaled
back in England. A new Civil Camouflage Assessment Committee
was meant to bring a more consistent policy and conserve valuable
materials – instituting degrees or grades of camouflage. 'The
present state of static camouflage is being reviewed,' states one of
Joe's 'most secret' memos from 1942. 'The object is to enable the
War Office to assess the importance of camouflage for military
property in comparison with property of other service and civil
departments and to calculate accordingly the disposal of material
and labour, limitations of which are controlling factors.'[2] It was all
about balancing priorities, but it was also an attempt to make
camouflage more efficient. Joe was now able to advise on proposed extensions or building works ahead of time, and in some
cases, as at Southern Command, he designed the layout of a new
War Department depot to incorporate camouflage from the outset.

His workload didn't seem to change. Steel wool was used for
top-priority sites – secret army wireless stations and bomb stores.
'This morning inspected a very hush-hush design. M&E have just

got another 500,000 sq yds job from AM [Air Ministry].' The growing sophistication of aerial photographic interpretation meant camouflage had to work even harder, and for once it felt like the Germans were lagging behind. 'The Germans have lately developed a great weakness for large-scale and often apparently pointless static camouflage,' Joe noted. He had been shown photographs of the Focke-Wulf works in Rotterdam where 'a housing etstate' had been built over the factory roof and a fake park created nearby. All of this was entirely pointless since 'the harbour predicts the position and it is mainly a night-bombing target'.[3] Similarly, other photos taken over one of the large German cities showed very poor attempts to hide a lake. Joe was delighted, not just by the growing evidence of German incompetence but also by the British ability to detect it.

In February 1942 he was dispatched by the War Office to Northern Ireland, to advise one of his old students, Michael Farrar Bell, on the camouflage of base installations, coast defences and anti-aircraft batteries ahead of the arrival of the first American troops who were to take command thereafter.[4]

Steel wool remained the most effective and efficient static cover, and what now became clear was that it could hide not just vital equipment but also, crucially, works and men. The pressure was growing for a second front in Europe. After Dunkirk, Churchill had set up commando units to conduct raids and harass garrisons in German-occupied territories. By 1942 they were the poster boys for the British military. There's a sketch of Lord Louis Mountbatten on the cover of *Time* magazine from that summer, his likeness depicted against a backdrop of flames. 'Mountbatten of the Commandos,' reads the caption, 'His boys in blackface will see the day of wrath.'[5]

As head of Combined Operations, Mountbatten was tasked with co-ordinating a series of commando raids along the North Sea and Atlantic coastlines of enemy-held territory, and ultimately planning and preparing for the re-invasion of Europe. *Time* describes 'Lord Louis' as one who now personifies the second front and gives a detailed account of the recruitment and training of commandos: 'They must know how to stalk, unseen, in woods, fields, mountains . . . Commandomen must learn to kill. They prefer to kill quietly . . . For night attack, they black their faces and shoes, wear black uniforms, partly for camouflage, partly for the effect on enemy morale.'[6]

Commandos were like snipers and stalkers of old, and every raid required weeks of careful reconnaissance, the painstaking study of land maps, ocean charts and weather cyles, and in-depth tactical planning. Steel wool provided an ideal cover for them. Peregrine Churchill had always stressed its value in offensive as well as defensive operations and now he could prove it. He created an 'enormous cover' for the Combined Operations attack on the French coast, to conceal the assembly point of the Commando Forces.

Dated from June 1942, the cover was more successful than the raid it supported. Operation Rutter was first scheduled for July, with Combined Operations wanting to test if it would be possible to capture a fortified seaport large enough to be used afterwards by invading troops. Dieppe was seventy miles from Newhaven, close enough to allow a surprise attack with a force approaching under the cover of darkness, and well within range of Fighter Command's aircraft.

Army commandos were reinforced by Canadian troops and after weeks of training they embarked. But bad weather stalled their advance and German bombers spotted them in the Solent, so the operation was postponed. Some thought it should be cancelled. General Montgomery, in charge of the South Eastern Command, worried about security breaches. 'All the troops had been fully informed of the objective of the raid; it was reasonable to expect that it was now a common subject of conversation in billets and pubs in the south of England.'[7] Montgomery, however, was summoned to Egypt to command the Eighth Army and promptly removed from the picture.

The rescheduled raid, Operation Jubilee, took place on 19 August but resulted in a massacre. Out of a combined landing force of 6,100, about 4,100 were reported killed, wounded or captured. The main reason for this disaster? The woeful inadequacy of Allied intelligence. They had completely underestimated the extent of German defences, and the Germans themselves were on high alert, having been tipped off by French double agents. British press reports tried to play down this humiliating defeat but there came a powerful backlash. Questions were swiftly raised about the purpose of the raid, the poor organisation, the lack of intelligence. There was even the suggestion that Canadian soldiers had been knowingly sacrificed, and that Allied commanders saw Commonwealth troops as more expendable than those in the British Army.

Churchill would later rationalise Dieppe as a costly but crucial precursor to the next stage, an exercise that brought home the realities of a cross-Channel assault. Any future attack would need far greater intelligence, advance saturation bombing, tanks to support the first wave of assault troops and, most importantly of all, a complete rethink about the point of invasion.

All of this meant static camouflage was still important. As Peregrine forged ahead with his large-scale covers, so did Eugene

Mollo, who had been drafted into the Army as a lieutenant. As an acknowledged expert in 'structural concealment' and large-scale covers he'd soon be lecturing on it at Farnham. 'Whether or not the Germans really covered vast stretches of the country with concealment, as suggested by Solomon J. Solomon, Lt. Mollo said he didn't know ... but he knew such structures were possible. Screens must be sited to merge with adjacent countryside. Overhead covers give men "added sense of security".'[8]

T *is for Tracks, which will photograph light,*
And disclose your activities; keep them
from sight

The survivors of Dieppe[1] were brought by ambulance to Basing-stoke. Mary watched them come in, an endless stream of men on stretchers, soaked, bloodied, overcome with pain and exhaustion. She wanted to help but didn't know how. In the end she retreated to her small office. Joe had spent the last three years telling her to get some perspective. Finally she had it.

'I have complete faith in you. I love you devotedly. I am sure you will find your place and your use. You are the most wonderful person I have ever met, more wonderful than anything I could have imagined.'

Through the early months of 1942 Joe had written to her daily, encouraging her, and she kept his letters in her desk drawer, close to hand, but she was now in a place that he couldn't often get to, and she was surrounded by people with years of medical training. It was a long way from anything she had done before. Out of her depth, Mary kept on swimming, sending pleas to the draughtsmen of RE8 to come up with some decent designs for her poor patients to work with, asking Joe for suggestions.

It seemed ridiculous to expect the battle-weary men of Dieppe to show an interest in stitching, but many had already surprised her with their eagerness. They liked her, they called her the 'craft

Left: Joe Gray on 'aerial reconnaisance',
c. 1940.

Below: Joe Gray with
Captain Kenneth Dalgliesh,
York, 1941.

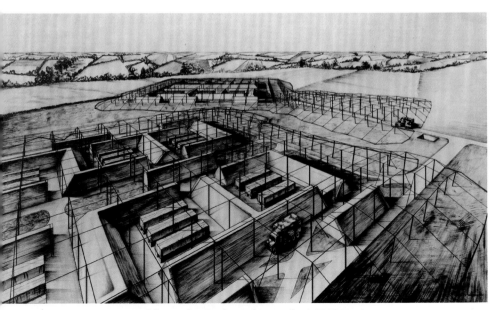

Drawing of frame for steel-wool cover by M&E Equipment.

Above: Joe Gray letter,
24 September 1940.

Right: Incendiary,
drypoint etching, 1940.

Below: Gray letter,
24 April 1941.

Blitz, Dawn, drypoint etching, 1940.

The Bells of St Clements, drypoint etching, alongside original sketch from 13 May 1941.

Steel-wool dummy trees under construction, *c.* 1941.

Steel-wool dummy farmhouse, *c.* 1941.

Joe Gray inspecting dummy gun, Sound City studios, 1941.

Lieutenant Eugene Mollo supervising the painting of steel wool, *c.* 1942–3.

Joe Gray with Mary Meade and Johnny Churchill (*above*), and (*left*) with Mary Cookson and Mary Meade, on the steps of 12 Lansdown Crescent, Bath, 1941.

Joe and Mary Gray on their wedding day, London, 20 September 1943.

Camouflaged pumping station for PLUTO, *c.* 1943.

PLUTO pumping station covered with netting and steel wool, Dungeness, Kent, *c.* 1943/4.

Grumble, York Aerodrome, 1941.

Waves, undated, oil on canvas.

lady', which was an acccurate enough description, and she was a good teacher.

'Occupational therapy involves any kind of mental or physical activity, medically prescribed, for the purpose of aiding recovery from disease or injury,' reported *The Times*. 'Work of this kind was found to be of very great help to soldier patients during the last War suffering from both nervous and physical disabilities.'[2]

Mary hadn't had formal training as a therapist but she came with recommendations from the Crafts Council and the Royal College of Needlework, and she was a kind and curious mentor. She looked good on paper, and so did Hackwood House, her grand new background. 'Johnny says there should be a painting of his in the hospital. It is set onto the wall so he doesn't think it could be removed easily. He did it for Lord Camrose after he bought the house from Canyon.' Lord this, Lord that. The connections were still there to be made. Camrose was a newspaper man and had used Hackwood as his country retreat before handing it to the Canadian Army for the duration of the war. It now housed 200 beds and acted as both an army hospital and a general emergency hospital, with Nissen huts sprawling over the vast lawn like giant metal caterpillars.

The official name was 'No. 1 Neurological Hospital'; sometimes they just called it 'No. 1 Nuts', since, as in the last war, not all wounds were physical. The great number of Mary's patients were suffering 'psychoneurosis', often the result of 'battle fatigue'. There were also those who had been seriously injured or disabled, with broken backs and shattered limbs. The idea was that an active engagement in a craft could aid both their physical and mental rehabilitation. Mary's patients felt marginalised, most were exhausted, all seemed depressed. But whatever brought them here, she tried to remind them what they could still do.

The hospital was continually growing, always busy with troops shipped in and out. Joe terrified himself with the prospect of Mary treating handsome wounded RAF pilots. 'As far as that is concerned I have no doubt that a lot of these people will fall temporarily or really in love with you. Troops in hospital usually do. As far as that is concerned I leave my honour in your hands (very 'ot!).'

His tone was jovial but it was no joke. Bath had been safe in more ways than one and now Mary was surrounded by men. Some of them were single, possibly eligible. The nature of her work meant close, daily contact. She was attractive and clever. Suddenly Joe saw her as other men might.

They were apart for much of February. Off in Northern Ireland Joe drank himself into a poetic stupor, imagining a future where he'd be dead, 'at the bottom of the Irish Sea', and blessing her 'for all the wonderful ways you have been to me and all the wonderful times we have had together'. He was sure she would marry a doctor, or someone young and virile.

'I wrote you some marvellous letters when I was away and then in a mad moment I thought you didn't really love me at all and tore them all up. Actually when I did that I had just come down from a very bad flight in awful weather and suddenly thought you were probably dancing about with Bloody drunken Canadians and had forgotten all about me. However, that was unworthy of me and unworthy of you.'

Mary wasn't and hadn't, of course. It was a ridiculous notion. Her life wasn't half as glamorous as Joe imagined. She was lodging with an elderly couple in a little house on Cliddesden Road, and she cycled to Hackwood each day, come rain or shine.

Joe rushed there once he'd returned to England and made a point of visiting the hospital and shaking hands with the doctors and nurses, determined to make them aware of his existence, but then he beat a hasty retreat. Basingstoke was 'a stuffy sort of place' and not somewhere he'd want to visit again. 'I felt it would be impossible to meet you in Basingstoke like a comparative stranger. I can't do it anymore darling.'

It was his turn to feel jealous. He was no longer at the centre of Mary's world and it made for a difficult adjustment. She had a tendency to overexert herself, and was now always rushing. She forgot to wear a scarf and caught a terrible cold. It happened once, it happened twice. She lost her voice and couldn't talk. Joe saved money to buy her a better coat, and begged her to take care of herself.

'Your success cannot be measured by the quantity of finished work. Don't forget – a negative result for you may be a very positive one from the medical point of view.' But Mary wanted perfection, the kind she couldn't have in her life. She wanted decent results from all her patients that offered concrete proof to the doctors. Feeling more than a little sidelined, Joe acted like a child. 'I was sorry if I was difficult but I can't camouflage what I feel and I won't try to. I am at the moment in a very vulnerable position, and very sensitive to what you say . . . You must let me do things in my own way. I won't do things in anybody else's way. I am trying to do my best for us and I will do what I said I would do.'

His own work was now more focused on lecturing at Farnham: 'I walk around the room, don't use notes or stand on the platform, but talk informally most of the time.' He was arming men with the knowledge required to use camouflage in offensive as well as defensive strategies. There was much focus on special schemes. 'The attacker can be deceived by means of dummy positions and dummy minefields, he can be misled by alternative positions.' The development of decoys, or 'devices of visual misdirection', was the order of the day.

'Consider what might be dummified,' Joe scribbled in his note-book.[3]

Was that even a verb?

'Of course it is no good posting this, so you will read it tomorrow night! Lucky Popcorn – and clever Popcorn to think out how to tell you how much he loves you in a room full of people and nobody having the slightest idea (perhaps!).' He'd wait for the colour to rise in her face, reassuring himself of the effect he still had. 'I love watching you reading my letters – in public places, surrounded by strangers and here we are in our own private world and none of them know anything about it or us.' For so long Joe had kept everything hidden, but now he needed proof.

He also suggested a new background. Cecil Schofield had rented Moulsford Grange for the duration of the war, a charming Queen Anne property with gardens stretching down to the Thames, tucked away in a picturesque Oxfordshire village. Schofield lived there with his wife Valerie, and the taciturn Peregrine as an irregular lodger. 'There is no possible misunderstanding about us,' Joe assured Mary. 'Both Cecil and Valerie and Peregrine know all about us and sympathise.'

Mary visited Moulsford with Joe for a few days' leave and Valerie fussed around them happily, glad to have more people to look after. Joe thought Cecil a fantastic fellow – gregarious, generous and charismatic – but Mary found him slippery as an eel. She felt he exploited Joe and she also didn't approve of how he took Valerie for granted. There was some talk of other women.

'Cecil & V seem to have a workable arrangement which suits him, though it wouldn't suit many people,' Joe concluded, by which he meant Valerie spent a lot of time at home whilst Cecil gallivanted off in the blackout.

For Joe, this felt like a life long past. He was a reformed character, no longer adrift. He just wanted to be with Mary. 'I wish to God we were married, meantime we have a lot to be thankful for. I might be in Libya or God knows where. I keep thinking about Moulsford. I never imagined before we met, that such a complete union was possible. It is all very wonderful.'

There are photographs of them all together one fine summer's afternoon. Joe, in uniform, has gained weight. He squints in the sunshine, smiling and chatting to colleagues and friends. Mary looks as thin as ever, smokes constantly, and has her hair tied up in a Liberty scarf. Peregrine is also there, hovering in the background, hands tucked into the pockets of his suit. He too is slim but has that unmissable Churchillian jowliness. Cecil Schofield, meanwhile, is still turning away, escaping out of every picture. He is handsome and elegantly suited. His wife, Valerie, is also impeccably dressed. She is much smaller than Mary, with soft round features and blonde hair curled up under an elaborate hat. She wears a fox fur round her neck despite the gloriously sunny day and holds her baby proudly, who is clad in swathes of white lace and frowning as if embarrassed. John Mollo, Eugene Mollo's son, identified Valerie instantly. 'I remember they were awfully flash. If I'd dressed an actress in a wartime film like that I would have been hooted off the set!' And he is an Oscar-winning costume designer so he knows whereof he speaks.

Moulsford was meant to be Joe and Mary's escape, but every weekend came with qualifications, corrections and amendments.

Both Cecil and Valerie and Peregrine do think a tremendous lot of you and they all do really sympathise with the present position. There is no doubt they both have many good qualities and are both kind and hospitable. I regard Cecil's fights and intrigues with 'big business' with great interest and considerable appreciation and amusement.

I told the Ministry of Supply the other day at Cecil's request that he [had] withdrawn his claim to a patent in favour of me, being the original inventor. I am rather anxious that you should not form an adverse opinion of Cecil, although neither you nor I could appreciate his personal or private affairs. I was particularly worried for fear that you – when I told you about Cecil – would perhaps 'do a Mary' on the lines that 'these people think that Grumble and I are like Cecil etc.

Joe was desperate to reassure Mary that whatever Cecil was up to, there could be no comparison, but she had her suspicions, and with good reason. The patent for steel wool camouflage was never withdrawn – Cecil Schofield's name is all over it, to this day. Joe always called Mary naive, but they both were. Joe took too much on trust and Cecil would play him at his own game, softening him up with the occasional handout. The already muddied waters thickened.

The war, the war, the war, how it had consumed and exhausted them. Joe was so weary of his flitting around the country and living like a gypsy. His dilapidated office 'lie-low' ('lilo' or 'lylow' – he always spelled it in a different way) had been patched up one time too many, and so in desperation he risked his last bit of money on digs in Bayswater Road, a drab upper-floor room that he begged 'Mrs Grumble' to make homely. He thought they could pass as a married couple but it didn't quite work out. He knew it then. Enough was enough.

I rang up the solicitor but he was engaged tonight. So I went to the Grosvenor and saw old Levy and said: 'Look here – what we want is proper evidence and could you fix it and would the hotel mind and so on' and when he had finished laughing – which he did, he said he would fix it alright if we liked and no need to take a flat, and he always knew we were two 'innocents abroad' and that seems the most practicable plan, my darling. So the Grosvenor it is. From the manager down they are all genuine friends. We must see what the solicitor says.

Joe steered towards the tried and tested route to divorce, where he'd be 'caught' in a hotel room with another woman and give Nancy grounds for divorce. Mary agreed to play 'the other woman' for one time only. Joe reassured her about everyone being most understanding and the staff counted as friends.

A.G. is taking it well. I am very glad that the B. Reids are to handle it as they have a personal interest and are really anxious to help and it makes it much easier for A.G., dealing with people she knows intimately. Mrs B. Reid says most of the expenses are at the beginning and says we should let A.G. have between £30 and £40, say £35 or £40. She says we can rely on the expenses being reduced to a minimum – I don't think there is any doubt about that. A.G. says she thought everything would not be more than £50. I posted the money and am busy composing the initial letter which must be short and to the point.

All that was required was one final deceptive display at the Grosvenor. After that there'd be no need to hide, and no excuse either.

U *is the Use you make of dummies*
   So the enemy can never trust what he sees

By July 1942 Rommel's men had been brought to a standstill in the desert, but the Allied Forces of the Eighth Army were in disarray and their position perilously weak. Auchinleck had kept the Axis at bay but the prime minister, obsessed with a further offensive and frustrated that it hadn't yet happened, replaced him with General Harold Alexander.

Alexander had commanded the vital rearguard during the retreat from Dunkirk before succeeding Auchinleck at Southern Command, where he too had been close to Edward Seago, with the two enjoying painting trips together. Unsurprisingly, Seago concluded that all generals were 'frustrated artists' at heart.[1] If regular soldiers remained sceptical about camouflage, the higher ranks were becoming more receptive. General Bernard Montgomery took control of the Eighth Army under Alexander, and although he professed no artistic ability, he had cultivated his own image expertly. 'Monty' well appreciated the need 'to mystify the enemy'[2] and brought in Geoffrey Barkas early on.

'They told me about concentration areas and enough about scale, about periods involved, about axis tracks, about the main cover plan . . . I was asked what Camouflage could do and what it could not do – in short I was asked to produce a plan. You can imagine my delight. This was what we had all been working for. It was pie!'[3]

Plenty has been written about El Alamein, this crucial battle in the war, and opinions vary wildly as to the significance of the part played by camouflage, yet there's no doubt the impact of the initial attack was stronger thanks to an elaborate deceptive cover plan.

Using all their knowledge and resources, the desert camoufleurs did everything to hide the build-up of troops and artillery in the north, and instead gave the impression that an attack was being mounted in the south, and at a later date. They first had to hide 2,000 tonnes of fuel in the north that would be required by Monty's troops by laying the fuel cans along the inner walls of existing slit trenches. This could be done at night and in daylight the trench looked exactly the same with no discernible thickening of shadow. The next challenge was to hide food, ammunition and other stores, but this was done in a brilliantly roundabout way. The camoufleurs first dumped waste materials (discarded packing cases and such) under camouflage nets, making them appear to be ammunition or ration dumps. The Axis noticed these but, as no offensive action immediately followed and the 'dumps' did not change in appearance, they were subsequently ignored. This allowed the Eighth Army to start building up supplies in the forward area unnoticed, by slowly replacing the rubbish with ammunition and rations, again under cover of night.

It was also vital to give a false impression of the actual timing of the assault. Barkas was asked if he could create something like Steven Sykes's dummy railhead at Misheifa. He came up with the plan to build a dummy water pipeline leading south, which would clearly not be ready at the time of the assault. This made German reconnaissance think that the attack would occur much later than

planned, and much further south. Peter Proud organised the digging of the pipeline (essentially a line of empty oil drums that were
repeatedly laid in a ditch, then at night the trench was filled in,
and the same fake pipe was advanced). The staging of dummy
pump houses, filling stations, artillery and equipment manned by
straw men further reinforced the illusion.

The job of hiding the real artillery and creating a false show of
them was woven into one, in a sense. Wavell's 'Sunshield' covers
for tanks were still very much in use. A similar idea was adapted
for field guns: a fabric and wood cover called a 'Cannibal' literally
hid the gun to make it resemble a more innocuous truck. There
were to be 722 Sunshields and 360 Cannibals used in the campaign, along with 500 dummy tanks, 150 dummy guns and 2,000
dummy transport vehicles, swapped around like pieces in a game
of chess. In the north, the build-up was concealed by first erecting
empty sunshields. Then real tanks were moved and installed under
the sunshields at night. Where the tanks had been resting, a battalion of dummy tanks replaced them.

Although there's evidence that the Axis had discovered this new
method of disguising tanks, the element of uncertainty kept
Rommel at a disadvantage. He couldn't be sure what was real and
what was fake and didn't want to make a serious mistake, so
divided his already depleted armies accordingly.

Montgomery's Eighth Army moved into attack position on 23
October 1942, the night of the full moon. The battle lasted twenty
days and there were serious casualties on both sides, but it was the
first great offensive against the Germans in which the Allies were
victorious. Evidence gathered later from enemy documents and
prisoners of war showed that the camoufleurs' schemes had

worked – it was only in the very last moments before the attack that the Germans grew suspicious of activity in the north.

Churchill was jubilant and quick to claim the victory as one for camouflage: 'By a marvellous system of camouflage, complete tactical surprise was achieved in the desert. The enemy suspected – indeed, knew – that an attack was impending, but when and where and how it was coming was hidden from him.'[4]

Churchill's championing of camouflage in itself subtly camouflaged the fact that El Alamein was a tough, bloody, prolonged battle with mistakes on both sides. But he had the success he wanted: a sign that the tide was turning in his favour.

V is for Vision, this means more than sight,
Use a strategy to keep your scheme tight

It is often only from a distance that patterns can become visible. When Maureen married John, nobody approved. They said it wouldn't last. When my mother married my father, she'd known him a matter of weeks. It created quite a scandal. Patricia Barclay introduced Philip Horlock to her parents just days before their wedding. She was using what General Alexander called 'the battle-winning factor': surprise.[1]

The hasty marriage came about as Philip had already accepted a job in Australia. He was training to be an accountant, just as John Barclay had been when he first met Maureen. Patricia would not endure any kind of separation and was determined to go with him. If two people loved each other, then why shouldn't they be together? She didn't see how everything was repeating. John and Maureen had moved to Northern Rhodesia (now Zambia) after the war, wanting to make a better life for themselves and their daughters.

Patricia and Philip were married in Ndola in 1962. There is a poignant Polaroid of the two of them, taken just days before their marriage. They look young and terrified, sitting close on a sofa but fighting to stay separate, hands held captive in laps. Above them looms a vivid churning seascape that almost expresses the whirlwind of emotions. It is of course a Joseph Gray.

Maureen loved her years in Africa but with hindsight she worries that the move made the rift with Joe permanent. She feels guilty that her daughters didn't get to know their grandfather. She never spoke to them about him, filling her house with his pictures instead. She didn't know what to say, how to explain him, and so she stopped trying.

'I just thought: what you don't know, you will not miss.'

She regrets that now, not trying harder to stay in contact, but she felt it was what he had willed.

Patricia was the only granddaughter Joe ever met. When she was born on 25 October 1942, the war in North Africa was but a few days old. Maureen was still in Paisley with her in-laws. Joe remained in London and heard news of the arrival of Patricia Maureen Barclay via telegram. He didn't mention this momentous event in his letters to Mary. It was slightly jarring to consider himself a grandfather. He had no savings, no security, very little in the way of possessions. He didn't even have a home. He had been forced to move out of Bayswater Road after falling out with the landlady over rent. She had asked him either to take a larger room or rent two rooms, in light of the fact that 'his wife' was spending so much time there. Angered and embarrassed, Joe had declared his hatred for the area, scattered crumbs 'in every damn mousehole', hastily packed and left.

So 1943 would be the year of fresh starts.

Again.

Early in the year John, Maureen and baby Patricia settled into a flat on Elm Grove in Wimbledon. Nancy, who had been in touch sporadically, chose this as the moment to visit. She arrived one February morning, her manner as brisk as the weather. She had not come directly from Bedford, having spent a day in London already, but these details were swept aside whilst she inspected her charming new grandchild.

She apologised for not coming sooner and expressed her relief at finding everybody well. Maureen was struck by how young her mother looked. She was glowing, and moved with a new lightness, fussing happily around the kitchen as if it were her own.

It was later, when they sat together – mother, daughter and granddaughter – that Nancy delivered her news.

'I have been up to the courts.' She rested a hand lightly on Maureen's knee. 'To see about divorcing your father.'

The irony was that Maureen didn't hear – her deafness had become quite chronic during the pregnancy and she was distracted by the baby. Nancy repeated the words slowly.

'I am divorcing your father.'

Maureen, pale and tired, turned towards her mother.

'Divorce?'

The word sounded strange, almost foreign.

Looking Nancy in the eye, holding her new baby in her arms, she didn't understand.

'But *why*?'

Nancy lifted her chin and glanced towards the window, showing off that fine and ageless profile.

'Ah well,' she said.

She could have given any kind of answer: she could have blamed it on the war, their changing circumstances, growing older. She kept her head held high.

'The thing is. He wants to marry Mary Meade.'

To Nancy this was the best explanation, and so it would become the only one. She hoped to dispose of the business quickly, without further discussion, and perhaps shock Maureen into silence. At first it worked, but how quickly shock turned to horror.

'Mary Meade?' Maureen was blinking fast. 'Mary Meade from *The Needlewoman?*'

Nancy gave a little sigh. 'That's the one.'

Mary Meade. Miss Mary Meade. Maureen's mind tumbled back to 1938 – four years, five years, how long had it been? '*Oh please do call me Mary.*' Joe had sent her there. '*Are you at all artistic?*' The woman she had worked for. It was incomprehensible. How could she have missed it? How? Questions crowded into her mind as she watched her mother, now leaning back, relieved to have got it off her chest.

'Come now. We have been living apart for some time.' Nancy absently stroked her daughter's arm, turning back, managing a slight smile. 'You knew that.'

Maureen stared down at her baby and slowly shook her head. 'I thought that was because of the war.'

'And it *was*. But your father has made his choice.'

His choice. Such careful wording. Little Patricia, sensing the sudden change in atmosphere, began to fret, and Maureen pulled her baby closer. To comfort the child was a consolation, just when she herself was feeling so small and helpless.

'Please don't be upset.' Nancy had a knack for shutting conversation down. 'And you must not worry about me. You have your own family now.'

But Maureen was reeling. Yes, she had her own family now, yet the foundations on which that family was based had vanished. She felt terrible. Mary Meade.

If Maureen wanted to ask her mother more questions, this wasn't the time. It was over. It was done.

But it wasn't – how could it be? Later, she paced the flat, brooding over the news. How foolish she must have been not to have guessed this, not to have known. She blamed her deafness, the pregnancy, her lack of sophistication. She didn't know what to do at all, apart from wait for John to come home from work. She was almost looking forward to telling him so that at least *he* could share her consternation.

It would be a long wait before she heard his key turn in the lock.

She ran into the corridor.

'You won't believe this. My mother is divorcing my father.'

John, briefcase in hand, gave a small sigh.

'Oh. *That.*'

Maureen blinked.

He knew.

'You *knew*?'

He squeezed past her. 'I did.'

This was another shock, almost as bad as the first. He knew and he hadn't told her.

Why?

The fact was John Barclay did not have an easy relationship with his mother-in-law. He had endured her disapproval, ignored her meddlings and grown increasingly weary of what he called her 'manoeuvrings'. But on this one matter they had reached an understanding.

He set down his briefcase and turned back to Maureen.

'Your mother and I, we thought it best not to tell you until after

Patricia was safely delivered. We didn't want you getting upset about it all.'

John reached out to his wife, placing his hands on her arms. Maureen had miscarried their first child and he had wanted, above all, to protect her and the baby.

'I knew how upset you'd be. You will always come first. You and the baby mattered more. I am sorry.'

Maureen turned away, dazed. How secrets could be contagious.

'You kept this from me!'

John turned her back to face him. He bowed his head and held her gaze.

'I give you my word I shall never ever do anything like this again.'

John Barclay would keep his promise. He proved himself, time and again, to be a devoted husband, determined to build a solid, loving family. This would be the first and last time he would ally himself with Nancy.

But for Maureen the shock of her parents' divorce would reverberate for years. She wasn't sure what upset her more: the fact of their divorce or the deliberate deception. She was a grown woman, but they'd treated her like a child. Perhaps they still thought of her as one, since they hadn't really watched her grow up. John was acutely aware of the pain this caused his wife and never forgave Joe or Nancy their game-playing. ('Maureen honestly had no inkling. It took a long time for her to get over it.'[2])

Joe didn't come to meet his first grandchild. He sent a charming note wishing everyone well, but left it to Nancy to expose and explain the details of his 'affair'. He was both embarrassed and ashamed. He had been trying to do the right thing, over and over, trying to keep everyone happy. It had not worked.

For years Joe had delayed and procrastinated, but now, when he was finally fulfilling his promise to Mary, he went into hiding from his own daughter. To John Barclay it smacked of cowardice, and as he became increasingly impatient with his wife's parents, the idea of moving away and starting over grew in appeal.

Joe thought keeping his distance meant keeping a promise, keeping his composure. He understood what it meant to Nancy. She needed Maureen more than he did, and Nancy could be there for Maureen in a way that he couldn't. The bond between mothers and daughters should not be interfered with. Joe had seen it up close between Kitty Meade and Mary.

But Maureen wanted to hear from her father, and when she didn't her hurt intensified. Without a full explanation she was left to imagine all sorts. For a long while after she'd learned of Joe and Mary's relationship she feared the very worst – that it was her doing. She assumed that the relationship must've started when she was working at *The Needlewoman*, and that she had unwittingly brought her father and Mary together. She was therefore to blame for the disintegration of her parents' marriage. It seemed entirely plausible in the context of what she knew.

As is often the way, one secret spawned another: Maureen voiced her worries to no one, for fear of upsetting her own mother.

In September 1943 a decree absolute set Nancy and Joe free. Nancy didn't publicise the news, although she had a week of leave and was spending it with Maureen, tidying and reorganising their new flat in Camp View. It was a larger space, with wide windows looking out onto Wimbledon Common, and an extra bedroom, which was just as well since Patricia was no longer a baby and another was expected. It was a Sunday, traditionally a day of rest, but Nancy couldn't stop cleaning. Maureen was exhausted just watching her. She wasn't in the mood for guests but one would soon be here. Dick Orr-Ewing was coming down from Scotland and had expressed a desire to see Maureen and John, and to meet Nancy's first grandchild. John remained rooted to his armchair, reading the newspaper. He didn't see the point in making a fuss.

Fortunately, Dick wasn't the type to need one. He arrived like a warm breeze, giving Maureen a fatherly embrace and tickling Patricia under her chin. He brought presents and compliments for everyone and settled himself in amongst them with his usual easy charm. Maureen thought he looked extremely well. She noted the paradox – how war robbed people of life whilst giving some a fresh chance at it.

John, meanwhile, gave Dick the sort of look he reserved for suspicious objects on station platforms.

Peering at Dick over his thick spectacles, he cast his newspaper aside.

'So tell me. How long will you be in London?'

Dick smiled.

'Just long enough to get married.'

A silence like a gasp of breath. Maureen had heard perfectly. Confused, she glanced over at her mother, then she looked back at Dick, who reached over and clasped her hands in his.

'I have asked your mother to marry me. I hope that's all right.'

Maureen smiled back, though still she didn't understand. This was the first time she'd heard anything about it.

'It's good news, I hope.' Dick's look was now rather imploring.

Maureen turned to John. Had he known, as well? But no, John gripped the arms of his chair, his eyes wide and his mouth open. He was utterly lost for words.

'Yes!' Nancy exclaimed brightly. 'I am delighted. Dick asked me to be his wife. We are to be married tomorrow.'

John sunk further into his chair. '*Tomorrow?*'

'Now that *was* extraordinary,' Maureen remembers. 'There I was, pregnant, with my own mother acting like a teenager. Dick was the same. I have a clear memory of him lightly skipping down the stairs from our flat, singing: "We're getting married in the morning!"'

We have come out to lunch at a nearby hotel. It's a stone's throw from her nursing home but too far for her to walk. I have pushed her here in a wheelchair, swaddled in blankets like a child. Although it is a bright winter day, she feels the cold terribly.

'You must have been surprised.'

'Well, *yes*,' Maureen sighs. 'Of course I'd known him a long time. Such a lovely, good-hearted chap. You couldn't *not* like him. But it came out of the blue. All I remember later on is John saying that Dick would look after Nancy – and how that was a relief – and he was right. Dick looked after everyone. Your mum and her sisters adored him.'

This I know is true. Dick was there jiggling babies on his knee, playing games, reading books and telling the wildest stories. If ever I ask my aunts about Dick, they lift their heads and smile. They can talk about Dick endlessly, his humour and his patience. Dick was more of a grandfather than Joe ever was, and a more devoted husband to Nancy than she could have wished for. He adored her.

They were married on 8 September without fuss or family members. There was no party afterwards or any formal announcement. Nancy used Maureen's address on their marriage certificate, which seems a bit rich considering Maureen *wasn't* there. But what surprises me most is the date. Nancy and Dick were married two weeks before Joe and Mary. When I tell Maureen this she stares at the tablecloth.

'I didn't know that.'

She says it in such a measured, quiet way. It's perhaps the only way she can say it. She takes a long pause.

'I was sure Joe had already married Mary.'

'No,' I reply. 'Were you told that, or was that just what you assumed? Joe waited. I think he was always trying to do the right thing, so he let Nancy go first.'

I do now believe this. Yes, Joe procrastinated terribly, but in all of his letters he stressed the need to do things 'in the right way'. He wanted Nancy to be looked after, so he let her take the lead and sort out her affairs. The moment she married Dick, that's when he was free.

It is ironic: for all Joe's interest in appearances, he lost control of how he was seen. He would forever be the unfaithful husband, the wayward artist, the gallivanting camoufleur. He was of course all of those things, but he was more.

As we start our meal I mention my theory about Joe and his pension to Maureen.

'He'd seen it, in the last war. People had no money. He wanted Nancy to be taken care of, even as his widow. Once she married Dick, she wasn't his responsibility.'

Maureen dabs at her mouth, not saying anything. I can't tell what she is thinking. I want to reassure her I am not trying to redeem or excuse Joe, I am not trying to make some comforting illusion, but I feel it needs to be said. Then I catch her smiling. After a few minutes' silence she takes a sip of wine.

'The thing is,' she begins.

She presses her fingers on the tablecloth, dabbing at the knife and fork. I've noticed she often does this when she is trying to order her words. She will play with her napkin or straighten the cutlery.

I lean in.

After a long moment, she levels her eyes on me.

'He did say something about that . . . it was when I took Patricia to Marlow, all those years later, and we had that awful discussion about art. Well, he took me to one side and we walked around by the flowerbeds, and he said: "You should know, you do know, don't you? . . . Dick was there before Mary."'

I press my hands into my knees. 'Dick was there before Mary.'

Maureen nods and lifts her finger. 'Yes. He said: "Dick was there first. You realise that, I hope." He wanted me to know.'

I sit back. It is of course what I had suspected. I can see them: Nancy and Dick, leaning close at the card table, lingering in the corridors of the Sutherland, eyes meeting, fingers touching. Dick was there first. But what catches me out is how Maureen can confirm it. The way she is looking at me now, with eyebrows raised, puzzles me. Is this some new memory bobbing to the surface or an old one she's long locked away? She gives a little sigh and shake of her head. I wish she had told me sooner, but no, I don't think she would have. I had to get there on my own.

I stare at our half-eaten food.

'Of course,' she goes on. 'By that time it barely mattered.'

I disagree. I think it mattered a great deal. It was the last time Maureen saw her father alive, in the garden in Marlow, and he had finally told her the truth.

'Joe put Mary off time and again,' I say. 'He did that so Dick and Nancy could sort themselves out, and he took the blame and kept it secret.'

Maureen smiles. 'He was good at that.'

Looking back, it all makes sense.

Maureen lifts her hand again. 'I remember on Norfolk Square ... I told you that time Dad was so angry, rapping the railings with his stick. He was friends with Dick, they *had been* friends. "Touch of the tar-brush" was what he said. Where did that come from?' She nods. 'Oh yes. He *was* angry.'

I picture it so vividly I feel I could be there. I had long wondered if Joe had met Mary when he was writing about camouflage and that these two deceptions wove together. But Dick and Nancy were the inspiration for everything. How to hide in plain sight – Joe learned from the best.

His marriage had barely survived the move south. Nobody could have fixed it. It was a relief, perhaps, that Dick was there, waiting for his life-changing event, *his* watershed moment. Meeting Nancy was like the strike of a match. It made things easier that Joe actually liked Dick. I am sure he could imagine Nancy happier with a respectable engineer, a good soldier who wore his heart on his sleeve. Dick was solid, and Dick was persistent, and most importantly Dick was *there*. It's something I haven't considered enough, how the very act of being there can come to mean so much. My grandmother has always been there for me, the rock and root of everything. Now I've built a family of my own I understand what's needed. I'm far from perfect, but I'm there. When you love someone, you have to stay, you have to listen. There is a certain surrender, an abdication of self. Dick would become Nancy's constant companion.

And Joe hoped that by giving Nancy a second chance, he might get the same. When he met Mary, when he spent his first night with her, he pretended he was free because he knew Dick was in love with Nancy. But he wasn't free and he wouldn't be, not until Nancy committed to Dick.

Two weeks after Nancy married Dick, Joe married Mary. There was no need to wait around. Joe could pretend it had all worked out just as he had planned. Hadn't it all come right in the end? Standing back and looking from a distance, everything was fitting into place.

A few days before Mary Meade became Mary Gray, her mother wrote to Joe. 'You know I wish you both the very best and mind you are good to my Mary or else I can be simply horrible beyond words!!' It was her final warning to him, but she signed herself with affection, 'Mrs Mumbles'. Yes, Joe had talked everyone round. James Meade wasn't able to go to the wedding because he was then working in Washington, so Margaret took his place.

'Mary was married yesterday,' she wrote.

The ceremony took place in the Chelsea Register Office, which was rather shocking for your mother, and she still can't feel that it's quite legal. Your cousin Toby gave the bride away, and young Churchill was best man. I was best girl! After that we all went to the Waldorf Hotel for a reception – about 60 people – a few relatives, a few Bathonians and a good many in uniforms from Gray's office. It was all very successful and Mary looked very well and happy.

Jack Sayer, Dalgliesh and the other members of the 'crazy gang' were there. Sayer overheard Mary reminding Joe: 'You've got to go round and talk to your guests, not just stand up at the bar grinning the whole time.' She knew Joe's ways well enough. Though perhaps Mary didn't anticipate her own family members, not being used to alcohol, becoming quite drunk and having to be 'deposited on a secluded sofa and dosed by a delighted Johnny Churchill with cups of black coffee'.[3]

I have several photographs of Joe and Mary from their wedding day, all taken out in the street. Joe is in uniform and grinning broadly, his arm interlaced with Mary's. She wears a dark beret, a coat that is neatly nipped in at her waist, and a rather luxurious fox fur draped around her shoulders. Her coat and dress stop just at the knee, showing off those splendid legs.

There is another photograph of Joe and Mary with Johnny Churchill, and then another of Joe flanked by the two Marys, then a final one of all four of them togther. There are no photographs of any other guests or of the reception, so I consider once more this neat quartet. Joe and Johnny and their two Marys, they look so smart and still young – Joe looks far younger than his years – and full of promise. It's a bright, clear day and everybody is smiling. At last, everybody is smiling.

GOOD RECEPTION

Let us drink to the Bride –
Come, fill ev'ry glass! –
And may she decide
That her newly formed Class
(In a class by himself is our Joseph)
Will achieve, if not honours, a Pass.

Let us drink to each Guest
As they come in the door,
All perfectly dressed – and sober, what's more.

May the drinking of healths with such fervour
Deposit but few on the floor.

Let us drink to Joe's Bank –
Here's dust in their eyes!
Though Joe's little prank
May cause them surprise
May they boost up his overdraft promptly
To a truly phenomenal size.

Let us drink to the Flat
And its prevalent hue –
We understand that
Will be Jubilee blue.
('tis sited next door to a Brewery
Which is almost too good to be true.)

Let us drink to Joe Gray
As he gropes for his train
At the dawn of each day
And at nightfall again.
And may missing the latter by seconds
Not be found over-hard to explain.

Let us drink to the Clock;
In its hands, moving round,
May a copious stock
Of Good Fortune be found –
And may all of the hours it points to
In happiness greatly abound.

20 SEPT 1943

Written:

'With best wishes from The Old Firm
Foule – Wyatt – Sayer – Dalgliesh'

POSTSCRIPT

Though after some glasses
We're down on the floor
We drink to a Grayling
Or Graylings Galore;
For Josephs are scarce
And there ought to be more![4]
[F.J.C.Wyatt]

W is for Waste. Please do not forget
Steel wool is harder to replace than a net

Joe settled into married life, or rather settled *back* into married life, but his life in camouflage wasn't over. Steel wool had a final but crucial role to play. The possible re-invasion of Europe had been on the agenda ever since Dunkirk but it wasn't until May 1943 that Churchill and President Roosevelt gave it their full attention.

The point of invasion was hotly contested. The Pas de Calais, the narrowest point in the English Channel, seemed ideal. But Mountbatten, still in charge of Combined Operations, was completely opposed to it, pointing out that it was far *too* obvious.[1] The Germans, he argued, were anticipating just such an attack and were rapidly building up military strength in considerable depth throughout the Calais area. But they had little motivation to do so further west, and had allotted nothing like the same fortification and military manpower to the defence of the Normandy beaches in the Baie de la Seine. The Chief of Staff to the Supreme Allied Commander (COSSAC) team identified this area as a possible entry point, and so began the tireless gathering of intelligence. Aerial reconaissance mapped the area carefully, British frogmen slipped ashore, commando raids brought back prisoners, and members of the SOE parachuted in, all determined to grasp the fullest picture of what was waiting on the ground. There would be no repeats of what had happened at Dieppe.

Operation Overlord was the codename given to this most crucial attack of the Second World War. It was a masterpiece of planning, shielded by an equally complex cover plan called Bodyguard (a nod to Winston Churchill's observation that 'in wartime truth is so precious that she should always be attended by a bodyguard of lies'[2]).

A deception plan for the cross-Channel attack, named Operation Fortitude, borrowed from the example of El Alamein and spun several separate stories. Firstly, everything was done to give the impression the assault could take place in any one of the occupied countries of Northern Europe, so that German troops would be drafted away from the action – this was called Fortitude North. The second thread came into play once it became clear that a cross-Channel assault *would* happen: everything then had to be done to convince the Germans that it would focus on the Pas de Calais rather than Normandy – this was Fortitude South. Thirdly, it was vital to convince the Germans that the attack would take place weeks later than it was actually scheduled.

Fortitude North aimed to fuel Hitler's obsession with the tactical value of Norway, and to this end a team of British officers were dispatched to the upper reaches of Scotland to fill the airwaves with fake radio transmissions. This was complemented by the arrival of armies of dummy tanks and gliders, and the appearance of surplus ships and decoy landing craft lining the Firth of Forth, all of which created the impression of the build-up of an Allied 'Fourth Army', making ready to attack.

Fortitude South was another crucial distraction, intended to give the impression of heightened activity in the areas around

Dover and Folkstone instead. The Camouflage Development and Training Centre held practice camps and exercises teaching men how to improvise the impression of 'false strength' or 'phantom brigades'. The First US Army Group (FUSAG) was really just that – a skeleton formation formed for purely administrative purposes – but the Germans were made to believe it was the main Allied threat and would be landing around Calais. Although camouflage was used to conceal its camps, it was deliberately inadequate: 'concealment measures will be conspicuous and uneven' and 'the occupation of camps will be emphasised by smoke from cookers and incinerators'.[3] It was even recommended that wood was the best and cheapest fuel to burn since this gave a thicker smoke.

Alongside these activities, dummy landing craft appeared in the Thames and Medway estuaries, while the airfields of Kent and Essex filled up with plywood gliders just waiting to be spotted. Sound City designers also built hundreds of dummy landing barges made of canvas and wood that floated on empty oil drums. They were towed to the sort of place you might expect a landing craft to be anchored, left for a few days, then moved again, to give the impression of activity.[4]

But the centrepiece of the illusion was a dummy oil-storage facility and docking station built near Dover, designed by architect Basil Spence and constructed by Sound City staff. This installation, stretching for miles along the shoreline, consisted of pipelines and pumping stations, jetties, truck bays, troop barracks and anti-aircraft defences. Official inspections by King George V and General Montgomery were noted in the press but precautions were taken to keep the Luftwaffe above 30,000 feet, from which height it was impossible for enemy cameras to pick out any obvious flaws. The Germans had every reason to believe that this was a terminus for an underwater pipeline that would eventually lead to Calais, heralding an imminent invasion of that area.

Of course, such ingenious distractions were nothing if the true build-up of troops wasn't kept under cover, and all the time this was going on in the west and south-west of England, with camps and tanks dispersed in wooded areas or under static covers, tracks and tents constantly darkened, and smokeless cookers recommended. (So conscious was Major Seago about the need to conceal the build-up of troops in Southern Command that he even vetoed the playing of football matches.)

A real fuel pipeline with pumping stations was also going to be needed, something steel wool proved key to hiding. Pluto ('Pipeline Under The Ocean') was intended to ensure a supply of petroleum as soon after D-Day as possible. This took the form of a complex system of pipes and terminals, with pumping stations at Dungeness in Kent (codenamed 'Dumbo') and Shanklin and Sandown on the Isle of Wight (codenamed 'Bambi'). One pipeline ran from the Isle of Wight to Cherbourg, the other from Dungeness to Boulogne.

Ashley Havinden, a camouflage adviser for Southern Command, was placed in charge of 'Bambi', and later 'Dumbo'. A protégé of the sculptor Henry Moore, Havinden was a hugely successful art director at the advertising agency W. S. Crawford. Once recruited into camouflage he had paid close attention to the deceptions at Tobruk and applied its many lessons to his new project. Hiding sites of this scale was no simple task – 'Dumbo' alone consisted of thirty storage tanks thirty feet long served by thirty diesel pumps – and Havinden not only had to camouflage the huge concrete tanks, but also the pipelines and any evidence of the works in progress. Large-scale netting covers were first installed to allow men to work underneath – which were later replaced by steel wool covers. Another solution was to retain the exterior of abandoned holiday homes and garages but transform their interiors completely.

'Captain Ashley Havinden and his camouflage officers did an outstanding job here. Behind the unchanged smiling façades of "Mon Repos", "Happy-Go-Lucky", "Sea Breezes", "Sans Souci" and a host of others were massive pumps and engines, and the owners would indeed have been surprised had they been able to walk into their erstwhile carefree resorts.'[5] Extending the pipeline down to the coast, steel wool came into its own, creating a seamless cover over which shingle could be piled.

Eugene Mollo was drafted in to work with Havinden on the Isle of Wight, responding to a need for static covers. Steel wool covered parts of the cross-Solent pipe ('Solo') that ran from Thorness on one side of the Isle of Wight, through the Pankhurst Forest to a 62,000-gallon reservoir tank that sat on high ground by Shanklin. The bomb-scarred appearance of Shanklin's seafront was then adapted: 'Amongst these ruins we built our pump-houses and laid our lines, simulating on a new elevation twelve feet higher up the debris and wrecked dwelling rooms . . . and hiding our mechanisms beneath this false floor.'[6]

At Sandown, a little north of Shanklin, a partly demolished granite fort hid pumping machinery. The mound of the fort was partially excavated to accommodate the pumps and a switch house was covered in painted steel wool.

Camouflage discipline was also crucial. Men worked under steel-wool covers, which could be painted any colour to blend with the setting and season, but even if work went on under cover and at night, any sign of activity – tracks, tyre marks, moved shingle – had to be carefully restored by first light. Fortnightly inspections by RAF aerial photographers made sure there was no visible irregularity that might give German Intelligence pause for thought. Men of the Pioneer Corps recalled: 'Camouflage to us pioneers was a source of great annoyance, arguments, cursing and extra work, but as the days passed, and after the attempted bombings of Jerry had failed at both sites, we fully realised the importance of first-class camouflage.'[7]

In August 1943 a memorandum stated that the manufacture of steel wool would cease. All camouflage officers were ordered to take care that 'existing stocks are only used on work of high priority'.[8] Havinden marked it with an 'X'.

Early in 1944 he called together Lieutenant Mollo, Captain Dalgliesh and Peregrine Churchill to discuss the overhead covers for Pluto's bulk storage tanks (so all men who had had a close association with Joe, if not Joe himself). Air reconnaissance reports revealed that covers of green steel wool and natural coir merged well into surrounding grass and shingle. It was noted the steel wool should be added to, since it was better than coir, which produced shine. It was also recommended that the flatness of steel wool could be broken up with false clumps of scrub, composed of green steel wool attached to built-up clumps of Dannert wire.

Michael Farrar Bell, fresh back from Northern Ireland, joined the newly created 21st Army Group, which controlled all ground forces in Overlord. He was initially attached to No. 1 Oil Construction Group in the Isle of Wight. 'My work was to develop a large cover two acres in area, under which the construction of petrol storage tanks had to proceed unseen by enemy air observation.'[9] He credited Joe as his adviser, and *Camouflage and Air Defence* a treasured resource. Unsurprisingly, Farrar Bell made use of steel wool for these covers, and 'within three weeks of the D-Day landing I had erected seventeen more covers at Port en Bessin and subsequently put up over a hundred of them in France, Belgium, and Holland'.[10]

Joe's precious material had really come into its own, and there was a legitimate fear that there would be insufficient stocks. A War Office notice ordered that all remaining supplies were reserved for Overlord, and the minute the underwater pipeline emerged in Cherbourg it was cloaked in steel wool, with brush and salvaged German material laid over the top.

But if Joe's material was everywhere in evidence, where then was Joe? He was now spending long hours in the office, writing reports and attending meetings, and advising on the 'winding down' of the camouflage schemes he had once started in earnest. Mary had found them a little house in Marlow, and he was eager to get back there every night. Younger officers were attached to the 21st Army Group Camouflage Service and from December 1943 began to leave England to report for camouflage duties on the beaches of Normandy. Joe wasn't considered fit enough for such a role, and for once he didn't mind. He dispensed notes ('little masterpieces') to those who were going, offering advice about the use of multiple decoys and dummy positions, or having several different plans 'ready-made' for different phases of the operation.

There were five beach areas – Utah, Omaha, Juno, Gold and Sword – and a staff captain was assigned early on to each so they could become accustomed to the terrain. The camouflage officers who had learned on the job were now able to hit the ground running, and this was as well since they faced a huge task – concealing stores, equipment and, of course, men.

Operation Neptune, launched on the night of 5 June 1944, saw thousands of troops, weapons and equipment set sail for Normandy flanked by a vast squadron of fighter planes and destroyers. As part of the deception plan Lancaster bombers flew in a ship's convoy formation north of the armada to drop 'chaff' (strips of aluminium foil) that would create an echo in enemy receivers and imply that there was a large flotilla heading for the Pas de Calais. Balloons and radar reflectors operated by the Navy also helped the illusion to succeed. With enemy air and sea forces sent to interrupt an imaginary fleet, the real force was left free from attack. So began the fabled Normandy landings.

Surprise was achieved but there was still much fighting to be done. Back from the desert, Steven Sykes was attached to No. 5 Group at Sword Beach and set to work concealing stores against German shelling. As Allied troops advanced he began making sniper hoods and painting yards of hessian for screening, in what seemed like a throwback to the last war. Basil Spence, now responsible for Sword Beach, employed various camouflage tactics including smoke screens. All officers stressed the importance of keeping up camouflage discipline.

The Normandy campaign was the first in which large numbers of troops wore camouflage uniforms. Up until then this had mostly been reserved for the elite troops. In Britain paratroopers were given the Denison smock (a disruptive leaf-like patterned outfit), whilst the US Army favoured a dappled green design with a darker variation on the reverse. This had started being produced and distributed to GIs in 1942. Germany was the most prolific developer and user of camouflage uniforms, however, with both the Army and the Waffen-SS being issued with various designs. The trouble was, all camouflage uniforms shared certain characteristics and it proved hard to distinguish between Allied and enemy units. After many outbreaks of 'friendly fire', soldiers on both sides didn't see them as quite such a protective coating.

D-Day marked both an end and a beginning. Some of the Farnham camoufleurs felt nostalgic already. 'I am sorry in some ways that I can no longer count myself amongst the exclusive band of happy and ubiquitous camoufleurs!' wrote Havinden, when his project had reached completion.[11] But in Normandy, the fighting was drawn out. Spence was horrified to watch British tanks destroy two beautiful churches at Ouistreham and Hermanville. In his dugout that night, when he was asked about his ambitions after the war, Spence expressed a desire to build a cathedral. He would later design and build the new cathedral in Coventry, linking it to the bombed-out ruins of the old one. Two former comrades – John Hutton and Steven Sykes – would contribute different aspects to the interior design. Camouflage had brought together artists, designers and architects, and in years to come they wouldn't be easily parted. Many would collaborate on exhibitions like Britain Can Make It in 1946 and the Festival of Britain in 1951, and they positively colonised departments of the Royal College of Art.

Everyone was making plans for a future they now felt they deserved, although Eugene Mollo felt it bordered on an obsession. He was ultimately relieved to spend less time with the 'rarefied' group at Farnham. 'His main complaint about them,' reported his son, 'was that they spent too much time planning what they were going to do after the war.'

And what was that? I asked.

'Oh,' he replied. 'To set up something called the "Arts Council".'[12]

X *is for Extras, there will always be some,*
But think economically to get the job done

Joe and Mary, finally married, settled down to life in Marlow. They rented out the larger part of their new home, leaving themselves a small annexe with a studio. Joe commuted into London and on the nights when he worked late or had appointments he stayed at the Constitutional Club, 'a very Colonel Blimp sort of place' that Dalgliesh had got him to join. He wrote long letters home. It was just like before, only now he had somewhere to return to, a secure place in the world. He was still pinching himself to be sure.

Tuesday, Oct '44
My dear P.F.

It is now 11.30pm – which doesn't mean I have just come in! I have spent about two hours writing to old *M* . . . I think I know exactly what he wants and I am sure Jagger – whose paintings I dislike – will be able to give him exactly what he wants.

Before the war Joe had wanted to make his name as a portrait painter, but now he was passing over work, directing commissions to the prolific portraitist David Jagger instead. It seemed rather odd. 'I dare not do it!' he told Mary. 'The results would be ultimately disastrous.' He was too long out of practice.

But if he wasn't going to take commissions, how would they live?

Of course, Joe had a plan. Joe always had a plan.

Owing to various misunderstandings I didn't meet Cecil until late. He was slightly tight. He refused to discuss such sordid things as pounds but was wide awake on facts and business. His attitude was: "We owe everything to you, as long as we have any money – just say what you want." So I said: "What about £25 to start with?" and it was immediately handed over. I believe Cecil is perfectly sincere, ie: that everything he has got is at our disposal.

But what about if he loses everything?!!

Cecil Schofield was not the best man to pin one's hopes to. The longed-for and talked-about future had arrived. This was real life, not some fantasy. Joe had to get back to painting and yet he faltered. His easels and paintbrushes were waiting, a studio was ready. He was scared.

Before the war he had had such big ambitions for his painting, and all of them had come to nothing. How many times had he tried and failed to sell a picture, or gone begging to his bank manager? Those memories hadn't gone away. He had no 'good old days' to return to. Camouflage had become much more than a stop-gap, and now it wasn't needed. Did that mean he wasn't needed? He wasn't sure how to cope. Yes, he was once the man who could catch a perfect likeness, but he had spent the last five years doing the opposite. It was a world of twists and turns, and he couldn't keep up.

Everyone at the Board had a job to go back to, and the army

men like Wyatt were happy to retire. Joe fell somewhere in-
between. Wyatt encouraged him to apply for an award for steel
wool. It was, after all, *his* invention.

'What is safe and appears to be is the fact that I will get £500
or £600 gratuity when the War finishes. Secondly, I should get
some thousands from the steel wool award.'

There was plenty of proof it had been widely used and to great
effect. Joe wasn't greedy, but it was nice to think that he'd get
something back. Joseph Gray: war artist, etcher, portrait painter,
camouflage officer, *inventor*.

It had a nice ring to it.

Schofield was already busy on other schemes. A man with an
eye for opportunities, he and Peregrine were already developing
new projects, inluding a design for liquid-soap dispensers. Steel
wool was consigned to history as far as he was concerned. But not
for Joe. Camouflage was the world he knew, a world of shadow
and greyscale, full of rich textures. The art world, by contrast,
looked hard and impenetrable. He wasn't sure of his audience,
what they wanted and whether he could deliver it. It was all
slightly terrifying.

So Joe had another idea. He was going to publish *Camouflage
and Air Defence* with an updated introduction, explaining about
steel wool and its part in the war effort. 'The idea now is that the
book shall be published as a classical work under my name –
M&E not mentioned at all – or if mentioned only indirectly.' How
about that? Joseph Gray: war artist, etcher, painter, camouflage
officer, inventor and author.

Except his publishers' enthusiasm was short-lived. There were
animated discussions, first impressions looked good, but the finished manuscript was judged overly technical and too specialist for

a wide readership. Joe's theories and ideas were interesting, but there was some uncertainty over whether the moment had passed.

How quickly Joe Gray had gone out of fashion all over again.

He had finally married the woman he loved, but he was not allowed to settle. It was rather like being up in a plane again, looking down on the world, seeing endless possibilities but all of them out of reach. His colleagues were encouraging him in various directions. 'Your etchings are superb,' they told him. 'Your draughtsmanship first-class.' He was very good at listening to other people's advice; he'd smile and nod wisely like the Grumble they all knew. Sayer sketched him time and again as a sleepy-eyed owl, but Joe only ever drew himself as a stout and scruffy colonel. It was unanimously agreed that his cartoons were the best. 'Joe would seize upon some small incident or remark that had amused him and grabbing a piece of scrap paper would produce a side-splitting and outrageous drawing in about three minutes. His favourite target was Dalgliesh, always shown with a wildly waving empty sleeve and an exaggeratedly red nose.'[1]

Could that even be made into a profession?

I went in with my air reports and found [Wyatt] chuckling over Dalgliesh's scrapbook of my drawings. He said – 'What are you going to do after the War, Gray?' I said – 'I thought I would finish the War first, Sir, and then think about it!' He said 'My dear boy you are quite obviously a tremendous draughtsman and certainly the greatest humorous draughtsman in the country – nobody can touch you. Your style is absolutely unique – and people understand that sort of drawing nowadays.' Very 'ot. That's what Beddington always said.

Joe tried to sound buoyant but his enthusiams were scattering like seeds on the wind. He reasoned he'd try harder once he was out of uniform. Everyone had exciting plans. Freddie Beddington was off to work as a director at Wildenstein's Gallery. Sayer was to return to the world of advertising and illustration. Johnny and Little Mary had set up their own interior design business. There seemed to be an endless round of retirement parties. Honours were bestowed, toasts made. Joe wondered when it would be his turn and reminisced with whoever was available. To his colleagues he seemed immensely confident and contented, but as he looked around he wondered if they too weren't a bit scared. 'The galleries have gone all ultra modern . . . What I want to set me up is a cracking one man show . . .'[2] Joe heard this kind of talk all the time, and from men much younger than him. He was now fifty-four, which wasn't really very old, but he suddenly felt ancient.

In the autumn of 1944 he wrote to one of his younger colleagues: 'Old Wyatt has gone and Sayer, Berry and I are just winding up. Berry will have to stay on to wind up his decoy sites but I understand otherwise RE8 will close officially about 17th Nov. I will then go into the pool or I hope on leave for five weeks or whatever it is and then get my "bowler hat". I think there is a good hope of the latter owing to my age and other signs of senile decay!'[3]

War hadn't been easy but it had provided him with a steady routine, given him some of his best friends, and it had afforded him an escape from an otherwise precarious existence. Jack Sayer saw it only too well, that it wasn't going to be easy, this adjusting to 'the horrors of peace' after what had been 'a very good war'.[4]

'*I say! What a war!*' declared Joe.

Yes, it had been. It really had been.

THE CAMOUFLAGE BLOKE

The camouflage bloke
Is a bit of a joke;
If he says he works hard he's a liar.
He counts all the files
And puts 'em in piles
And watches 'em daily grow higher.

All the morning, I own,
He answers the phone;
And some of the callers grow surly
When told, at midday,
That the great Major Gray
Isn't in, though he swore he'd be early.

His job, after two,
Is dispensing Drambuies –
That afternoon very soon goes if
(In spite of the Colonel)
he's told the nocturnal
And latest adventure of Joseph

When the Drambuie sinks
In the bottle, he thinks
With longing of hill, dale and dewpond.
So out comes the car –
That man will go far,
(But only because he's well coupon'd.)

He writes a report
(Remarkably short)
Of places he claims to have been to,
But on his return
One never can learn
If a roof is saw-edged or a lean-to

But the travelling claim!
Ah, that's not a game;
He labours to make it grow higher. The
   camouflage bloke
May be quite a joke
But <u>here</u> without doubt he's a liar!⁵

Y *is for You, sir, on whom will depend*
  The success or the failure of all in the end

I never wanted to be an artist but I did want to write about them. After I left university I printed out endless copies of my CV and marched up and down Bond Street, attempting to leaflet my way into the art world. My first job was in a contemporary gallery where the walls were pristine white and the staff wore blackest black. An artist had recently exhibited a cast of his head made out of his own blood. During a power cut it had leaked onto the gallery manager's Gucci loafers. She was feeling most out of sorts, and I soon realised that wasn't the only reason why. The couple who actually ran the gallery were in the midst of an acrimonious divorce and could never be in the same room at the same time, so I often sat on my own, in charge of a silent telephone. It could have been depressing had it not been for their incredible library, and I passed the time making notes on my favourite artists, creating my own personal index of appropriated expert knowledge.

Six months later I was relieved to be accepted onto the Graduate Trainee Scheme at Christie's. It gave a handful of recent graduates the chance to work their way around various departments in the hope that, by the end of the year, they would find themselves a permanent position. Although I worked incredibly hard I never fitted in there. I was lacking what Joe might've called 'camouflage and push'.

I spent my first months in Old Master Paintings, widely regarded as a baptism of fire. The specialists were either descended from aristocracy or spoke as if they were. (I remember a lot of shouting and slamming doors, hysterical assistants trotting about in kitten heels – 'Have you spoken to the *Marquess of Bute*?') Some of the commotion revolved around Charles Beddington. He was revered by his co-workers as having the best eye in the business. It would be a long time before I realised he was Freddie Beddington's nephew, and all his art books had been bequeathed from his beloved uncle.

The connections were still there to be made, I just had to look a little harder.

I was offered a job in the Modern and Impressionist Paintings department. At the time it was considered very flashy, as were all the men who worked there. I still didn't fit in – I couldn't talk fast or feign confidence – but I could write. What I enjoyed most of all was sitting in the basement with the pictures, researching a painting's history, confirming provenance and finding a context. Yes, I loved the storerooms, the making everything accurate.

Does that sound familiar?

I was soon penning the texts to be published in the catalogues. I had no talent for selling art, that was plain from the start. I'd listen to the senior specialists on the telephone, wooing their clients in various languages, and knew I'd never be like them. That doesn't mean I looked down on what they did. I just didn't think I'd be as convincing. Also, a strong part of me still felt that art shouldn't have a price tag and be bought and sold like a commodity. To put all that effort into a creation and then wait for the highest bidder. It was my aunt Kitty who made me see things a little differently.

Of Maureen's four daughters, my mother, Patricia, is the oldest, then there's Fiona, Catriona (who we only call Kitty) and Victoria. Kitty is a chef with her own catering company and lives and works in London. From time to time I'd sneak her into the sumptuous pre-sale events, and we'd weave our way around the invited guests and chuckle at the improbable canapés. These were prosperous times for the Impressionist department and I was still young and green, utterly dazzled by the glamour of it all. I remember very clearly Kitty standing in front of one of Monet's *Rouen Cathedral* series, a sun-dappled view of the building's façade, which was valued at $5.5 million. (It would sell for over double that amount.)

She was laughing and shaking her head.

'What's so funny?' I asked.

'It's incredible.' She turned to me. 'An acutal *Monet*, and it has a price tag on it!' She threw her hand up casually. 'It's just something you or I could buy.'

I saw what she meant. We were talking about a 'priceless' artwork but there it was without any barrier to stop me leaning over and touching it, and there was the label I had just placed next to it, with its lot number and estimate price. Art can sell for a little or a lot, but the very act of selling (or being sold) levels the field.

I suppose the only way to retain control is to refuse to sell your art, for any price at all.

Jack Sayer visited Joe and Mary from time to time after the war. 'The Grays established themselves very comfortably in one of the small, old houses lining West Street in Marlow. There was a long and rather dishevelled garden at the back where Joe had a fair sized studio crammed with portfolios and canvases.'[1]

Mary went back to teaching needlework, this time at Wycombe Abbey girls' school, where she proved memorably eccentric, as all the best teachers are. And Joe finally knuckled down to his painting. It was an ideal setting, the new beginning they had talked of for so long. But having spent much of his early life painting to order, Joe now refused to take this path again. He would spend hours outside, sketching the countryside and painting on river-banks. His initial reluctance to accept portrait commissions was understandable since he hadn't painted seriously for nearly a decade. He reminded anyone and everyone that he needed time to get his eye in, a period of adjustment, before he committed to any-thing. But it became like a compulsion, this turning down of work. Much of the 1930s had seen him hustling for sales, trying desper-ately to find an audience for his art. Back then he would have readily turned his hand to any commission. He was a trier, what-ever else. But now so much time had passed. It felt like a lifetime. Joe had spent too long out of step with things. When he visited the Tate he felt quite overwhelmed by what he saw. He stared and stared at a painting by Jack Yeats: 'very exciting colour – but what happens to painting that depends almost entirely on colour and hasn't a solid basis of form? The only permanent colours are the earth colours and these he never uses.' Retreating to an earlier gallery, Joe sought solace in the Constables.

The procrastinations multiplied as time passed. Joe was back at work, but quite what this work amounted to was difficult to grasp. When friends visited he continued to talk of the great things he would do, and there was a growing number of canvases gathering in his studio, eager for his attention. It looked and sounded promising.

He kept in touch with his old friends from camouflage, too, and on regular trips into London he would go round the galleries and have lunch at the Arts Club. Wildenstein's was a favourite haunt, where Freddie Beddington was creating a name for himself as a great promoter of young artists. 'I went round to Wildenstein's and was very pleased with the show, which is first class,' Joe told Mary after one such visit.

A most marvellous Manet a wonderful Daumier, and a glorious Fragonard. Freddie was the super Bond Street dealer – very good indeed – introduced me to the manager who knows what he's talking about. I said I <u>might</u> let them see my stuff after I had worked a year.

Freddie said he had just seen some of my etchings next door (Fine Arts Society) in their exhibition 'Rembrandt and Modern Masters'. Freddie was nicely enthusiastic – but, of course what I am going to do in Marlow with P.F. will knock everything I have already done . . . All the same I have got the personal contact with everybody who counts in the art dealing business, and it is now only necessary to produce the stuff!

Freddie remained a loyal friend. He went out of his way to help struggling artists in the years after the war, pushing them into the spotlight alongside works by more established painters. There were people who could have helped Joe if he'd asked. The well-known art critic Reginald Wilenski was practically his neighbour. They'd sit and talk for hours about Manet, Degas or Dutch still life.

'Is he *somebody*, dear?' Kitty Meade would ask, and he was.

Talking about painting could be almost as time-consuming as the act itself. Joe would tell amusing stories and keep everyone up late into the night, he'd happily listen to people's opinions, but still he wouldn't sell them a picture. He'd make excuses, create a diversion. And he'd never part with a single canvas.

Maureen reasoned that her father didn't need to sell work because Mary had enough money to keep them. ('*Nancy* wouldn't have let him go on like that. She would have insisted that he get down to it and sell his work, but Mary allowed him to carry on in his own way.') It was true Mary had a small income, but they lived frugally, renting out the larger part of their house and retaining only much smaller, rather cramped quarters for themselves. A bit more money would have been useful, and the fact was Joe had every intention of paying his way, he just didn't intend on doing it through his art.

Joe was convinced that the money, the *real* money, would come from steel wool. It was widely reported after the First World War how a Royal Commission – members of a 'small and exclusive club'² – would meet to remunerate those persons who had contributed significantly to the war effort. There was an award for the invention of a smoke-producing apparatus, the invention of an aircraft camera, and £2,000 (and an OBE) had gone to Norman Wilkinson for dazzle camouflage.

Joe hoped that, now the war was over, he would receive some form of recognition for his endeavours. Watching Cecil Schofield get rich on contract work with various ministries had built his hopes up, and all his old colleagues now encouraged and supported him. If he put in a claim for steel wool, he was sure to win a financial award as well as official acknowledgement. There was no longer any need for the cloak-and-dagger secrecy. He wanted everyone to know the part he'd played: how he had argued the case for camouflage, and how he had created a new kind of covering material when Britain had most needed it.

Camouflage had obsessed Joe for a long time – and it never really went away. He began compiling a dossier of information, recording the facts and figures that might otherwise have been sealed in files or lost to obscurity. He wrote to all his old contacts, asking them to verify the sequence of events, the dates and other details. The file slowly expanded over the course of five long years – almost as long as the war itself – as Joe rewrote old notes and sourced new photographs. He gathered together memorandums, past correspondence, drawings and plans. He annotated an old version of *Camouflage and Air Defence*. He made detailed lists of persons of influence to act as referees – from publishers, industrialists and engineers. Most wrote back quickly, several wrote twice.

Eugene Mollo, Arthur Sayer, Frederick Beddington, Francis Wyatt, Peregrine and Johnny Churchill, Norman Wilkinson, Michael Farrar Bell – they all supported him. They praised Joe for his extraordinary commitment to the cause of camouflage. Freddie Beddington talked of Joe's 'enthusiasm, imagination and years of effort' and confirmed that 'had steel wool material not been available in large and ever larger quantities, covers and schemes carried out . . . could not possibly have been executed.'[3] Joe's old brigadier hailed the development of steel wool as an 'outstanding achievement', and Peregrine Churchill went so far as to say that Joe's pre-war research meant structural camouflage was applied in time to meet the threat of German air attack. There were reams of documents on the production and distribution of steel wool, and case studies to show how effectively it had been applied.

How quickly life was shaped around 'the claim', 'the claim', 'the claim'. Just as Joe amassed canvases, so he piled letter upon letter, references, certificates, reports on production. Everything was copied in triplicate and filed in various places. He and Mary talked of it in hushed tones but with growing excitement. It genuinely worried her brother. James Meade offered to buy a few paintings to make life just a little bit easier, but Joe put him off with his usual excuses, assuring him the steel wool money would come through soon enough. James's young daughter Charlotte would visit in the school holidays. Joe and Mary taught her how you didn't need money to have fun, but there was always hope that money would come.[4]

Cecil Schofield had vanished from Joe's life, but he still retained the patent for steel wool, which became a thorny issue. He eventually wrote a lengthy statement, saying Joe was the 'true inventor': 'I am glad to feel that I and my late firm made a very vital contribution to the war effort in the great camouflage constructional engineering business we created, but that was concerned with the use of "Steel Wool" camouflage material, rather than its origin . . .'[5]

Joe submitted all these papers along with the first draft of *Camouflage and Air Defence*, a freshly authored 'Note on Research', and a brief history of RESB outlining the role and responsibilities of civil camouflage officers from 1939 onwards.

By now everyone was talking about it. They acknowledged what he had done and they wanted him to be rewarded. Was it wrong to feel excited? There was always a risk.

In July 1953 the Ministry of Supply wrote offering Joe £2,000. It was exactly the same figure that had been awarded to Norman Wilkinson several decades earlier. The wording of the letter was succinct and business-like. There were no congratulations. There would be no press announcement.

Everyone felt the aftershock. James and Margaret Meade were

bitterly disappointed on Joe's behalf. They felt he deserved far more, and that he had been wronged. After that, there was always the feeling Joe had been done out of his invention.

Even Joe, the eternal optimist, struggled to find a silver lining.

His vast dossier, his 'claim', now resides in the Imperial War Museum. He put it in a box and tried to forget it, just as other camoufleurs were busy trying to remember. Geoffrey Barkas, Jasper Maskelyne, Jack Sayer and Julian Trevelyan wrote up their experiences. They were ready to lift the lid on camouflage and record their endeavours for posterity.

For Joe it was too late. He had wanted to secure his place in this history. He had used 'the claim' to defer decisions, deflect commissions, to avoid going back to his old life as a jobbing artist. That initial hesitancy was a temporary solution, but then it became a resolution. For most of his life Joe had wanted an audience, but after two wars, two marriages and countless setbacks, he stopped. Perhaps, after all, concealment was better.

An artist has to make his mistakes in public – Joe felt he'd made enough. The disappointment over steel wool was the last. Perhaps he had expected too much, but his optimism was inbuilt – he couldn't have got this far without it. It would persist in its own way, but he'd no longer seek an audience other than that which he found in his own home. He carried on painting, every single day, and he stopped worrying where it would take him. Each painting had a fresh potential and he could keep that alive for as long as he liked.

In his head, he could still achieve great things. In his head, the best was always still ahead.

Z *is for Zeal with which you apply*
These few simple principles – do have a try

Despite early predictions to the contrary, Maureen and John Barclay enjoyed a long and happy marriage. Neither of them had come from stable or straightforward families, but they created one of their own. John had a dry Scot's wit, a gravelly laugh and a formidable repertoire of put-downs. With four daughters he was quickly outnumbered, and he was surprised by how much he loved it – a calm centre in an often turbulent sea of women. He and Maureen returned from Africa in 1973 and settled in Verwood in Dorset, in a house that was essentially an extension to the cottage where Dick and Nancy were living. That John organised the building of this extension personally is testament to his love for his wife. Two years later Dick died and Maureen became Nancy's carer. John, meanwhile, lived at the other end of the house and kept himself busy brewing beer and building endless wooden chests to be dispersed amongst his grandchildren.

John Barclay was also a man of books. He read constantly. When he became less physically active he would spend hours researching his family history, and on the request of his youngest daughter, Victoria, penned his own life story. John enjoyed writing – long before he began his biography he was a fastidious keeper of diaries. Every night before bed he would sit at his small writing desk, take up his pen and record the day's events. He never missed a single entry.

Growing up, I was naturally curious about what my grandfather wrote, but I knew well enough not to pry. I also kept a diary, the contents of which I guarded fiercely. What I found strange, however, was that where I went to great lengths to hide my personal jottings and even kept them under lock and key, my grandfather's diary remained open on his desk, in full view, all day long. As far as he was concerned, there was no need to hide things away. John Barclay had no secrets.

But when he died in 2002 the careful balance in our family was disrupted. Maureen had always been so fit and able. It was a shock to discover her husband was not. The one thing John had hidden was his failing health. I had by then escaped Christie's and was working as a curator at the Tate, doing the job I'd always said I'd do. I was organising a large retrospective exhibition of the painter Lucian Freud, which meant long hours in the gallery. I'd have to go in very early in the morning, the time Lucian preferred to meet, to discuss how the show was taking shape, what pictures should go where, and what colour the walls should be. As my grandfather was rushed to hospital for what would be the last time, I was standing in a gallery with Lucian discussing the importance of finding a particular shade of white. It couldn't be too bright but neither should it be dull. It required a touch of dusk yellow, a hint of earth red, a dash of dove grey. I was amazed at the subtle differences and how much it came to matter.

At the time I was living with a painter who had, for several years, been based in America. Our relationship had taken shape around lengthy emails, letters and late-night phone calls, and for a long time we had seen each other only sporadically. It was exhausting and when I look back I cannot help but wonder if I wasn't trying just a little too hard to fall in love with an idea and not a person. When you see someone infrequently and they live far away, it's easy to let your imagination make up the distance. I wanted to love an artist, and perhaps the only way I could do this was from a distance and on paper. But now my artist was living with me and reality had come crashing in. He hated the fact that I was always working, and spending all this time with an older artist of great note, and an older artist noted for seducing much younger women. He needn't have worried, but still our relationship was becoming strained. In the months before the exhibition opened he persistently told me how much he disliked Lucian's work, and would offer a running critique on what precisely was 'wrong' with it. But he'd also spend hours in his small studio just across the Thames, brooding over his own paintings, which had yet to find an exhibition. I began to feel a little torn in two.

I loved my job and I loved working with artists; I also knew I was good at it. I admired Lucian – his work ethic, his perfectionism – and it didn't matter that he could be difficult, since I was used to difficult. I had worked with plenty of artists before and many had become trusted friends despite their exacting standards. But Lucian was different. For him, closeness was carefully guarded. There were flashes, of course. He liked to talk and he was very good company, but he liked most of all to have control. I did not know his telephone number, and even if I had, I would not dare call him.

But one day Lucian telephoned me. It was an afternoon, not long after the exhibition had opened, and he asked me to stop in at his house on my way home from work. There was something about the American print run of the catalogue to be discussed.

Evening visits were common since Lucian worked in shifts, switching between different portraits in the morning, afternoon and then later at night. I have never known an artist to work so hard and within such a timetable.

The very next day I was planning to travel down to Bournemouth to see my grandfather. He was by now very seriously ill and I knew that he might soon die. So as I left work that evening my mind was already far away. I was weighed down with worry over what tomorrow would bring. It must have been obvious, because within minutes Lucian asked me what was wrong. I explained about my grandfather and how the whole family was gathering to be with him. I felt rather embarrassed, but it mattered far more than any catalogue, or any exhibition, in that moment.

Lucian listened quietly.

'So you are a close family?' he asked.

'Yes,' I replied. 'But it wasn't always that way.'

Then, almost seamlessly, I moved from talking of my grandfather, the sensible, caring accountant, to Joe, the insolvent artist and his fractured relations. Lucian was intrigued to hear about my great-grandfather, and we talked then for a long time about artists and families, and the complexities of the two. It was strange to be discussing such personal things when for months we had been meeting in draughty galleries and talking mostly of lighting and lenders, but it felt important.

I had rarely mentioned Joe to other artists until then – there seemed little point, since nobody had ever heard of him – and I wasn't particularly interested in reviving Joe's reputation. But Lucian talked about the disappointments and difficulties of making art, the obsessive pursuit of making things real.

'It is all a quest for truths,' he said. 'You hold out for what you don't know.'

That's when it struck me. I had spent years in the company of artists, and I had prided myself in the work that I did for them, yet all the while the one artist that really mattered would always elude me. He wasn't great, he wasn't famous, and he was already gone.

The next morning I travelled down to Bournemouth to say goodbye to my grandfather. He was conscious but heavily medicated, recounting fragments of family history with some urgency. He would die the following night.

'I'm going to miss you all so much,' he said, in a sudden flash of clarity. We reached the hospital just minutes too late. I remember seeing him lying peacefully with the covers up to his chin.

The nurse explained: 'I'm so sorry, he's just gone.'

Maureen reached out to stroke his pallid face. I knew her heart was broken, but she didn't cry then. She simply ran her hand along the side of his cheek, the gentlest touch that lingered.

Back at home later, we stayed awake, keeping her company into the small hours, drinking John's whisky and remembering his finest moments. Maureen was devastated but she stayed very calm because she understood something. Yes, John Barclay was gone and we missed him terribly, but we knew very precisely what and who we missed.

A few days later Lucian called again, and I sat on the pavement outside Tate Britain and told him what had happened. I explained about the midnight rush to the hospital and our all-night reminiscing. He said it was good that we were all together and I agreed, saying something about how, even though we no longer had my grandfather, we would still have each other.

Lucian was quiet for a moment, then he said: 'I'm aware that I have rather kept family at a distance.'

I was struck by this admission, since I had met many of his children, and they all seemed well within his reach, and of course he had painted them.

'Is it because of your work?' I asked.

'I don't know,' he paused. 'But I have always felt it was better to leave everyone wanting more.'

Those words rang around my head.

When my grandmother talks about her father her eyes will fill with tears. She misses him because she has always missed him, and her grief is like a human presence – shifting and visceral. He is there but he is also not there; in his paintings, in her memories. The truth is, Joe has left us all wanting more.

It wasn't long after John's funeral that I remembered the diaries he'd written so religiously. There must have been so many, and I imagined that Maureen would have kept them safe. Choosing my moment carefully, I asked my mother where they were and what was to be done with them.

'Mummy shredded them,' came her reply.

I stared at her, open-mouthed.

'She didn't think we'd gain anything from reading them, and she was worried we might find something we didn't like.'

I couldn't quite believe that Maureen had felt the need to tidy her husband's memory since his death. I was amazed there might be anything in those pages that would make us think less of the man we had loved. I was also confused. Why shred everything of my grandfather's but hold onto so much from Joe? I am thinking of the big black file on his steel wool claim, the memos and notes on research that now spill all over my own little desk. What about the portfolios crammed full of 'working drawings', cartoons and figure studies that have been passed to me for 'safe-keeping'?

Maureen had lost Joe years before. She blames herself for moving to Africa and not staying in touch, and so she holds on to every scrap of paper he ever wrote or drew on. She is pained by her father's absence, but this absence has been everything. Now we look at his pictures, we hear her stories, and we fill in the gaps for ourselves. He is good and bad, sloppy and precise, selfish and genuine, loyal and a liar. He is given the most marvellous retrospective that is still in constant flux.

'I wrote him a letter and posted it under the sitting-room carpet when I was nine,' recalls Victoria. 'I wanted to tell him I liked his paintings.' Their house in Africa contained many of Joe's oils and etchings, but there were no pictures of the man himself. We perfected him in his absence. To my mother, who was the only granddaughter to meet him, he was precisely what an artist should be – fascinating, idiosyncratic, obstinate, charismatic. Mary, too, 'the artist's wife', had a magical aura. 'I felt intimidated by her – I decided she was *bohemian* . . . posh but sort of slumming it for the sake of art. I never felt that I matched up to her standards, I thought that was why I was never introduced to any of *her* family.'

Maureen had visited Joe and Mary a few times over the years. There had been occasions when she'd been back on leave from Africa, but she'd always travelled alone to Marlow. Why she had kept Joe a secret from her children is something she still struggles to explain, but after years of being kept in the dark herself, she was perhaps more disposed to the idea of it. She also wasn't sure where she stood with Joe and Mary, and she wasn't sure how they'd respond to four lively granddaughters. Afraid of upsetting the balance of things, she once again kept quiet, repeating what was now a clear pattern. Thus it was only Patricia, when she was almost an adult herself, who would be taken to meet her grand-father.

It was very strange for Joe. He had spent years seeking some kind of official acknowledgement and now it was being asked of *him*. The idea of another artist in the family, his young grand-daughter, didn't sit too well. This was when he muttered those famous lines.

'Art? What has *art* ever done for *us* as a family?'

Maureen shakes her head, as if still smarting from the exact intonation. She took it to mean so many things and didn't try to reply. My mother, happily oblivious to all that had gone on, was quick to brush it aside. Joe and the elegantly dishevelled Mary were too fascinating to resist. After that she would go to Marlow as often as she could, though she never mentioned this to her younger sister, who remained in Africa. Of course she still wanted to be an artist, and those weekends only made her want it more.

'But according to Joe, there were too many art schools churning out too many artists. He was worried they had no real prospects and it was all *too hard*, competing in the marketplace.'

The fact that Joe was against anyone else in the family studying art shows his disappointment. Underneath all that cheerfulness, there were shadows.

'I never saw that,' my mother assures me.

But just because you can't see something doesn't mean it isn't there.

Joe put on a good show. The trouble was, he never had one. He would paint every day, but with no exhibition deadline there was never a reason to finish anything. Patricia became accustomed to a merry-go-round of pictures on easels. A painting would be put aside for months, only to be taken up again and focused on exclusively. Joe worked on some canvases for years, going back over them endlessly, blending colours and adding details, scraping off paint and starting again.

Abbott Thayer, the 'father of camouflage', was notorious for constantly making adjustments to his paintings. A work might be almost near completion and then suddenly packed away for months or even years, and finishing a picture became horrendously difficult. Even when he had sold a painting it was not unusual for him to write and ask to have it returned so that he could make improvements, and he was known to go to the train station at night, uncrate a painting destined for a client and work on it by lantern light. With his personal standards set impossibly high he was always doomed to fall short. He was also frequently misunderstood. In later life he took issue with restorers who attempted to alter the appearance of certain canvases, explaining that any 'imperfectly executed part' was 'tuned to, harmonized with, every other part of the canvas'.[1] It's as if he were still thinking about camouflage.

In August 1939 Joe wrote to Mary about his painting *North Sea*, 'a supreme masterpiece' according to Freddie Beddington. It was shut away for the duration of the war and then installed in his studio in Marlow and renamed *The Wave*. Charlotte Lewis, James and Margaret Meade's daughter, remembered him working on it. 'Joe was obsessed with this painting. At one stage whenever I went there it had either been resurrected or was in a state of semipermanent alteration . . . Sometimes Joe would ask me to come to the studio and stand me in front of the painting, sweep his closed hand over the sea and then open it up to reveal paper fish he had cut out!'[2] There was one very significant later painting. Joe decided to paint the Henley Regatta. Charlotte's brother Tom was to be rowing for his Oxford college so the event had special significance. Joe threw himself into it, determined to capture each detail and even borrowing Tom's cap and blazer to match the colours. It took him far longer than he'd expected and the finished painting, shockingly bright and crammed full of life, is unlike any of his other works. It is more like one of his old battle paintings.

Not long after this, Joe suffered his first heart attack.

My great-grandfather had been through two wars; his body was finally failing. But I will not think of Joe as old or slow, struggling to get down the stairs and squeezing out each breath. I want to keep him with Mary, smiling in the sunshine in his garden in Marlow. Now I visit my grandmother at the nursing home and wheel her outside so she too can feel the warmth of the same sun. We chit-chat about the usual things, then she recounts a 'set piece' or two about Joe. Occasionally tiny details emerge that I had otherwise missed, but the basics remain unaltered.

My only worry is what will happen now. Perhaps, once every story is told, there won't be the same need to discuss Joe. By going back over him constantly I am keeping him alive. I want him to have hope, potential, even after all this time, and I want Maureen to feel it. Because I am terrified of losing her, too.

Few artists achieve financial security, and critical success is even more elusive. Joe was in his fifties when the war was over. Wasn't there still time? I saw it enough in my years at the Tate – artists who aren't recognised until later in their life, or who slip into obscurity for a decade, can enjoy a sudden career resurgence. It is part of the excitement, it is part of the promise of creation. Looking back now, I see those immediate post-war years as wasted. Joe was preoccupied by his steel wool claim – it distracted him for too long. He wanted something that would last longer than an exhibition, and that is understandable, but it's ironic to want to be recognised for how well you hid things. Did he spot the paradox? I look back at the tired and yellowed pages of *Camouflage and Air Defence*, the book he never published. In each draft he has made revisions in pen and pencil. It remains a draft forever, never quite finished or finessed. This was the first time he left something unfinished, and after that it became a habit.

If *Camouflage and Air Defence* had been published things might have been different. Instead, years after the war was won, Joe was juggling his canvases, going back to them constantly, adding and editing, like an author unable to lay down his pen.

When Joe stared at each painting what did he see? Did everything have to be 'harmonized' and blended into one? Camouflage became art and the art became camouflage.

The little house in Marlow became overcrowded with pictures, two or three deep resting against each wall. Joe never knew when to stop. The purest form of painting was the action itself. If he stopped, where would that leave him? He had to paint like he had to breathe.

'When is a painting finished?' I keep asking my artist friends. They all agree finishing is the hardest part, an intrusion of sanity, a terrible breaking off. To step back from a canvas needs conviction. 'For, fleeting, momentary reasons, a finished painting seems to be the best painting one can do at that exact moment, and for its own reasons it just stops,' says one.[3] 'It's finished when it stares back at you and says so,' replies another.[4] Nothing was so clear for my great-grandfather.

'If you won't sell or show, who are these paintings for?' Patricia asked him once.

'That is simple,' he replied. 'They're all for Mary.'

Mary smiled. 'Yes, but I'd rather have a bit of money!'

Joe either didn't hear or pretended not to.

My mother feels certain Joe wasn't insecure about his work. Although he painted over some, he never cursed or complained, he just continued.

'He was definitely a perfectionist. But he didn't *suffer*. There were no theatrics. I never saw him get angry or upset.'

Still, I am not convinced. Was it all part of another deception, a self-deception? Doesn't an artist need an audience? Without that confrontation, how does the art *live*? I have met many artists who have told me resolutely, insistently, that they only make work for themselves. I imagine it starts that way but surely in the end you want a conversation.

I prod and push my mother for more answers.

'Joe must've had a plan,' I insist. 'He was always thinking ahead. I am certain he must've intended something to happen to all these paintings.'

My mother is silent. This is rare.

'Perhaps,' she admits. 'I did suspect that maybe he thought he would be recognised only after his death and then Mary would know she had been right to support him all these years and also reap the benefit.'

I remember a letter from 1948, when Joe tells Mary he has written his will: 'after all I might leave valuable patent rights – not to mention valuable works of art, etching plates, etc!' Is this the key? I want clear answers so that I can understand, but then I wonder why I'm pushing so hard for clarity.

At this moment a writer friend shows me a copy of Stanislaw Lem's *Memoirs Found in a Bathtub*. It is a darkly funny tale about an aspiring secret agent in search of a mission, trapped within a strange and confusing bureaucracy where everyone he meets leads him in a different direction. There is a passage underlined, a conversation between the protagonist and another agent.

'Using your argument, we'd have to conclude that everything is code.'

'And so it is, absolutely everything. Code or camouflage. Yourself included.'

'You're joking.'

'Not at all.'

'I'm a code?'

'Or a camouflage. Every code is a camouflage, not every camouflage is code.'

'Perhaps, I said, following it through, 'if you are thinking about genetics, heredity, those programs of ourselves we carry in every cell . . . In that way I am a code for my progeny, my descendants. But camouflage? What would I have to do with camouflage?'[5]

Joe often talked of legacies – perhaps that mattered most. But I fear it's another camouflage. His art would be revealed only once the artist himself had disappeared. Isn't *that* the perfect camouflage?

Retrospective

It was a sunny afternoon in May, the year was 1963. Victoria Barclay, aged thirteen, skipped up the steps to her front door. After the rancours of a school day she was glad to be home. The house in Ndola was light and airy with every surface finely polished. She called out a hello but nobody answered. This was strange. It was late afternoon and her mother's car was in the garage. Victoria traced her fingers along the wall of the long corridor leading to the bedrooms. Just out of her reach were etchings of moody Scottish Highlands, a landscape that seemed as unfamiliar and distant as the moon. She headed for her parents' room, searching for signs of life. Then she heard noises coming from another bedroom further down the corridor, the room that belonged to her older sister, Fiona. She tiptoed quietly and peered through the half-open door. There sat Maureen in one of her immaculate sundresses, usually crisp and starched yet today crumpled like paper. She was clutching a telegram and tears streamed down her face. Victoria had never seen her mother so distressed.

She ran into the room and threw herself down at her mother's feet.

'Oh Mummy, what's wrong?'

Maureen looked up from the telegram, eyes red and swollen.

'My father's dead.'

She almost choked on the words.

Victoria rocked back on her heels, startled.

'But,' she said, struggling to understand. 'Your father? I didn't even know *he was alive.*'

It was a bleak February night in 1966 – bitterly cold and raining hard. They hovered on the pavement outside the gallery, their shoes and tights already drenched. Light and noise spilled out onto Bond street, and passers-by, surprised at the hubbub, asked who was exhibiting inside. The name Joseph Gray didn't mean anything to them.

Maureen, flustered from running so late, gripped Victoria's hand and propelled her through the door. She had brought two of her daughters – Victoria, now sixteen, and the newly married Fiona – as moral support. Fiona's husband David had driven them to the gallery in his battered little car, cursing the weather and London traffic all the way.

'We have missed the speeches,' Maureen breathed. She forced out a smile. 'But never mind, never mind.'

They pushed into the first room, and what a crowd it was.

The exhibition had been opened by the now Sir William Cold-stream, a kind-looking man surrounded by other guests. He was apparently the principal at the Slade School of Art and had been a friend and colleague of Joe's, but Maureen didn't know him. She didn't hear his kind words, nor would she meet Freddie Beddington, Jack Sayer, Kenneth Dalgliesh, or any of the camouflage chaps who had come along to celebrate. But they were all there, milling around and enjoying this small reunion. A few of Joe's old

RE8 cartoons had been hung alongside his oil paintings and etchings. Jack Sayer was annoyed to find they had already been sold. So much, in fact, was already sold.

Maureen, confronted with an enormous and anonymous crowd, began to panic. The rooms were crowded to suffocation, but through the throng she glimpsed Mary. Mary Gray, the artist's wife, now his widow. She was talking and gesturing, smoking constantly. She looked as nervous as Maureen felt.

'Come and meet Mary.' Maureen pulled Victoria along to be introduced.

The two women embraced.

'Thank goodness you are here,' said Mary. 'It would have meant so much to Joe.'

It was the first time they had seen each other since since he had died and there was now a surge of understanding – how they missed him. Maureen tried to look delighted as she admired her father's work and sat for a moment beside Mary. The photographs that were taken would be convincing. Maureen had chosen her outfit carefully: a matching pale blue suit with navy trim, accessorised with a single string of pearls. With her hair freshly coiffured she looked almost regal. She had her father's eyes and the same thick brown hair; did anyone make the connection?

Mary squeezed her hand, glancing around at the walls.

'It's rather like *my* children are leaving home.'

Maureen nodded gently. They were losing Joe all over again and neither particularly liked it. Moving away from Mary, she clung to the edges of the room and tried to focus on the paintings. She wanted to feel proud but instead she felt empty.

'Aren't they marvellous?' someone said. 'To think he kept them hidden. He was so naughty, he would not show.'

Maureen knew about her father's refusal to show work. It was just another part of him she wouldn't understand. Then came a tightening in her chest as she realised something else. She looked at the pictures again, anxiously reading the labels, walking around each room.

Victoria was happily adrift, staring in wonder at this well-dressed adult world, caught up in the laughter and conversation. Then she felt her mother's grip close around her arm.

'We have to go.'

Victoria turned, confused.

'Why? We've only just arrived!'

Maureen shook her head, swallowing back tears. 'No.'

Fiona was beside them quickly, sensing something wrong.

'It's rather hot, is it the heat?' she asked. 'Shall we step outside?'

Maureen raised a hand to her temple, ducking her head as tears welled up.

'We have to go,' she repeated. 'Now.'

Fiona ushered her mother towards the door, glancing round for David.

Once they were outside, the tears came quickly.

'What is it?' Fiona wrapped her arms around her mother. 'Tell me.'

Maureen shook her head, her voice shrank to a whisper. 'They're all sold.' She made a circular gesture backwards. 'They are all sold.'

Victoria twisted her head to look back into the room and realised for the first time what those small red dots beside each painting meant. It was true. Everything *had* sold.

In the darkness of the street Fiona and Victoria watched on in horror as their mother crumpled before them. Her shoulders were heaving and she wept bitterly, almost unable to stand. They stroked her arms, trying to shield her from prying eyes and hoping the storm might pass. But it was unrelenting.

David, embarrassed, rushed to fetch the car.

The photographs from that night are preserved in a makeshift album, along with press cuttings from the show. There are also some large black-and-white photographs of several of the oil paintings. I look first at the snapshots, tacked to the page with curling Sellotape. There's one of Maureen seated beside Mary, another of her standing with Fiona by a seascape, and yet another of her with an older couple. Mary is smiling, she wears darker colours and holds a cigarette, with her large black handbag spread across her lap. Looking at these snapshots, it would be hard to guess that anything was amiss. How easily we hide our feelings for a frozen instant. We want to make happy memories, because the reality resists easy explanation.

'She felt completely overwhelmed,' Victoria remembers. 'We were late and I don't think she had expected such huge crowds of people, every room was packed. It was incredible, but also bewildering, because there were so many faces she didn't know.' Victoria shakes her head and smiles sadly. 'Then she saw the dots. She was seeing all these pictures, they were a part of Joe, and already they had been lost to her.'

Fiona agrees. 'I remember the tears. I think all the memories of the difficult times during the thirties came bubbling up and she said how often it was that an artist wasn't recognised until after their death . . . it was all so very sad. Mum, as Joe's daughter, should have been in the spotlight, and it could have been a wonderful celebration of Joe's life, but it didn't work out that way.'

Having missed Joe's funeral, his memorial exhibition was Maureen's first real chance to mourn, so of course it hit her hard.

When I broach the subject with her I make sure there is sherry, but she remains calm and composed.

'Yes, I was devastated. It was awful. But you know I went back the next day, when it was less busy, and Mary said there were other paintings that hadn't sold and so we fixed it up.' She offers me a consolatory smile. 'I felt better after that.'

Yes, the exhibition was a sellout, which is presumably what Mary wanted. I venture to suggest that Mary must have felt very proud, since at last Joe had made her some money. My grandmother shrugs non-committally.

'I don't recall.'

'Actually, I don't think it was ever about the money,' Fiona corrects me. 'I remember quite distinctly that Mary had put a high price on the paintings, because deep down she hoped they *wouldn't* sell. The reason she held the exhibition was simply to recognise Joe's talent and achievements, to show him off. She became quite agitated when they sold so quickly.'

I should have known. What Mary wanted was for the work to be seen and for Joe to be remembered as a good artist. And he was. The reviewers made comparisons with Augustus John and Matthew Smith. 'One feels that with a little more luck or push he would be in line with the familiarly known English artists of the first half of our century.'[1] The *Arts Review* commented: 'When he paints the English countryside he absorbs the whole scene but at the same time he remembers all that he has learnt from 19th-century French painting, its beauty and colour, directness of touch and the quality of texture.'² And so it was that Joe's work was seen and judged and bought, only after he himself had gone.

Perhaps he wasn't so bad at endings, after all. Mary wasn't with him when he died. Her mother was, though. Kitty Meade had become a fixture at their Marlow home, keeping Joe company whenever her daughter was out. They were sitting together in a companionable silence when he had his second heart attack. Kitty would never be able to explain what it was that made her look up, but as she met Joe's eyes for the last time he gave her a wave as if he knew.

'Dear Joe. It helped me a great deal,' Kitty reflected. 'I wasn't afraid of death after that. He really took the sting out of it.'

Then she died too.

Mary had lost the two people she was closest to. It opened her up to a new kind of loneliness she hadn't known before. The house in Marlow had always been cluttered but now objects blocked her in mentally and physically. She wasn't ready to surrender yet, and so by 1970 she had sold up and moved back to London. The idea was she could return to her old life in Chelsea, take up some hobbies, see some old friends. Unexpectedly, my aunt Victoria became a new one.

Having glimpsed Mary at Joe's memorial exhibition, Victoria hadn't anticipated they would ever get along, but she was working at the United Nations and Mary thought that sounded rather grand. Victoria was soon invited to Sloane Avenue Mansions for afternoon tea, to a tiny flat where every inch of wall space was covered with Joe's pictures. Victoria finally got to know her grandfather at one remove, and whether her mother liked it or not, she too would turn out to be a very good artist.

Mary did her best to fill her time creatively, she saw her nieces and her nephew. There were theatre trips and evening classes. But London had changed, it was fiendishly expensive and life moved too fast now for her to keep pace. As the years slipped by objects piled up around her, and she held on to them, hoping to feel more in control.

Eventually it became too much. Mary felt she was trying to recapture something long lost. By her eightieth birthday, she had returned to Marlow, to a new house in a familiar context. She was comfortable there and for many years kept up with a regular stream of visitors. Yet slowly and surely the clutter crept up. The stairs became a problem; they were narrow and steep and Mary found she simply couldn't manage them. So the top floor was abandoned. Objects piled higher and higher down below. Charlotte remembers a house where memories spilled out of every cupboard, where the extraordinary and the banal gathered dust together. There were bags of whale-boned undergarments in excellent condition, hundreds of knitting needles of different size, length and colour, art books of some value, magazines of little value, scraps of material, cuttings from old newspapers. So many things were accumulated without reason, or with a clear reason that was then forgotten. And amidst all this there were Joe's paintings, stacked haphazardly, rearranged sporadically, a living presence beside her.

Maureen had tried hard to hold onto the fragments of her father. Did she ever realise Mary was doing the same? Mary didn't just keep all of Joe's paintings and etchings, she kept all his sketches, cartoons, letters, cards and lists, a book of his 'bons mots'. Delicate little drawings in ink were folded between torn scraps of paper bearing a few squiggled lines. If one thing mattered, everything mattered. It was simple.

I wonder if I shouldn't leave her here, in her cluttered home in Marlow, an eccentric and entertaining hostess. She never cleaned or tidied up if there were people to talk to. She poured them a drink and they'd stay past midnight. She'd be remembered fondly, as a true original, but she became more cantankerous after Joe died. She could always be brittle, a maker of scenes, and as the years passed there was a growing risk that you could say or do a small, seemingly innocent thing and be met with a barrage of rebukes, usually dispensed over a genteel arrangement of cucumber sandwiches. Mary embodied contradictions just as Joe had done, only Joe had softened her edges.

It wasn't much fun, growing old without him.

My mother was living in Australia, and so missed Joe's funeral and final exhibition. But she wrote to Mary, telling her that she had at last enrolled in art school, and informing her of the births of her two daughters – Sarah Anne and Mary Kathleen. I'd like to pretend that Mary Gray was secretly pleased to hear that her name mirrored mine – but her response was unambiguous: 'I don't know why you have called her that, I have never liked *either* of my names.'

I wasn't keen on those names either. There were no other Marys in my class at school, which I took as a bad sign. I remember a friend telling me only old ladies were called Mary. Well, Mary Gray was now that. Victoria visited regularly, finding her both fun and infuriating depending on the day. But after one particularly difficult visit Victoria withdrew, hurt by Mary's razor-sharp tongue.

'I don't know how long we didn't talk for and I don't even remember why, and of course I felt bad about it because she was old and vulnerable and alone. So one day I just thought it was silly and I picked up the phone and broke the silence. When Mary answered she sounded much like her old self.'

'I'm glad you've called,' she told Victoria. 'But you must come down to Marlow tomorrow. As soon as you can, in fact.'

Sensing an emergency, Victoria did as she was told. When she arrived, however, things seemed quite normal – the house was as untidy as always and Mary full of life. She ushered Victoria into the kitchen and made her a cup of tea. Then, without further ceremony, she made her announcement:

'I am moving into a home tomorrow. I have had my name down for some time and now they have a room and I should take it.'

Victoria was amazed. 'Where?'

Mary smiled faintly. 'The Old Vicarage, a place in Moulsford, it's a lovely little village. I used to go there with your grandfather . . .' Her eyes glazed over. She lost herself momentarily in a memory she couldn't and wouldn't share.

Victoria had no idea what Moulsford meant and in that moment she did wonder if she knew Mary at all. But what confused her so completely was the state of the house. There was no sign of anything being packed up, there were no cases or trunks or boxes. She wanted to ask about it but then, as if understanding, Mary led her silently into the front room.

It was the largest in the house but there was no space left to walk around. It was literally stacked wall to wall with canvases, mostly undated, many unfinished. There were also hundreds of drawings, sketches and prints crammed into portfolios propped in corners, and still more lying across a battered table where dust had been dredging for what looked like a decade. It was an extraordinary sight.

'You'll have to find a place for these,' Mary said matter-of-factly. 'After all, I cannot take them with me!'

Just as Maureen would do decades later, Mary was downsizing, finally shedding some of her skin.

Victoria, gripped by panic, managed a nod. 'Are you quite sure about this?'

Mary shrugged. 'Of course. I will only have a small room.'

And there it was. Joe was finally coming home.

It was too much for Victoria. She called Kitty in a panic. Kitty was the sensible sister, the problem-solver, who woke every morning before dawn to deliver cakes to London eateries. Quickly, Kitty hit upon a plan. She rearranged the next day's deliveries and adapted her little red van for the transporting of art. Collecting Victoria the next day, they drove straight to Mary's to get to work, not yet realising it would take them several days.

'We were both in shock. We never realised how much Joe had left.'

I had never realised it either. I had grown up with Joe's pictures all around me and yet I didn't question why. I suppose if he had been successful, commercial, well known, we wouldn't have been left with much. They would have been hung in other people's homes, and we'd never have had the money to buy them back.

Imagine that.

Joe never let go of anything and now we have done the same. Maureen rallied together with her daughters: Patricia, Fiona, Kitty and Victoria. Everything was discussed and examined. Joseph Gray was lost to us, but *a* Joseph Gray was different. They were framed and hung on walls. They weren't hidden in attics or stacked up in spare rooms. They became the first things installed in a new home – a good-luck charm. When my sister Sarah and I set up home together in London we were each given a vivid sea-scape. We placed them side by side in our sitting room, and they looked so out of place people always asked: 'Where on earth did *they* come from?'

Now I have Joe's haunting self-portrait staring out at me from the wall of my little study. We size each other up for a few minutes most days and I find myself gazing at the curve of his ear or the cleft of his chin. I haven't framed all his pencil sketches – there are just too many. Delicate watercolours vie with torn figure studies. There are scribbled cartoons of fat old men dozing contentedly, drawn quickly on the back of memos about anti-aircraft defences. There are pencil portraits, sketches of shrubberies and trees. Some are so small and rough they could surely be discarded. I wouldn't dare.

Joe once asked what art ever did for us as a family. He didn't expect an answer and at the time nobody offered one. Now I feel better equipped to try. Art has brought us together and kept us together. It has given us a language in common. It has allowed us to talk about the things Joe didn't, to question things, to try things. It has challenged us, it has offered us connection, and it has given us comfort. Time will not alter any of that.

Art?

The truth is, we couldn't be without it.

An Ending

It's important to know when a picture is finished – that precise moment when adding to it would be to destroy it. A life is not so definite. We don't know when it will end and we rarely have control; we only hope to make sense of it and console ourselves by creating things around it.

I've been rereading Kurt Vonnegut's *Bluebeard*. I read it years ago but now I find myself drawn in once again. It is the story of Rabo Karabekian, a painter who served in US camouflage during the Second World War. ('We were so good at camouflage that half the things we hid from the enemy have to this day never been seen again!'¹) Afterwards Karabekian turns his back on realism and finds success as an Abstract Expressionist, but he is constantly tormented by the question of whether he can actually draw. As the years pass he hides away, spending long hours working on a final masterpiece. His intention is for it to be exhibited only after his death. Eventually, at the insistence of a beguiling new house guest, Karabekian changes his plans. His master work is unveiled and hugely acclaimed. The artist's talent is recognised and so he has his happy ending. And the mysterious painting? A vast panorama of all the horrors seen on the last day of the war, a precisely rendered picture, 'so realistic it might have been a photograph'.²

Joseph Gray achieved no such mastery over reality. He became lost in his own camouflage, and he was real, which makes the ending bittersweet. He never recaptured the eye-watering accuracy of his earliest works, and he never found the recognition he pretended not to want. Of course he's not alone. There are many artists in the world and only very few achieve the credit that they deserve. But they make their mark in their own way, they persevere. Maureen thinks her father was an undiscovered genius. I don't think that's true. Joe was a good artist and he painted some astonishing works – his battlefields still give me goosebumps – but it was in camouflage where he excelled.

As a man he was self-centred, proud and stubborn, loving and deeply loved. After he died the letters poured in. 'Dear Joe. We are terribly distressed at the tragic news. We counted him a very dear friend and were proud to do so.' There were hundreds; Mary kept them all. I am still opening folders, finding loose pages from undated letters. I have read them once and filed them away but now I read them again, just to be sure I haven't missed something. I suspect I will keep on doing this. Nothing feels very finished.

It seems fitting that I return to the house where I grew up, a house perched high on a cliff and facing out to sea. When my mother met my father she knew two simple facts about him: that he was training to be an accountant, just like her own father, and that he loved the sea, just as Joe had done. My father was only happy living close to water. When we moved back to England from Australia we swapped one coastline with another. Dad had no interest in art but Joe's seascapes suited this house, his house, and echoed the views out of each window.

I was thirteen when he fell ill and Maureen came to stay. She looked after Sarah and I whilst Mum stayed close to the hospital.

Maureen cooked and cleaned and took us to school, pretending everything was fine and hoping it would be so. In the end she broke the news that Dad had died. I only had to see the gentle grief etched on her face to know, and I thought, at first, that I might die too. Maureen held me together, literally, and her strength surrounded and supported me in that first terrible year of being fatherless. I saw something then in her then, the sum of a certain kind of loss. I was missing things I didn't yet know; I wouldn't grow up under my father's gaze, fight him or feel his support. Maureen showed that it was possible, and she bridged the growing gap between me and everyone else in the world.

Back then Sarah and I lived in the attic rooms and kept the curtains closed. Now we are long grown up, and we have made homes and families of our own. The attic is crammed full of battered toys, photo albums, antiques, paintings, books – the accumulations of many different lives. I didn't marry an artist, much to my mother's relief, but her own pastel landscapes hover on the stairs, a reminder that, despite Joe's advice, she went to art school and for a time worked as an artist. Her student portfolios are stacked away in a cupboard, swaddled in polythene. I used to go through them constantly when I was younger, intrigued that my own mother had this special talent, this other identity, this secret life. There was a stunning screenprint of a tiger prowling through grassland – the long stalks of grass mimicking and merging with his stripes. I can see him now, almost invisible but for those piercing eyes. Mum made multiple impressions, testing out different colours. I didn't know it then but it was my first lesson in camouflage.

It was my mother who taught me that art was difficult. When I was ten she had wanted Sarah and I to sit for our portraits. We took it in turns, sitting very still for an hour after school each night. We were desperate to see what she was doing, to jump up every minute and assess her progress, but she would do everything to shield us from her efforts. As the days passed her frown wouldn't shift. She would shake her head, and brush back tears of frustration. They weren't ready, she would say, they're not right.

I don't know what happened to those portraits – they were thrown away or painted over – but I realised that capturing a likeness wasn't easy. I also decided that I wouldn't like to be an artist. Artists were idealised in our family but they were not ideal family members. They were too obsessed with their work and needed to spend all that time alone with it, ignoring everything else, often for little reward. Why do it? Of course, I now understand that to make someone see through your eyes is more than a little alluring. It is like the telling of a story.

Now, when I visit my mother with my children, she puts us in the two spare bedrooms on the first floor, so we are close together. The largest one is light and airy, and that's where I am now. On the walls all around me are Joe's paintings. I cannot escape them, not that I'd want to.

I stare at a painting I have looked at so many times before. It is a long and narrow landscape of trees beside a river, rich in autumnal colours, framed in heavy, dark-stained wood. My children are busy elsewhere and so, rather furtively, I take it off the wall. It feels strange to do this, almost like I am trespassing. This is a painting that has always known its place and I imagine the roots of each tree have sunk into the wall and now hold it secure. In fact, it comes away quickly. I blow off the dust and turn it over. When I worked at Christie's the specialists would always look at the back of a painting first, searching for clues of provenance and history.

'Every painting is a puzzle,' is what they used to say.

All I find here, though, is *Orange Willows* written on an old label on the reverse. I return the picture to face me and prop it against the bed. It must be a view of the river at Marlow. The trees are rust coloured, but how can they be willows? Their branches do not droop or sway in the wind as willows should. Instead they shoot outwards, bursting like explosions – star shells. The sky shows an ominous low line of black cloud. It is evening and a storm is coming, or perhaps has already arrived. My eyes scan the murky green of the bank. This one at least is signed and dated: 'Joseph Gray 1948'.

Recently, Maureen asked me if I knew why or when Joe stopped signing his paintings.

'I can't help wondering if he did it on purpose,' she said. 'Because if he didn't sign them then they weren't "authenticated", and perhaps he thought they couldn't then be sold. It was his way of holding onto them.'

It's an interesting idea: to sign and date a painting is the 'finishing touch', and it's also about laying claim. I am reminded of something closer to home. There's a museum of local history near our house, and in the cafeteria can be found a rather moody mural depicting the town seafront. What's strange to me is that I saw it develop through many stages, in my own home, years ago.

'*You* painted that,' I remind my mother when we chance upon it during one visit.

My words come out like an accusation and she looks suitably guilty.

'Yes, I did. Oh dear. It's not at all like I wanted it to be . . .'

She tries to usher me away but I stand fixed firm. I scan the mural from left to right, feeling distinctly uncertain. There's no signature, but I know she painted it.

'It's very odd,' I say. 'It's not how I remember.'

Mum gestures at the smudged silhouette of buildings.

'It wouldn't be! It was completely different. I put in all the details of the houses here, there was a lot more in the foreground, and the sky was a completely different colour.' She pauses, lets out a small sigh. 'It was commissioned by a local designer and when I presented him with the end result *he* said it was too detailed and so he painted out over the houses with dark paint, and made me change the sky! I was furious and disowned the whole thing.' She shakes her head. 'I mean, honestly, that taught me not to work to commission. But don't tell anyone! I didn't know it had ended up here. How strange.'

How strange indeed, and I'm afraid I've just told everyone.

Back in the spare room and I turn to one of Joe's large, proud still lifes. As Joe grew older and became less mobile he painted endless still lifes of flowers from his garden. This one is a glorious mix of roses, chrysanthemums, irises and forget-me-nots in a tall vase set on a blue cloth. I wonder if there's anything on the back and try to take it off the wall, but it's heavier than I expect. It comes free – nail and all – and for a minute I am swaying with it, about to fall backwards and have it come crashing on top of me. It takes some effort to steady myself and bring it safely to the floor, then I catch my breath.

This still life and I, we glare at one another for a few minutes. I scrape my eyes across its whole surface, taking in the lively curls of paint. It's better and more detailed than the willows. I can see

Joe's brushwork exactly. I've looked at these pictures so often that I think I know them, but I've only ever seen them on the wall, in a frame. I turn the painting around to see the back, hoping to find a few clues there. But whilst the painted surface is full of life, the clean, bare back gives me nothing at all. No date. No title. Not even a label on the frame. All I have is a messy hole in the wall, where it broke free of the plaster.

Abandoning the still life, I wander downstairs, past etchings of empty northern landscapes and the London Blitz. I have paused on the stairs from time to time and stared at these prints, deciphering the mesh of narrow lines. After Joe died Mary offered a selection of his prints to the British Museum. A curator came to visit but showed little interest in the work that she'd so hoped he would admire, calling my great-grandfather an etcher 'remembered by few'.[3] In the end he only accepted Joe's etchings because Mary offered him something he *did* value: a rare 1925 lithograph by Louis Lozowick that she had acquired years earlier. On learning of its importance, she gave it to the museum without hesitation. For her, the real treasure lay somewhere else entirely.

Now I am standing in what my mother calls 'the family room'. Here, staring down at the chaos of children's toys, are three of Joe's later paintings. Picking my way around Lego, I go to the one I like the least. It's a small, simple landscape – a field of harvested wheat, two neat rows of hayricks stretching towards a high horizon, bordering what resembles a cabbage field. In the distance there's a blurred line of trees bordering an angry, choppy sky. Joe liked stormy skies and painted them just like he painted the sea, turning clouds into churning foam. The air is heavy with moisture, weighing down on the land. And what of this land? When I look again at the rolling fields, I wonder why I am so sure of these crops. Because Joe made so many sketches of different vegetation, of course. I have little pencil sketches of cabbage patches, drawings of wheat, hops and barley, each carefully annotated as to the precise colour. I look again at the land. The colours are so closely blended that if I screw up my eyes the image disappears.

Just at that moment my mother comes in and stands beside me. We have lived with this painting for decades but we have never yet discussed it.

'He spent too long on it,' I tell her, 'the colours all seem to blend into one.'

'Yes,' my mother sighs. 'It's *mud*.'

She's right. It is the churned earth of a battlefield. I remember the bursting star shell willows upstairs. As Joe grew older, past and present merged. Every painting was still a battlefield. He had survived two world wars, of course he lived with ghosts.

My mother found art difficult – hours and hours of hard work, so much uncertainty for so little acknowledgement. I could romanticise memories of her sketching in the woods whilst Sarah and I built dens, but I'm aware of how frustrated it made her.

Growing up, I was never remotely artistic, although I found myself drawn to those who were. I admired artistic talent but it also made me anxious. I remember, even when I was very young, worrying about what made a painting 'good' or 'bad', and whether these things came through instinct or hard work. I preferred the certainty of words and facts and books, things that could be learned and quantified.

For all the years that I worked at the Tate, I never envied artists. I remember thinking how hard it must be, to spend all that time alone with an image or idea. I wondered how they did it. Ironically, it was only when I started writing that I began to understand. When you find something you love doing, it's hard to stop. When you want to get it right, you don't want anything else.

But there is a skill in knowing when to stop.

It is the thought of Joe's unseen canvases, stacked up in Mary's front room, that haunts me now. I cannot let Joe hide any longer, nor will I hide behind him. But I am conscious of where this began, with my grandmother wanting to get her stories straight. I'm worried that if I stop, Maureen will, too. I'm not ready for her to stop, and I do not want her to go.

So I turn to my favourite of all his paintings: a simple farm track curving up and over a hill, bordering a cluster of trees beside a hulking haystack. It's larger than all the other paintings – standing over three feet wide – and looks almost freshly painted. Why do I like it so much? It's a rich, blustery image, the style is fast and loose and the colours far bolder than anywhere else – cobalt blue and fiery red. Each tree trunk and branch is streaked in a medley of blacks, yellows, greens and browns. The sky has every imaginable shade of blue. Everything vibrates with life.

I love this painting the most – probably because it isn't finished. There are snatches of bare canvas amidst the leaves on the trees. They are like breathing spaces. Yes, there is still space left.

'What are you thinking?' asks my mother. I'd forgotten she was still here.

I smile and nod to the painting. 'You never had it framed.'

'It didn't seem to need it,' she replies. 'It almost escapes off the wall, doesn't it? It's like he painted it yesterday.'

This is absolutely true. It is fresh, vibrant, very much *alive*. It makes me question again what it means to finish. Perhaps what completes a painting is the viewer, because we each see something different in a picture, and so we carry the story on. There are no endings, just new beginnings. If I stop writing, I am merely handing the story over for someone else to start.

I hear the front door slam and the sound of my children coming in from outside.

'And this, of course.' Mum points to the painting beside it. 'This is the one I told you about. The one with the cat that kept disappearing.'

It is a tree in full blossom, set against a high brick wall. I am reminded of the story and I picture my mother at nineteen, sitting beside Joe as he paints it.

'What kind of tree is it?'

Mum pulls a face. 'You know, I can't remember.'

There are demands for food coming from the kitchen. I know we don't have long.

'Quick, help me take it off the wall.'

The label on the back reads *The Almond Tree, Marlow*. Turning it back around, I frown at this picture – at the thin dark branches stretching upwards into snow-white blossom. The brick wall behind the tree is traced in staccato dabs of red and brown. The brushstrokes look light, and again there is bare canvas. It doesn't look like a picture Joe went back to again and again. I ask my mother if this is definitely the painting she thinks it is. She smiles and points. There at the base of the tree trunk, to the left, I see a shadow: a smudge of greens and blacks, indistinct brushstrokes layered far too thickly. It jars with the delicate dappled strokes elsewhere.

'*Not* so well hidden, is it?'

And suddenly I am the one sitting on a paint-splattered stool, arms folded, frowning.

'Where's the cat?' I ask Joe. He shrugs coyly. It's a bit of a pantomime, our familiar routine. He smiles indulgently and rubs at his chin. Eventually, he will relent, I will make him paint the cat back.

Glancing at my mother now, I wonder what would have happened if she hadn't married and moved to Australia. Would the cat have stayed in the picture? Probably not. But maybe Joe painted the cat back in once or twice, just to be sure.

It takes the two of us to return the painting to the wall. Here it has sat for at least a decade, and will hopefully sit for decades more. Standing close, beside Mum, I think of all the times I have stood beside her at exhibitions, our elbows almost touching.

Before I can say anything else my oldest daughter bursts in, her copper curls swinging behind her. She is searching the floor for a crucial lost pencil, and she holds in her hand her newest creation, a drawing in need of the last dash of colour. When she sees us, her mother and grandmother caught in quiet contemplation, she stops suddenly and cocks her head.

'What *are* you two doing?' she asks, clearly outraged to find us existing without her.

I rest an arm on her shoulder and then point at Joe's picture, directing her sharp eyes to the base of the tree.

'Your grandmother and I, we are looking for something in this picture,' I say. 'I wonder if you can see it? It is something very special.'

She leans close. I wait.

'I promise if you concentrate hard you will find it.'

Because it's not what you see on a surface that gives the answers. Don't be afraid of the shadows. Screw up your eyes really tight. Lean in, open wide and look again.

There.

Those two small pointed ears, the curve of a tail.

Yes. You can see it.

You can really see it.

Notes

CAB = Cabinet Papers
CD, TC, CDTC = Camouglage Development and Training Centre
HO= Home Office
IWM = Imperial War Museum
PREM = Prime Minister's Office Records
TNA = The National Archives
WO = War Office

Jack Sayer, 'The Camouflage Game', refers to his unpublished, hand-written memoir, courtesy of Gillian Ward.

To avoid repetition, the majority of quotes from Joseph's letters to Mary are not noted. Unless stated otherwise, they form part of the Barclay family archive. Similarly, images reproduced form part of this archive, except where credited otherwise.

Preface
1 'London Press', June 1922, Joseph Gray to Andrew Paterson in a letter, 22 June 1922, from the Paterson Family Archives, courtesy Andrew Paterson Collection
2 *The Graphic*, 20 June 1916, n.p.

3 Tim Newark & Jonathan Miller, *Camouflage*, ex. cat. IWM, London, 2007, p. 56

4 *Ibid.*

5 Roy R. Behrens, *False Colors: Art, Design and Modern Camouflage*, Bobolink Books, Iowa, 2002, p. 171

6 'Notes on Concealment and Camouflage', The War Office, 1937, IWM collections WO 1732

7 Diary of 2nd Lt. David Cooper (September 1940–December 1943), IWM Archive 90/6/1

8 The original version of this poem can be found in IWM Archive Maj. D. A. J. Pavitt Documents.2790

1 A stands for Aeroplane . . .

1 J. Gray, 'The Fourth Black Watch in the Great War', *The Dundee Advertiser*, 11 December 1917, n.p.

2 *Ibid.*,14 December 1917, n.p.

3 William Linton Andrews, *Haunting Years*, The Naval and Military Press Ltd, Uckfield, 2001, first pub. 1930, p. 21

4 Gray, 'The Fourth Black Watch', 14 December 1917, n.p.

5 *Ibid.*, 17 December 1917, n.p.

6 Frank Rutter, *The Influence of the War on Art*, in H. W. Wilson (ed.), *The Great War*, vol. 12, ch. 263, www.greatwardifferent.com/Great_War/Kitsch/Art_01.htm

7 Gray, 'The Fourth Black Watch', 21 December 1917

8 *Ibid.*, 22 December 1917

9 *Ibid.*

10 *Ibid.*, 28 December 1917

11 *Ibid.*

12 *Ibid.*, 29 December 1917

13 *Ibid.*, 2 January 1918

14 Stuart Sillars, *Art and Survival in First World War Britain*, St Martin's Press, New York, 1987, p. 154

15 *The Dundee Courier*, 19 December 1918, p. 3

16 J. Gray in an undated letter, IWM First World War Art Archive ART/WA1/125

17 J. Gray in a letter, 27 January 1919, IWM First World War Art Archive ART/WA1/125

18 Gray, 'The Fourth Black Watch', 19 December 1917, n.p.

19 *Ibid.*, 3 December 1917, n.p.

20 Andrews, *Haunting Years*, p. 5

21 J. Gray in a letter to Mary Meade, 6 January 1941, Barclay Archive

22 Gray, 'The Fourth Black Watch', 5 January 1918, n.p.

23 *Ibid.*, 7 January 1918, n.p.

24 *Ibid.*

25 William Linton Andrews, *The Autobiography of a Journalist*, Ernest Benn Ltd, London, 1964, p. 92

2 B is for Bomber . . .

1 Quoted in Barbara Tuchman, *The Guns of August*, Dell Publishing, New York, 1971, p. 55

2 Gray, 'The Fourth Black Watch', 19 December 1917, p. 7

3 Letters to the editor, *The Times*, 27 January 1915, p. 9

4 *Ibid.*, 29 January 1915, p. 9

5 Reginald Ryves, *The Principles of Camouflage*, comprising 'The Optics of Skulking and Scouting'. First appeared in *The Field*, 16 September 1905. To which is added: 'Notes From My War Experience', July 1920 (printed for private distribution 1921), p. 7

6 Major H. Hesketh-Prichard, *Sniping in France*, Hutchinson & Co., London, 1920, p. 124

7 *Ibid.*, p. 157

8 *Ibid.*

9   *Ibid.*, p. 156
10 Olga Somech Phillips, *Solomon J. Solomon: A Memoir of Peace and War*, Herbert Joseph, London, 1933, p. 118
11 *Ibid.*, p. 117
12 Guirand de Scévola, *Souvenirs de Camouflage* (1914–18), La Revue, Christmas 1950, pp. 719–20, quoted in Elisabeth Kahn, *The Neglected Majority – Les Camoufleurs, Art History and World War One*, University Press of America, 1984, p. 14
13 *The Graphic*, 20 February 1915
14 Oliver P. Bernard, *Cock Sparrow – A True Chronicle*, Jonathan Cape, London, 1936, p. 197
15 Philip Warner, *Kitchener: The Man Behind the Legend*, Hamish Hamilton, London, 1985, p. 4
16 Solomon J. Solomon, *Strategic Camouflage*, John Murray, London, 1920, p. 54
17 Somech Phillips, *Solomon J. Solomon*, p. 139
18 Diary extract quoted in Somech Phillips, *Solomon J.Solomon*, p. 143
19 Bernard, *Cock Sparrow*, p. 197
20 *Ibid.*, p. 274
21 Solomon, *Strategic Camouflage*, p. 51
22 'Camouflage. Col. Solomon's "Fantastic Ideas"', *The Morning Post*, 28 May 1920, p. 3
23 'Strategic Camouflage', *Times Literary Supplement*, 6 May 1920, p. 279

3 C is for Camera . . .

1   As reported in *The Dundee Advertiser*, 1 April 1922, p. 2
2   *Ibid.*
3   *Ibid.*
4   Mabel Boase, *I Stir the Poppy Dust*, J. & G. Innes Ltd, Cupar, 1936, p. 21

5 The *Scotsman*, 7 June 1922, p. 8

6 'London Press', June 1922, quoted by J. Gray to A. Paterson in a letter, 22 June 1922, from the Paterson Family Archives, courtesy Andrew Paterson Collection

7 Undated letter to A. Paterson (assumed June 1922), from the Paterson Family Archives, courtesy Andrew Paterson Collection

8 J. Gray in a letter to Ernest Blaikley, 28 September 1932. IWM First World War Art Archive, ART/WA1/386

9 *Ibid.*

10 E. Blaikley in two letters to J. Gray, 9 and 16 February 1929 respectively, First World War Art Archive, ART/WA1/386

11 J. Gray in a letter to E. Blaikley, 27 January 1919, IWM First World War Art Archive, ART/WA1/125

12 J. Gray in a letter to E. Blaikley, 21 April 1930, IWM First World War Art Archive, ART/WA1/386

13 As reported in The *Scotsman*, 18 November 1922, p. 8

4 D is Deception . . .

1 J. Gray in a letter, IWM First World War Art Archive, ART/WA1/125

2 Gertrude Stein, *Picasso*, Dover Publications Inc., New York, 1985, p. 11

3 Richard Merryman, 'A Painter of Angels Became the Father of Camouflage', *Smithsonian*, April 1999, www.smithsonianmag.com/arts-culture/A-Painter-of-Angels-Became-the-Father-of-Camouflage.html#ixzz1EJFQnhZD

4 Patrick Wright, *Tank*, Faber & Faber, London, 2000, p. 57

5 Guirand de Scévola, 'Souvenirs du Camouflage (1914–1918)', quoted in Kahn, p. 19

6 Norman Wilkinson, *A Brush with Life*, Seeley Service & Co., London, 1969, p. 79

7 Norman Wilkinson, 'The Dazzle Painting of Ships' lecture, Victory

Meeting, Newcastle-upon-Tyne, 10 July 1919, reproduced in abridged form in ex. cat. *Camouflage*, Scottish Arts Council Touring Exhibition, 1988

8 *The Independent*, New York, USA, 3 May 1919, p. 160

5 E is for Enemy . . .

1 J. Gray in a letter, 28 September 1932, IWM First World War Art Archive, ART/WA1/386

2 *Dundee People's Journal*, 5 October 1918

3 E. Blaikley in a letter, 9 February 1929, IWM First World War Art Archive, ART/WA1/386

4 J. Gray in a letter, 28 September 1932, IWM First World War Art Archive, ART/WA1/386

5 E. Blaikley in a letter, 19 October 1932, *ibid.*

6 J. Gray in a letter, 28 September 1932, *ibid.*

7 'Mr Baldwin on Aerial Warfare – A Fear for the Future', *The Times*, 11 November 1932, p. 7

8 J. Gray in a letter, 28 September 1932, IWM First World War Art Archive, ART/WA1/386.

9 Harold Dickens's comments in his diary, courtesy Harold Dickens

10 J. Gray in a letter to A. Paterson, 24 July 1928, from the Paterson Family Archives, courtesy Andrew Paterson Collection

11 Boyd Cable, 'When War Does Come: Terrifying Effects of Gas Attacks', in Sir John Hammerton (ed.), *War in the Air: Aerial Wonders of Our Time*, Amalgamated Press, London, 1935

12 Joseph Gray, *Camouflage and Air Defence*, p. 1, IWM Archive Major J. Gray Documents.4273

13 *Ibid.*, p. 3

6 F is for False Work . . .

1 Brig. J. S. Wilkinson in an undated letter, IWM Archive Gray Documents.4273
2 J. Gray, 'Further Notes,' February 1948, Barclay Archive, p. 1
3 *Ibid.*, p. 5
4 Gray, *Camouflage and Air Defence*, p. 1
5 *Ibid.*, p. 1
6 *Ibid.*, p. 5
7 *Ibid.*, p. 5
8 *Ibid.*, p. 6
9 *Ibid.*, p. 8
10 *Ibid.*, p. 10
11 *Ibid.*, p. 9
12 *Ibid.*, p. 16
13 *Ibid.*, p. 17
14 *Ibid.*, p. 77
15 *Ibid.*, p. 19
16 *Ibid.*, p. 48
17 *Ibid.*, pp. 76–7
18 Brig. A. P. Sayer in a statement connected to Steel Wool Claim, Barclay Archive
19 STEEL WOOL CAMOUFLAGE MATERIAL, 'Gray's First Claim 8 Jan '46 and Comments', IWM Archive Gray Documents.4273
20 CID Report 130-B, 3/2/37, p. 3, TNA HO186/14
21 TNA HO186/390
22 F. J. C.Wyatt, *The Principles and Organisation of Static Camouflage*, London, 1944, pp. 27–8
23 John Spencer Churchill, *Crowded Canvas*, Odhams Press Ltd, London, 1961, p. 148

7 G is for Garnishing . . .

1   *The Embroideress*, vol. 5, parts 33–40, a collection of articles published in an album by James Pearsall and Co. Ltd, 1931, p. 848

2   Jane Waller (ed.), *A Stitch in Time – Knitting and Crochet Patterns of the 20s, 30s & 40s*, Gerald Duckworth and Co. Ltd, London, 1972, p. 10

8 H is for Hiding . . .

1   See discussions in C. H. R. Chesney, *The Art of Camouflage*, Robert Hale Ltd, London, 1941, p. 112

2   'Static Camouflage', p. 4, TNA CAB102/206

3   F. J. C. Wyatt, *Notes on Deficiencies in Camouflage Organisation*, October 1938, TNA HO186/390

4   Gray, *Camouflage and Air Defence*, p. 62

5   J. Gray, 'Notes on Research', February 1948, IWM Archive Gray Documents.4273, p. 6

6   J. Gray, draft 'steel wool' notes, Barclay Archive

7   J. Gray, 'Notes on Research', February 1948, IWM Archive Gray Documents.4273, p. 8

8   *Ibid.*, p. 9

9   Statement by A. P. Sayer, Barclay Archive

10   CID Report 1516-B, 9/2/39, p. 9, TNA HO186/14

11   ARP Handbook No. 11: Camouflage of Large Installations TNA HO186/964

12   Jan Gordon quoted in Chesney, *The Art of Camouflage*, p. 18

13   J. P. Sayer, *The Camouflage Game*, p. 5

14   C. S. Schofield in an undated letter to Ministry of Supply, IWM Archive Gray Documents.4273

15   IWM Archive Capt. A. E. Havinden Documents.7762

16   IWM Archive Maj. D. A. J. Pavitt Documents.2790

9 I is for Invention . . .

1 H. J. Barclay memoir, courtesy Victoria Barclay
2 Air Raid Precautions, set up in 1937 to protect civilians from bombing

10 J is the Job . . .

1 TNA WO 227/48
2 Eugene Mollo statement, Barclay Archive
3 'E' Committee memo from J. Gray, 20 November 1939 to the President, Royal Engineers and Signals Board, IWM Archive Gray Documents.4273
4 Memo from Brig. A. P. Sayer, RESB, 28 November 1939, IWM Archive Gray Documents.4273
5 IWM Archive Pavitt Documents.2790
6 Sayer, *Camouflage Game*, p. 7
7 Capt. Tom Van Oss in a letter home, 26 September 1940, courtesy Richard Van Oss
8 Buckley was a brilliant instructor and inspired great loyalty, but his temper tantrums became the stuff of legend. ('We all grew very fond of this intelligent, unstable Commandant.') See J. Lewis, *Such Things Happen: Life of a Typographer*, Unicorn Publishing Group, Stowmarket, 2002, p. 57
9 'Notes on Concealment and Camouflage', Military Training Pamphlet No. 26, Ocotober 1939, prepared by J. Gray, IWM Archive Gray Documents.4273
10 E. Mollo in an undated letter, IWM Archive Gray Documents.4273
11 C. S. Schofield in an undated letter, IWM Archive Gray Documents.4273
12 C. S. Schofield in an undated letter to Ministry of Supply, Barclay Archive

13 E. Mollo, 'Notes on S.A. Camouflage Material', Barclay Archive

14 C. S. Schofield in an undated letter to Ministry of Supply, Barclay Archive

15 E. Mollo in a letter, 25 September 1947, IWM Archive Gray Documents.4273

16 Lt. Col. F. Beddington in a letter, 12 September 1947, Barclay Archive

11 K is the Knowledge . . .

1 Sayer, *Camouflage Game*, p. 9

2 *Ibid.*

3 *Ibid.*, p. 14

4 *Ibid.*, p. 10

5 *Ibid.*, p. 3

6 *Ibid.*, p. 6

7 *Ibid.*

8 *Ibid.*, p. 3

9 *Ibid.*, p. 28

10 *Ibid.*, p. 22

11 Churchill, *Crowded Canvas*, p. 153

12 Celia and John Lee, *Winston and Jack: The Churchill Brothers*, Celia Lee, London, 2007, p. 315

13 Jack Churchill in a letter, 5 April 1940, Churchill Archives Centre, PCHL 4/10

14 Seymour Reit, *The Hidden War: The Amazing Camouflage Deception of World War II*, Corgi, London, 1980, p. 61

15 Churchill, *Crowded Canvas*, p. 160

16 Lewis, *Such Things Happen*, p. 55

17 Geoffrey Barkas, *The Camouflage Story: From Aintree to Alamein*, Cassell and Co. Ltd, London, 1952, p. 26.

18 Sayer, *The Camouflage Game*, p. 12
19 *Ibid.*
20 Barkas, *The Camouflage Story*, p. 31
21 Sayer, *Camouflage Game*, p. 14
22 *Ibid.*

12 L is for Lay-out . . .

1 Capt. T. Van Oss in a letter (with pencil drawing), 21 August 1941, IWM ARCH40
2 Sayer, *Camouflage Game*, p. 35
3 Lewis, *Such Things Happen*, p. 55
4 Capt. T. Van Oss in a letter home, 26 September 1940, courtesy Richard Van Oss
5 *Static Camouflage*, TNA CAB102/206
6 Capt. T. Van Oss in a letter to his wife, 2 November 1941, courtesy Richard Van Oss
7 Julian Trevelyan, *Indigo Days*, MacGibbon & Kee, London, 1957, p. 123
8 *Ibid.*, p. 122
9 Roland Penrose, *Manual on Camouflage for the Home Guard*, George Routledge & Sons Ltd, London, 1941, IWM 25160, pp. 4–5
10 J. Trevelyan in a letter to Maj. Edward Seago at Southern Command, 3 April 1941, TNA WO199/1630
11 Wright, *Tank*, p. 31
12 Jean Goodman, *Edward Seago: The Other Side of the Canvas*, Collins, London, 1978, p. 150
13 IWM Archive Pavitt Documents.2790
14 Sayer, *Camouflage Game*, p. 36
15 *Ibid.*, p. 11

16 Peregrine Churchill in a letter to his aunt, 12 July 1940, TNA PREM 3/81/1

17 Ben Williams in a letter, 7 August 1940, TNA PREM 3/81/1

18 TNA WO 199/1630

19 Sayer, *Camouflage Game*, p. 17

20 TNA AVIA 15/1495

21 'Minute Sheet – talk on Steel Wool', 3 December 1940, TNA AVIA 15/1495-360620,

22 Lewis, *Such Things Happen*, p. 61

13 M is for Maintenance . . .

1 Hermann Göring quoted in Juliet Gardiner, *The Blitz: The British Under Attack*, Harper Collins, London, 2011, p. 7

2 James Meade in a letter to his wife Margaret, 10 September 1940, courtesy Charlotte Lewis

14 N is for Nets . . .

1 Wilkinson, *A Brush with Life*, p. 121

2 *Ibid.*, pp. 118–20

3 Sayer, *Camouflage Game*, pp. 33–4

4 Godfrey Baxter, *The Fortnightly D.O.*, No. 10, January 1942, TNA WO 199/1630

5 Lecture notes of Capt. Hymes, IWM 83.9(41).0/5

6 J. Meade in a letter to his wife Margaret, 3 April 1941, courtesy Charlotte Lewis

7 First Aid Nursing Yeomanry. All female unit founded 1907, called yeomanry because they first rode horseback, employed in various capacities in WW2.

8 J. Meade in a letter to his wife Margaret, 18 May 1941, courtesy Charlotte Lewis

15 O is Opacity . . .

1 Prime Minister Winston Churchill in a letter to the Commander-in-Chief (Home Forces), 10 July 1941, TNA PREM 3/81/4

2 T. Van Oss, York, 3 July 1941, IWM Archive Pavitt Documents. 2790

3 'The Strategy of Concealment for Defence Against Tank and Dive Bombing Attack', TNA PREM 3/81/4

4 Geoffrey Baxter, The Fortnightly D.O., No.10, January 1942, TNA WO199 1630.

16 P is for People . . .

1 J. Meade in a letter to his wife Margaret, 30 May 1941, courtesy Charlotte Lewis

2 YMCA: The Young Men's Christian Association, founded in 1844, was involved in a wide variety of charity work. During the Second World War it initially provided mobile canteens and tea cars, offering food and drink to those made homeless in the Blitz.

3 An extract from the memoir by Felicity Sutton (née Fisher), a young artist recruited in London, artofdeception.org/more.htm

4 Churchill, *Crowded Canvas*, p. 12

5 J. Meade in a letter to his wife Margaret, 27 July 1941, courtesy Charlotte Lewis

6 *Ibid.*

17 Q is the Question . . .

1 Gray, *Camouflage and Air Defence*, p. 77

2 *Ibid.*, p. 42

3 Colin Dobinson, *Fields of Deception – Britain's Bombing Decoys of World War II*, Methuen, London, 2000, p. 26

4 *Ibid.*, p. 28

5   Gray, *Camouflage and Air Defence*, p. 43

6   Nicholas Rankin, *Churchill's Wizards – The British Genius for Deception 1914–1945*, Faber & Faber, 2008, p. 277

7   Gray, *Camouflage and Air Defence*, p. 77

8   Sayer, *Camouflage Game*, p. 43

9   War Office letter, 9 December 1941, Appendix C, TNA WO199/1629

10 Barkas, *The Camouflage Story*, p. 96

11 A. Wavell, handwritten note dated 23 April 1941 with original sketch of the idea of the 'Sunshield' cover.

12 Steven Sykes (quoting a letter from Barkas), *Deceivers Ever: Memoirs of a Camouflage Officer*, Spellmount, Tunbridge Wells, 1990, p. 95

13 *Ibid.*

14 Sykes, *Deceivers Ever*, p. 54

15 Trevelyan, *Indigo Days*, p. 159

16 See www.maskelynemagic.com. Richard Stokes's excellent website cuts the Maskelyne myth down to size, comparing and contrasting the material in Maskelyne's 1949 memoir *Magic – Top Secret* and David Fisher's *The War Magician* and including interviews with desert camoufleur John Codner and Maskelyne's son, Alistair.

18 R is for Regularity . . .

1   Quoted from Jerrard Tickell, *Moon Squadron*, Allan Wingate, London, 1956, p. 66

2   Capt. T. Van Oss in a letter to his wife, 2 November 1941, courtesy Richard Van Oss

19 S stands for Siting . . .

1   *Life*, July 1941, p. 48

2   Memo, 21 January 1942, TNA WO199/1629

3   J. Gray, lecture notes, Barclay Archive

4 M. Farrar Bell in a letter dated 1947, IWM Archive Gray Documents.4273

5 Cover *Time* magazine, 8 June 1942, vol. xxxix

6 *Ibid.*, p. 25

7 Bernard Law Montgomery, Viscount Montgomery of Alamein, *The Memoirs of Field Marshal Montgomery*, The World Publishing Company, Cleveland and New York, 1958, p. 70

8 'Structural Concealment in the Field', a lecture by Eugene Mollo, 16 January 1943, CDTC, IWM Archive Havinden Documents.7762

20 T is for Tracks . . .

1 About 600 went to Basingstoke from Dieppe, according to Larry Heide, *The Mennonite Saga: With Medics in World War II*, ebook, 2014.

2 *The Times*, 1 February 1939, p. 19

3 J. Gray, draft lecture notes, Barclay Archive

21 U is the Use . . .

1 Goodman, *Edward Seago*, p. 158

2 Lieut-General Bernard Montgomery, *Legion* Magazine Archives, on August 1942

3 Sykes, *Deceivers Ever*, p. 97

4 Hansard, Winston Churchill, House of Commons Debate, 11/11/42, vol. 385, cc37

22 V is for Vision . . .

1 As quoted in Rankin, *Churchill's Wizards*, p. 367

2 H. J. Barclay memoir, courtesy Victoria Barclay.

3 Sayer, *Camouflage Game*, p. 40

4 'Good Reception', 20 September 1943, Barclay Archive.

23 W is for Waste . . .

1   Adrian Searle, *PLUTO: Pipe-line Under the Ocean*, Shanklin Chine, 1995, p. 41

2   Rankin, *Churchill's Wizards*, p. 394

3   Camouflage Report – Overlord, TNA WO199/1314

4   Lt. Col. White, quoted in Juliet Gardiner, *D-Day: Those Who Were There*, Collins & Brown, London, 1994, pp. 75–6

5   Sir Donald Banks, *Flame Over Britain – A Personal Narrative of Petroleum Warfare*, Sampson Low, Marston & Co. Ltd, London, 1946, p. 187

6   *Ibid.*, p. 183

7   R. Parker and B. Scothen quoted in Searle, *PLUTO*, p. 48

8   C.D. & T.C. memo, 27 August 1943, IWM Archive Havinden Documents.7762

9   M. Farrar Bell in a letter, 1 December 1947, Barclay Archive

10 *Ibid.*

11 A. Havinden in an undated letter to R. Buckley, IWM Archive Havinden Documents.7762

12 John Mollo in a letter to the author, 30 June 2010

24 X is for Extras . . .

1   Sayer, *Camouflage Game*, p. 15

2   IWM Archive Pavitt Documents.2790

3   J. Gray in a letter to Maj. D. Pavitt, 4 November 1944, IWM Archive Pavitt Documents.2790

4   Sayer, *Camouflage Game*, p. 45

5   Poem by Jack Sayer, Barclay Archive.

25 Y is for You . . .

1   Sayer, *Camouflage Game*, p. 44

2 'Inventions used in War', *Dundee Evening Telegraph*, 28 November 1936, p. 7

3 F. Beddington in a letter, 12 September 1947, Barclay Archive

4 Charlotte Lewis in a letter to the author, 28 April 2008

5 C. S. Schofield in a letter, 8 October 1947, Barclay Archive

26 Z is for Zeal . . .

1 Quoted in Ross Anderson, *Abbott Henderson Thayer*, ex. cat. Everson Museum of Art of Syracuse, New York, 1982, p. 33

2 Charlotte Lewis in a letter to the author, 28 September 2008

3 Conversation with Nigel Cooke, 5 November 2011

4 Conversation with Gary Hume, 2 April 2011

5 Stanislaw Lem, *Memoirs Found in a Bathtub*, Harcourt Publishers Ltd, 1986, pp. 60–1

Retrospective

1 *The Daily Mail*, 23 February 1966, p. 18

2 *Arts Review*, 5 March 1966

An Ending

1 Kurt Vonnegut, *Bluebeard*, Dell Publishing, New York, 1987, p. 278

2 *Ibid.*, p. 298

3 Antony Griffiths in S. Coppel, *The American Scene – Prints from Hopper to Pollock 1905–1960*, ex. cat. British Museum, London, 2008, p. 8

Select Bibliography

Andrews, William Linton, *The Autobiography of a Journalist*, Ernest Benn Ltd, London, 1964

Barkas, Geoffrey, *The Camouflage Story: From Aintree to Alamein*, Cassell and Co. Ltd, London, 1952

Behrens, Roy R., *False Colours, Art, Design and Modern Camouflage*, Bobolink Books, Iowa, 2002

Bernard, Oliver P., *Cock Sparrow – A True Chronicle*, Jonathan Cape, London, 1936

Blechman, Hardy, *Disruptive Pattern Material: An Encyclopedia of Camouflage*, Firefly Books, 2004

Chesney, C.H.R., *The Art of Camouflage*, Robert Hale Ltd, 1941

Churchill, John Spencer, *Crowded Canvas*, The Hollen Street Press, London, 1961

Dobson, Colin, *Fields of Deception – Britain's Bombing Decoys of World War II*, Methuen, 2000

Edmonds, James E., *A Short History of World War I*, Oxford University Press, 1951

Forbes, Peter, *Dazzled and Deceived: Mimicry and Camouflage*, Yale University Press, 2009

Gardiner, Juliet, *The Blitz: The British Under Attack*, Harper Collins, London, 2011

Gardner, James, *The ARTful Designer: Ideas off the Drawing Board*, Lavis Marketing, 1993

Gibbs, Philip, *The Realities of War*, Hutchinson & Co. Ltd, London, 1920

Goodden, Henrietta, *Camouflage and Art: Design for Deception in World War II*, Unicorn, London, 2007

Hartcup, Guy, *Camouflage: a History of Concealment and Deception in War*, David & Charles Ltd, Devon, 1979

Hesketh-Pritchard, Hesketh Vernon, *Sniping in France 1914–18: With Notes on the Scientific Training of Scouts, Observers, and Snipers*, Hutchinson & Co. Ltd, London, 1920

Hynes, Samuel, *A War Imagined – The First World War and English Culture*, Pimlico, 1992

Kahn, Elizabeth L., *The Neglected Majority: Les Camoufleurs, Art History, and World War 1*, University Press of America, 1984

Lee, Celia and John, *Winston and Jack: The Churchill Brothers*, Celia Lee, London, 2007

Lewis, John, *Such Things Happen: Life of a Typographer*, Unicorn Publishing Group, Stowmarket, 2002

Malvern, Sue, *Modern Art, Britain and the Great War – Witnessing, Testimony and Remembrance*, Yale University Press, New Haven and London, 2004

Maskelyne, Jasper, *Magic – Top Secret*, Stanley Paul and Co. Ltd, 1949

Miller, Jonathan and Tim Newark, *Camouflage*, ex. cat. Imperial War Museum, 2007

Rankin, Nicholas, *A Genius for Deception: How Cunning Helped the British Win Two World Wars*, Oxford University Press, 2011

Reit, Seymour, *The Hidden War: The Amazing Camouflage Deception of World War II*, Corgi, London, 1980

Searle, Adrian, *PLUTO: Pipe-line Under the Ocean*, Shanklin Chine, 1995

Shell, Hanna Rose, *Hide and Seek – Camouflage, Photography and the Media of Reconaissance*, Zone Books, New York, 2012

Sillars, Stuart, *Art and Survival in First World War Britain*, St Martin's Press, New York, 1987

Solomon, Solomon J., *Strategic Camouflage*, John Murray, London, 1920

Phillips, Olga Somech, *Solomon J. Solomon: A Memoir of Peace and War*, Herbert Joseph, London, 1933

Stansky, Peter and William Abrahams, *London's Burning – Life, Death and Art in the Second World War*, Stanford University Press, 1994

Stroud, Rick, *The Phantom Army of Alamein: The Men who Hoodwinked Rommel*, Bloomsbury, London, 2013

Stein, Gertrude, *The Autobiography of Alice B. Toklas*, Random House, New York, 1933

Sykes, Steven, *Deceivers Ever – Memoirs of a Camouflage Officer*, Tunbridge Wells, Kent, 1990

Thayer, Abbott and Gerard, *Concealing Colouration in the Animal Kingdom: An Exposition of the Laws of Disguise Through Color and Pattern; Being a Summary of Abbott H. Thayer's Discoveries*, Macmillan, USA, 1909

Tickell, Jerrard, *Moon Squadron*, Allan Wingate, London, 1956

Trevelyan, Julian, *Indigo Days – The Art and Memoirs of Julian Trevelyan*, Scolar Press, 1996 (first publ. 1957)

Tuchman, Barbara, *The Guns of August*, Penguin, 2014 (first pub. 1962)

Whatley, Swinfen and Smith, *The Life and Times of Dundee*, John Donald Publishers Ltd, Edinburgh, 1993

Wilkinson, Norman, *A Brush with Life*, Seeley Service & Co., London, 1969

Wright, Patrick, *Tank – The Progress of a Monstrous War Machine*, Faber & Faber, London, 2000

Acknowledgements

I am enormously grateful to Adrian Harvey, curator of the Andrew Paterson Collection, who shared early letters between Joe and Paterson, and many of Joe's working drawings and war sketches. Adrian cemented my contacts with both the Black Watch Museum in Perth and the Highlander's Museum in Fort George, where Joe's work is held, and created the website www.josephgray.co.uk, which has brought forth many new sources. People whose relatives served with or knew Joe have generously shared documents, artworks and memories. Charles Beddington, Paul McCririck, John and Louise Mollo, Richard Van Oss, Julius Strathmore Schofield, and Sally Ashburton (née Churchill) have all offered insights into the fascinating characters in this story, and I was lucky to meet James Meade and interview him several times before his death. Harold Dickens, the grandson of Joe's London print dealer, H. W. Dickens, kindly shared his grandfather's original diary, documenting a decade of their transactions. I am also indebted to Gillian Ward, the daughter of Jack Sayer, who gave me a copy of her father's charming and perceptive memoir, *The Camouflage Game*, which is widely quoted in these pages.

As I tracked Joe up and down the country, I visited many archives, public record offices and museums. I'm especially grateful to David Powell at DC Thomson and Tommy Smyth, the archivist at the Black Watch Museum. Thank you also to Celia Lee for her knowledge of all things Churchill, and for introducing me to Chris and Christine Halsall at RAF Medmenham where Peregrine Churchill's photographs are housed and where Johnny Churchill once worked, and to Henrietta Goodden, whose own excellent book on art and camouflage has been hugely inspiring.

When I first began writing Joe's story I wasn't sure of the shape it would take. Darian Leader helped at every stage with his thoughtful prompts and queries, and his loving support has meant the world to me. Once I began writing I was encouraged along the way by many people: Ailah Ahmed, Chloe Aridjis, Devorah Baum, Marie Darieussecq, Nigel Cooke, Natasha Fairweather, Antony Gormley, the late Guy Hartcup, Gary Hume, Rachel Kneebone, Vicken Parsons, Anya Serota, Ian Strathcarron and Sarah Wood to name but a few.

The idea to make Joe's story into an ABC came from the archives of the Imperial War Museum. I altered later verses of this poem to fit my own agenda – but the original copy remains in the files of Major Denis Pavitt. Thank you to all the staff of that museum who dealt with my endless visits and enquiries, and a special thank you to curator Sara Bevan, who was always happy to usher me into the stores, just as Ernest Blaikley did for Joe.

This book was a long time coming but I'm eternally grateful to Mathew Clayton, Anna Simpson and the great people at Unbound for their enthusiasm and committment, and to all the supporters who generously funded the project. Several are family members, or extended family, and have helped make the book what it is. Charlotte Lewis, Mary's niece, entrusted me with private letters and diaries that first brought her to life. Tom Meade, Mary's nephew, gave a new perspective and showed me yet more of Joe's paintings. My aunts Victoria Barclay, Kitty Richardson and Fiona Paice were constantly revisiting the past on my behalf, and a special thanks must go to my mother Patricia Whitford for her tolerance of my interrogations.

But of course the person I most need to thank is my grandmother, Alice Maureen Barclay, whose stories about her father first started me on this process. Although she didn't live to see this book physically published, I was able to read the draft to her in her final hours. She has left us now, but she is here on every page, as firmly as she is fixed in our hearts.

Index

Supporters

Unbound is a new kind of publishing house. Our books are funded directly by readers. This was a very popular idea during the late eighteenth and early nineteenth centuries. Now we have revived it for the internet age. It allows authors to write the books they really want to write and readers to support the books they would most like to see published.

The names listed below are of readers who have pledged their support and made this book happen. If you'd like to join them, visit www.unbound.com.

Maria Alvarez

Alison Baker

Ann Ballinger

Victoria Barclay

Anthony L. Bardlaugh

David Batchelor

Clare Batiste

Claire Bishop

Charles Boot

Mark Borkowski

Ben Borthwick

Susie Boyt

Hilary Burton

Nick Butcher

Chloe Campbell

Lizzie Carey-Thomas

Maureen Carter

Rupert Casey

Sabine Casparie

Edwin Cohen

Nigel Cooke

David Corfield

Rachel Currie

Anne da Costa

Jan Dalley

Marie Darrieussecq

Ann Davidson

Stuart Davidson

Harriet Fear Davies

Essie Davis

Daisy de Villeneuve

Stephen Deuchar

Marion Deuchars

Allison Devers

Simon Dimmer

Bridget Dommen

Doug Helena Sophie
    Hamish & Tilda

Lauren Elkin

Peter Englander

Dee Ferris

Thomas Ian Finnigan

Paul Forster

Robert Forsyth

Iain Forsyth & Jane Pollard

Emily Franklin

Sarah Ghai

Kamal Kishore Ghai
    (24/12/38 – 01/04/16)

Reeve Goldhaber

Dryden Goodwin

Antony Gormley and
    Vicken Parsons

Leon Grant

Andrew Grassie

Winnifred Gray

Charlie Greig

Carole Griffiths

Jane Grimes

Anouchka Grose

Lee Hall

Philip Harley

Adrian Harvey

Simon Haslam

The Hegarty Family

Linda Hepper

Philip Hewitt

Lucy Heyward and
    Fedja Klikovac

William Hill

Andy Holden

Colin Horlock

Catherine Howard-Dobson

Gary Hume

Joe Frankland Hume

Judith Illsley

Mike James

Katrina & Johnsy Johns

Penny Johnson
Al Johnston
Iris Kaltenbäck
Flea Keeble
Diggory Kenrick
Dan Kieran
Leanda Kroll
Ben Langlands
Rex Last
Kalina Lazarova
Boika and Elliot Leader
Imre and Janet Leader
Ninon Leader
Celia Lee
Cherry Lewis
Irwin & Sue Lipworth
Roy Long
Geoff Lowe
Rut Luxemburg
Hazel Macmillan
Francesco Manacorda
Gavin Marshall
Richard Mayston
Paul McCririck
Wendell McMurrain
Andrew Melomet
John Mitchinson
Andrew Mollo
Henrietta Moore

Jonathan Moore
Geneviève Morel
Richard Morphet
Jelle Mulder
Sandy Nairne
Carlo Navato
David Neill
Judith Nesbitt
Mary Newell
Maureen Nieber
Richard Noble
Par Olsson
Julian Opie
Francette Pacteau
Andrew, Jana, Katarina,
    Chris & Alex Paice
Michael Paley
Cornelia Parker
Iain Pears
Rowan Pelling
Flip Phillips
Justin Pollard
Matthew Porter
Jane Prior
Monique Proudlove
Barry Rees
Andrew Reeves
Lucy Reeves
Alexander Richardson

Catriona Richardson

Keith & Therese Riddle

Leonardo Rodríguez

Jane Rosch

Emma Royall

Renata Salecl

Tim Saxton

Bill Scott-Kerr

David Seager

Alice Seferiades

Nicholas Serota

Anya Serota &
    Simon Prosser

Stuart Shave

Mark Sladen

Alexandra Smith

Drew Smith

Michael T A Smith

Scott F Smith

Ali and Sarah Smith
    and Wood

Lili Soh

Christina Stanton

Catriona Stares

Chris Stephens

Polly Stokes

Katharine Stout

Ian Strathcarron

Chris Suslowicz

Eleanor Tattersfield

Nicole Taylor

Wolfgang Tillmans

Julia Trocme-Latter

James Tucker

Richard Van Oss

David Verey

Martin Voshell

Marina Warner

Andy Way

Andrew Weaver

Richard Whitford

Louise Wilson

Charles G Wood

Steve Woodward